# VOCATIONAL EDUCATION AND TRAINING
# FOR A GLOBAL ECONOMY

# VOCATIONAL EDUCATION AND TRAINING FOR A GLOBAL ECONOMY

## Lessons from Four Countries

*Edited by*

**MARC S. TUCKER**

HARVARD EDUCATION PRESS

CAMBRIDGE, MASSACHUSETTS

WORK AND
LEARNING
SERIES

Paperback ISBN 978-1-68253-389-5
Library Edition ISBN 978-1-68253-390-1

Library of Congress Cataloging-in-Publication Data

Names: Tucker, Marc S., editor.
Title: Vocational education and training for a global economy : lessons from four countries / edited by Marc S. Tucker.
Description: Cambridge, Massachusetts : Harvard Education Press, [2019] | Series: Work and learning series | Includes bibliographical references and index.
Identifiers: LCCN 2019019328| ISBN 9781682533895 (pbk.) | ISBN 9781682533901 (library binding)
Subjects: LCSH: Vocational education—Singapore. | Vocational education— Switzerland. | Vocational education—China. | Vocational education—United States.
Classification: LCC LC1043 .V616 2019 | DDC 370.113095957—dc23
LC record available at https://lccn.loc.gov/2019019328

Published by Harvard Education Press,
an imprint of the Harvard Education Publishing Group

Harvard Education Press
8 Story Street
Cambridge, MA 02138

Cover Design: Wilcox Design
Cover Image: Suttipong Sutiratanachai/Moment/Getty Images

The typefaces used in this book are Futura for display and Adobe Garamond for text.

# CONTENTS

# SERIES FOREWORD

*by Robert B. Schwartz and Nancy Hoffman*
*Work and Learning Series Editors*

With the publication of this volume, we are delighted to be inaugurating a new series of books for Harvard Education Press on the theme of Work and Learning. While the series may be new, the topic is not a new one for the Press. In the last few years the Press has published such titles as *Beyond the Skills Gap, Higher Education and Employability, Schooling in the Workplace,* and *Learning for Careers.* What is new, however, is the degree to which questions about the future of work and its implications for schooling at all levels have moved to the center of discussion among thoughtful policy makers and practitioners.

In the United States, while there is no consensus yet on what kind of education can best prepare our young people for an economy increasingly defined by the twin impacts of technology and globalization, there is a growing recognition that all young people will need some kind of education or training beyond high school if they are to get launched on a career path that can assure them economic self-sufficiency. The debate revolves around two questions: Is the attainment of a four-year degree really the only reliable route into the middle class? What mix of academic knowledge and skills, vocational or technical skills, and professional and social skills can best prepare young people for an uncertain future?

While the four-year "College for All" mantra has an appealing ring, the sobering reality is that only one young American in three attains a four-year degree by age twenty-five. Especially worrisome is that this percentage drops to about one in ten for those young people born into families in the bottom 40 percent of the wealth distribution. This suggests that if one is serious about promoting policies that can increase economic mobility and reduce the growing inequality in our country, we'd better figure out a way to get many more young people into the labor market that does not rely primarily on our four-year colleges and universities to equip young people with relevant skills and credentials.

This brings us to *Vocational Education and Training for a Global Economy*, a comparative look at how four very different countries—China, Singapore, Switzerland, and the United States—address the problem of how best to prepare young people for the world of work and careers. It is fitting that this first book in our Work and Learning series is a product of the National Center on Education and the Economy (NCEE) and of its founder and president, Marc Tucker, for this organization has throughout its thirty-year history been tirelessly focused on helping US policy makers learn from the policies and practices of higher-performing education systems. With the publication, since 2000, of international student performance data from the Organisation for Economic Co-operation and Development's (OECD) widely respected Programme for International Student Assessment (PISA), it has become increasingly clear just how mediocre the US education system is, especially in relation to the strongest Asian and European systems and to that of our immediate neighbor to the north, Canada. These PISA results have significantly increased the market for NCEE's work among state and local leaders, for it is now incontrovertibly clear that there are in fact lessons to be learned from higher-performing systems.

Full disclosure requires us to acknowledge that one of us (Schwartz) has had a long-standing involvement with NCEE, as a board member over two different periods of time and as a funder of its work. And it is no accident that Marc Tucker invited us to write two of the country reports in this volume, for we have been close allies in the effort to bring best international policy and practice in vocational education and training (VET) to the attention of US policy makers. We are honored to be associated with the work of NCEE and to initiate our Work and Learning series with the publication of *Vocational Education and Training for a Global Economy.*

# THE VOCATIONAL EDUCATION AND TRAINING SYSTEM YOU NEED DEPENDS ON THE KIND OF ECONOMY YOU WANT

*Marc S. Tucker*

Poor VET. In recent decades, in many countries, vocational education and training (career and technical education in the United States) has fallen on tough times. It is not hard to see why. Families ambitious for their children do not need to see the statistics to know that the returns to university education have been skyrocketing, both in money and status.

The effect on vocational programs that do not terminate in a bachelor's degree has not been benign. What happened in Denmark a few years ago says it all. A new prime minister, on taking office, decided to create a commission on the future of the Danish economy and the skills needed to drive it forward. The issue was so important to him that he chose to chair it himself. The commission concluded that the future of Denmark lay in high technology and that Denmark and Danes could only succeed in that future with advanced education and skills. Denmark, in the eyes of many of us who study these things, had at the time one of the finest vocational education and training systems in the world. But the commission report convinced Danish parents that their children would have no future if they pursued anything other than a university education, and VET enrollments plummeted.

In recent years, as VET systems in many countries have become the education of last resort, the option of students who have no other option, governments all over the developed world began to have second thoughts. Yes, it became difficult to find competent people to come to one's home to fix the plumbing, remodel the kitchen, and install more efficient lighting systems.

But it slowly became clear, in some countries, that much more than that was at stake. The whole economy was becoming unbalanced. In some places, young people with university degrees who could not find jobs roomed with their parents, unwilling to accept jobs they saw as beneath them, while companies in those countries were taking their work offshore to find the workers with the skills they needed at much lower wages. Companies with mushrooming demand could not meet it because they could not find the highly skilled technicians they needed to make and service their product. Hospitals that could find the physicians they needed could not find the technologically sophisticated staff to install, monitor, use, and service the complex medical technologies on which new and better diagnostics and treatments depended.

It was hardly surprising, then, that politicians in many countries found that they were striking a chord with the electorate when they said that perhaps not everyone needed a university education. There seems to be widespread agreement now on that point. But there is much less agreement on what the new VET system, one better suited to the modern economy than the old VET system, ought to look like.

The National Center on Education and the Economy (NCEE) has been studying the world's most effective primary and secondary education systems in the world for three decades. From the start, we have been observing how the VET systems in these nations have evolved in the face of tumultuous shifts in the dynamics of the global economy and rapid changes in technologies, particularly digital technologies. Some countries appear to have adapted to these changes very nimbly. Others, at their risk, hardly at all or, at best, very slowly. And still others in surprising ways.

We decided a few years ago to take a closer, more systematic look at these developments in a set of countries that are very different from each other in the nature of their economies and also in the design of their VET systems. The result was a series of monographs on the VET systems in four countries: Vivien Stewart wrote on the People's Republic of China (PRC); I wrote on Singapore; and Nancy Hoffman and Robert Schwartz wrote on both Switzerland and the United States. The first three were initially published as independent monographs by the NCEE's Center on International Education Benchmarking under the general editorial direction of the Center's director, Betsy Brown Ruzzi; these essays have been updated for inclusion in this volume. The fourth, on the US, is published for the first time here. We did not select these four countries because we think they have the world's best VET systems—although, if pressed, we would confess that we think Singapore and Switzerland would be very strong contenders for that title. We selected them because we think there is a great deal to be learned by studying them closely and comparing them even more closely.

Perhaps the most widespread image of a successful VET system in the world today is the dual-system model that is center stage in central and northern Europe, most notably in Germany, Austria, Denmark, and Switzerland. All of these countries' VET systems grew from the same medieval roots. Young people in those times were apprenticed to accomplished craftsmen who took them in, trained them to a standard set by the guild of which they were a member in exchange for their labor, and then, when they attained journeyman status, either employed them or sent them off to another master craftsman who would do so. The guilds kept their standards up and their numbers down to maintain the standard of living of their members. This system is the quintessence of an employer-based system of vocational skills training. It was not until the late nineteenth century that it was married to some formal schooling for the apprentices and that the government got involved. Later, the modern corporation began to replace the guilds in their central role as providers of training. For a variety of reasons, we see Switzerland as the best current example of the employer-based, apprentice form of vocational skills development.

Singapore may offer the world's best example of a school-based VET system. It is very closely tied to a well-developed, explicit, and articulated economic development plan, a feature that should be of particular interest to governments that also see VET as a key strategy for economic development. It may also reflect the greatest and most sustained effort to build a system based on careful study of all the other systems that have preceded it. The Singaporeans are the most adept benchmarkers in the world. In that sense, to study Singapore is to access a unique window onto all the other VET systems. Singapore's system has developed almost in lockstep with its evolving economic development priorities and, at the same time, with the evolution of its primary and secondary education systems. Indeed, more than in any other country we have studied, these three systems function in Singapore like three very closely aligned subsystems of one human resources system. So if the world is agreed that the dual system of apprenticeship in the firm combined with classroom study of theory is the best way to learn how to do almost anything, why would we want to analyze a school-based system, one in which most opportunities for students to actually do the work are in schools, not in workplaces controlled by employers? The reason is simple. We know of no country that has successfully built an employer-based system of apprenticeship that did not have guilds that took in apprentices in medieval times. If that is true and your country, state, or province is looking for a model that gets as close to the European model as possible, your best bet may be to study Singapore, not Switzerland.

These two countries are our candidates for world leaders in VET. They are also among the world's most successful economies, which lends some credence to the proposition that a strong VET system is a vital component of a strong national economy. Yet, the old caution that correlation is not cause applies here. And that is why we chose two other countries to study, the PRC and the US. These are the two largest and most dynamic economies in the world, but we would not nominate either of these countries for world leaders in VET. So if we maintain that a strong VET system is vital for a strong economy, what is wrong with our logic if these two economies lead the world in size and dynamism? There is something important to be learned here.

The case of China is fascinating. Prior to and during the Mao years, it never had a very strong VET system. Then Mao closed the schools and universities, so the country had hardly any education system at all for a long time, until Deng Xiaoping took over and began to build a new education system from scratch. Deng's economic development plan for China was very ambitious, but the country was practically bereft of the kind of skilled technicians required for his foreign-invested industrial development plan to work. Who would build the factories, bridges, airports, and all the other infrastructure that would be needed? Where would their skills come from? Later, when the PRC was becoming the "workshop of the world," turning out products that in some cases met the highest quality standards in the world, someone on the shop floor and among the supervisors had to have the high skills the company needed to meet the very demanding global quality standards that these firms had to meet to get the work. Where did they come from? We wanted to get some insight into how China had managed to develop the skills needed to become the workshop of the world. We also sought to understand where it wanted to go from here as it set out to wean itself off of an economy based on cheap labor and become an economy that could provide a solidly middle-class standard of living for its people based mainly on internal consumption in a country that was rapidly automating the jobs that its manufacturing workers used to do.

In an odd way, we saw the United States as similar to China in one respect. Like China, the US VET system is, by any measure, nowhere near as strong as those of Singapore or Switzerland. In both countries, VET is seen by parents and students as the education option for students who are not very good at academics. And like China, the US has a booming, dynamic economy. Yet, the education cultures of the United States and China are very different. Americans travel to China to find out why Chinese students do so much better than American students on international comparative tests of academic performance, passing plane loads of Chinese who are traveling to the US to find out how the Americans teach creativity and innovative behavior to their children (answer: They don't; it's in the culture).

When thinking about these issues, I am reminded of a phone conversation I had many years ago with Peter Drucker, the renowned management consultant. I was seeking Drucker's view as to whether it made sense for NCEE to try to persuade American policy makers to adopt the formal skills training systems we had seen in Europe and in the former colonies of Europe, systems that are based on formal systems of occupational skills standards developed by employers. I'll never forget his response. He got very angry and warned me in the strongest possible terms not to do any such thing. The glory of the American economy and of its labor market, he said, was its flexibility, its fluidity, which enabled it not only to turn on a dime but to do so with the expertise it needed when and where it needed it. One of the country's great assets, in Drucker's view, was the lack of formal qualifications of the kind developed in the countries that had had guilds from medieval times. He saw those standards as slow to change, exercising a very conservative influence on companies and the national economy at a time when countries would win or lose based on their ability to respond very quickly to shifts in markets, technology, and work organization. Better to have a system with few formal credentials and many opportunities to learn new skills quickly, from the firm or from a plethora of other providers.

If you take Drucker's perspective seriously—and I do—then it is possible that the wise policy maker needs to understand that while there is a strong argument for national systems for education and skills development that focus like a laser on the complex technical skills needed for particular occupations requiring less than a university degree, there is an equally compelling argument for building a system emphasizing not the development of the particular skills needed for particular occupations but, rather, the kind of broad education and knowledge that will make our workers nimble in an environment in which new digital technologies are likely to wipe out whole legions of jobs overnight with increasing frequency. If that is true, then perhaps Drucker was right, and it is dangerous for countries to build their VET systems on the models developed by the countries that have what many regard as the best VET systems. Or maybe not.

We chose these four countries not because we knew which models of VET would work best as the future unfolds but because we did not know and wanted to study a group of countries that would make us think hard about what would make sense now and in the near future. Our hunch when we picked these countries was that Drucker was both right and wrong—that the rigidities of the old European system were indeed a problem of increasing importance but that more recent developments there had gone some distance toward addressing those concerns; that Singapore was in the process of moving toward the best of the European system while still holding on to what it most prized about its own system; that China was most certainly aware of the shortcomings of its system and determined to overcome them in ways that would turn out to be very interesting for the rest of us; and that the United States, in its usual way, would start to muddle through to a unique version of the future that would fascinate the world.

But don't misunderstand me. These hunches don't lead to an on-the-one-hand-but-on-the-other-hand resolution of the issues I have briefly raised here. This book is not intended to be another set of case studies held together by little more than a common binding. The chapters are intended to help you think hard about what kind of VET system makes sense for your country in a very complex environment. In the last chapter I draw those threads together in an argument I hope will be helpful.

There is a lot at stake for the leading industrial countries. Well-regarded scholars tell us that more than half of the jobs now being done by American workers can be automated by currently available technology. National incomes are rising, but average real wages have not increased in decades. As machines take over the less-skilled jobs, low-skilled workers will have to acquire higher skills. And as higher-skilled jobs are taken by the machines, the humans who held them will have to learn new and even more complex skills or they will be jobless. Get it wrong and income disparities will increase to the point that countries' economies could fail and their social and political systems could be torn apart.

So while it's important to have enough electricians and carpenters, this is not about having enough electricians and carpenters. It is about having enough skilled technicians to run a successful economy, it is about greatly upgrading our education and training systems so that the adults in our societies have an opportunity to lead fulfilling lives with the dignity that comes from doing work that is valued by others, and it is about maintaining democracies that can easily come apart when some people have much and a growing number have nothing.

CHAPTER 1

# THE PHOENIX

## Vocational Education and Training in Singapore

*Marc S. Tucker*

One cannot begin to appreciate the enormity of the Singaporean achievement in vocational education and training (VET) unless we start at the beginning. For Europe, the story begins with the origins of the guild structure built by the artisans in medieval times. The current European model of VET is the result of a long, slow process of evolution that developed in tandem with the emergence of capitalism on the Continent. It was only in the very latter stages of that development that government came to play an important role in VET, and, even then, the other players made sure that government would be only a member of the team.

In Singapore, by contrast, government led the charge at every step. The story begins only recently, after World War II, when the fledgling government faced a sea of challenges to its very existence and chose to concentrate on economic development as its strategy for shaping a new national spirit and for meeting the urgent needs of its people. Singapore was not only extremely adept at promoting economic development but, from the beginning, made very aggressive investments in general education and made VET a keystone of their economic development strategy. Thus, for countries without a guild tradition, countries that are still at an early stage of the economic development process or are on their way but still well behind the leaders, the Singapore model may be more relevant than the European one. This is also true because, at every step, Singapore borrowed heavily from models all over the world, including the European model, as it developed its own unique system.

But it would be less than useful to confine this account to a description of the current state of VET in Singapore. That is because each stage of development of the Singaporean VET model was matched to the stage of economic development that Singapore was going through at the time. And each stage of development of the VET system can best be understood only in relation to the parallel development of the general education system. While I concentrate here on the policies and structures that define the VET system, I describe not only what it looks like now but also how it developed, stage by stage, in relation to Singapore's economic development program and its unfolding general education system (figure 1.1).

## A STUNNING SUCCESS STORY

When the Japanese advanced through East Asia as World War II began in the Pacific, the British built a major naval installation in Singapore to guard the strategically crucial straits through which the world's ships traveled between the East and the West, between the countries of the Indian Ocean and the Arabian Sea and those of the Pacific Rim. The greatest maritime power in the world situated the guns of its massive fort based on the assumption that the enemy would come by sea. But the Japanese came instead by land, through Malaysia. British cannons pointed in the wrong direction, and the fighting was all but over before it started.

After the war, the British tried to hang on to their colonial holdings but ultimately failed. Singapore, comprised of a series of little islands at the southern tip of the peninsula, had a population of only 1.6 million (today about 5.5 million). It declared independence and became self-governing in 1959. In 1963 it joined a group of formerly independent colonies on the Malaysian peninsula to form a new country, Malaysia. In the beginning there was talk of forming a common market in East Asia, which would have greatly benefited Singapore, but the Indonesians, newly freed from their colonial masters, the Dutch, felt threatened by the developments on the other side of the straits and cut off exports to the new Malaysian federation

**FIGURE 1.1    Schematic history of the Singapore system**

*Phase I: Low-Cost, Low-Skill Export Strategy (ca. 1945 to mid-1970s)*

| Economic strategy | General education | VET |
|---|---|---|
| Get on lowest rung of value chain. Offer low-skilled, low-cost labor to multinationals. Create attractive incentives to use that labor in highly competitive industrial parks with good infrastructure and first-rate port facilities. Create other incentives for multinationals to invest in skills of Singaporeans to get to next stage of economic development. | Great emphasis on improving quantity of provision: reduce adult illiteracy; increase primary school attendance; greatly raise number of primary school teachers (e.g., training them part time, putting them in classrooms part time); build schools; expand secondary schools; send small numbers to universities overseas to train for leadership positions; found university. | 1961 Winsemius Report highlights shortage of skilled technical workers. Great expansion of vocational education. Government requires all secondary students to get two years of vocational education, after which streamed into academic, commercial, or technical upper secondary. Industrial training centers and vocational institutes built. |

*Phase II: Capital-Intensive, High-Tech, High-Skill Export Strategy (mid-1970s to 1990s)*

| Economic strategy | General education | VET |
|---|---|---|
| "Second Industrial Revolution" (1981) to provide high-technology base for economy. Make Singapore attractive to high-value-added global manufacturing firms and provide new incentives for them to locate in Singapore. Produce home-grown senior and midlevel technical and scientific professionals to reduce need for expats. | Turn to emphasis on quality. Goh Report leads to introduction of New Education System: streaming at end of grade 4; much higher academic standards for English, math, science; radical upgrade of teacher quality; new Curriculum Development Institute; major effort to keep students in school beyond compulsory age with more choice and flexibility. | Economic Development Board creates French-Singapore Institute and German-Singapore Institute to create world-class models of VET. In 1980 only 5 percent of cohort entered universities and 8 percent polytechnics, but research scientists and engineers increased by a factor of five. There were few important changes in the regular vocation education system. |

*continued on next page*

### Phase III: Creativity and Entrepreneurship Strategy (1990s to Present)

| Economic strategy | General education | VET |
|---|---|---|
| Get to top of value chain: world-class producer of highly innovative, high-value, R&D-driven products and services. Develop Singapore-headquartered companies with regional and global reach. Turn Singapore into economic, education, R&D hub for Southeast Asia. | Thinking Schools, Learning Nation, then Teach Less Learn More shift schooling paradigm from rote learning toward complex skills and creativity. New National Institute of Education develops world-class teacher training system; human resources system rationalized; schools given more autonomy; students given more choice and flexibility. | Vocational education moved out of secondary schools into state-of-the-art postsecondary institutions installed in impressive physical facilities. Polytechnics greatly strengthened on factory school model employed in German-Singapore and French-Singapore Institutes. Apprenticeship program continued. |

and any hope of a common market. Because its business was trade, and no small amount of that trade had been with Indonesia, Singapore was in trouble from the very beginning.

Then, in 1965, Malaysia tossed Singapore out of the new federation. The Chinese, a majority in Singapore, were resented in that part of the world. Clever and resourceful in business and finance, they held a disproportionate amount of the wealth in the world between China and Australia. So the Malaysians pushed them out. When the leader of the Singaporeans, Lee Kuan Yew, announced the news to his people, there were tears in his eyes. No wonder. He knew that Singapore could not support its people. It had no raw materials. It was completely dependent on Malaysia for fresh water. Unemployment was very high. Most of the industrial plants were on the other side of the new border and now no longer accessible. A very large portion of the workforce was illiterate. Fewer than half had any formal education at all. In its whole population, there were fewer than a thousand college graduates. The Indonesians were hostile. The little cauldron of ethnic rivalries among its ethnic Chinese, Malaysian, and Tamil (Indian) residents threatened to tear it apart. And while Britain was taking responsibility for Hong Kong, it was not doing the same for Singapore.

Yet, Britain maintained its enormous naval base in Singapore, which meant that the tiny country was not defenseless against its far larger hostile neighbors to the north and south. The base provided employment to a large number of Singaporeans who would otherwise have been added to the already high unemployment rate, to say nothing of all the Singaporeans whose livelihoods depended on the people who worked at the base. In 1967, however, without warning, the British announced they would be closing that base. Those thirty thousand jobs—plus all the other jobs that depended on those employed at the base—disappeared. Singapore's economy went on life support. It was without expertise, jobs, or prospects—and it was now also defenseless.

Today, Singapore is one of the most successful economies on Earth. It has the third-highest GDP per capita. Though it is home to only 5.5 million people, it has the thirty-eighth-largest economy in the world. It has the world's busiest port. Its production growth rate for 2010 was the third-highest in the world at 15 percent. It is the Asia region headquarters for many of the world's largest firms, a leader in digital and electronics manufacturing, and a rising star in pharmaceutical and biomedical manufacturing. Though it has no oil of its own, it operates the third-largest oil refinery and is a net exporter of oil, making it a lead player in the global oil industry.[1]

For decades, Singapore has had one of the lowest unemployment rates and lowest inflation rates of any country in the developed world. Its stable economy and business-friendly reputation have made it a haven for global business for decades. Despite the prominence of Singapore on the global manufacturing stage, services accounted for 73 percent of its economy in 2010. It has become a giant of Asia's banking and finance scene and operates the world's fourth-largest foreign exchange market. It is home to more than two hundred asset management firms, having become an important factor in the development of the whole of Southeast Asia. Remarkably, it has become an increasingly important tourist destination. Tourism, sightseeing, and entertainment industries grew by 1,834 percent in 2010 alone.[2] And Singapore is also on its way to becoming a major supplier of education services to the region.

How did this happen? How did this small country move from a third world economic disaster to become one of the world's leading economies in just a few decades? And what role did VET play in these remarkable developments?

## SINGAPORE'S EVOLVING ECONOMIC DEVELOPMENT STRATEGIES

In the 1950s, during the years leading to independence and nationhood, most of the world's poor countries were, like Singapore, either former colonies or about to be former colonies. Generally, the colony's economic role had been to supply the mother country with raw materials and purchase the mother country's finished manufactured products (the mercantile system). Because the mother country set the prices for the raw materials and for the manufactured products, the colony was generally at the wrong end of this system of trade. The conventional wisdom in the international economic development community at the time was that the only way to break this dependency and to grow was for a colony to substitute its own manufactured products for those supplied by the mother country.

### Economic Development Phase I: Low-Cost, Low-Skill Export Strategy (1945 to mid-1970s)

The strategy of substituting the former colony's manufactured products for those of the mother country was not very attractive to Singapore's leaders because Singapore was much too small to constitute a market for its own manufactures. Though there had been some hope of a market in the rest of Malaysia before the separation, there was none after Malaysia slammed the door shut. Singapore needed another strategy.

Even before independence, and long before the British closed their naval base, Singapore's leaders chose another direction. In 1961, Prime Minister Lee Kuan Yew created the Economic Development Board (EDB), giving it a mandate to develop a strong manufacturing sector in Singapore that would reduce the very high rate of unemployment. But the market for those manufactures could not be limited to tiny, poor Singapore. It would have to be the whole world. Singapore would have to grow its economy by exporting what it made, and it would have to attract both the capital and the expertise needed to do that. The EDB worked with United Nations (UN) development expert Albert Winsemius, under the direction of Singapore's finance minister, Goh Keng Swee, a graduate of the London School of Economics. Together they created a plan to attract multinational firms to locate their manufacturing facilities in Singapore to take advantage of the low cost of labor, the strategic location, and the fine port facilities. Goh led the effort to develop a large tract of land on Jurong Island as a vast industrial park. Included in the development plan were all the residential facilities, schools, and transportation and port facilities needed by global firms to set up their factories and house their staff. The government provided very attractive tax incentives and devised other policies designed to attract global firms.

At first, not much happened, and Goh became the butt of many jokes. But, in time, Jurong was an enormous success and was followed by other vast industrial parks. Singapore was off and running. Even before Singapore became an independent nation in 1965, this city-state was lifting itself up by its bootstraps, working very hard to provide a workforce with the skills needed to make this low-wage, foreign-direct-invested manufacturing strategy successful.

### Economic Development Phase II: Capital-Intensive, High-Tech, High-Skill Export Strategy (mid-1970s to 1990s)

In the beginning, Singapore had the advantages that come with being first. Later, however, when other, larger nations—particularly China and India— implemented similar strategies, Singapore's leaders realized that success with a low-wage, foreign-invested manufacturing strategy meant competing with those nations on the price of labor. The strategy would only work in the long term if the government kept Singapore's wages down, and it might even force the government to push wages lower as more and more countries offered more and more cheap labor on the global labor market. But Singapore's leaders were determined to improve the standard of living in their country. They wanted to raise wages. So they needed another strategy.

This thinking led to the second stage of Singapore's industrial development. The government understood that the future for low-wage countries was a low standard of living; their aim for Singapore was to have a high standard of living. They knew that they would only have a high standard of living if Singapore could join the high-tech world, producing high-value-added products for which the world was paying high prices. The problem it faced was how to acquire the high technologies that held the key to its future. The answer was from foreign high-tech firms themselves: Singapore would become a high-tech, high-value-added manufacturing center by attracting the high-tech, high-value-added firms and then learn from those firms what they needed to know.

The question was how to do that. Part of the answer was a judicious mix of tax and grant incentives favoring such firms. Another part was making Singapore increasingly inhospitable to firms that had come just for low-cost labor. Singapore actually took the audacious step of raising salaries, sending the clearest of all messages that foreign companies should not locate in Singapore to get access to a low-cost labor force. Another such policy was around industrial job training. All firms were required to contribute to a job-training fund. They could get their money back (in fact, they could get even more than they had put in), but they had to write a proposal to the EDB. The winning proposals were those that showed how the money would be used to provide Singaporean workers on their staff with transferable high-tech skills that would enable them to add more value to the products they were making, a proposition that was very attractive to high-tech, high-value-added firms but very unattractive to low-value-added firms.

Many policies of this sort were implemented, and, over time, the proportion of low-value-added firms relying mainly on low-skill, low-cost labor declined, and the proportion of high-tech, high-value-added firms steadily increased, and with that increase came a rise in the standard of living of Singaporeans. Of course, this strategy, like the previous one, required a determined effort on the part of the Singaporean government to greatly raise the education and skill level of the entire Singaporean workforce to match the needs of an economy based on high technology, an economy requiring world-class skills in many domains.

One particularly important role in these developments was played by the National Computer Board (NCB), established in 1981. NCB's principal brief was to develop an IT-savvy workforce, but it also developed a plan to implement a culture of IT throughout the country, to provide high-speed links to the rest of the industrialized world and the same kind of infrastructure within the country. High-tech industrial parks were formed, as were alliances between Singapore's universities and polytechnics with leading universities and research centers worldwide. Every effort was made to establish Singapore as a global center of advanced information technology and research.

### Economic Development Strategy Phase III: Creativity and Entrepreneurship (1990s to Present)

As with the first phase, the strategy of the second phase of Singapore's development was successful only for a while. In time, other previously low-wage and often much larger countries followed Singapore up the value ladder to become producers of high-tech products for the global market. Once again, Singapore saw that its ability to provide a high standard of living for its citizens would fall victim to competition from lower-wage nations unless it could offer something they could not. Singapore's leaders knew just what that "something" was: innovative, creative products and services that would be in demand worldwide. Singapore would have to become one of the few nations making their living by inventing the future—and not just once but continuously.

The government, however, wanted more than that. It saw a future for Singapore as being not only the Asian headquarters of many premier global firms but, increasingly, the headquarters of Singaporean firms with a regional and even global reach. Just as Hong Kong had become the finance and management headquarters of the whole enormous Pearl River delta region in China, Singapore could become the nerve center of much of Southeast

Asia. The government knew, as well, that this sort of vision, a future that depended on Singapore's ability to lead advancements in many high-tech areas at once and manage a supply chain that extended to many nearby countries, would depend on this city-state becoming a major global center for world-class research and development, finance, technology, education, and creative design.

At this third stage of economic development, it was clear that everything depended on again making a giant leap in education and training. None of this could happen unless Singapore was able to convert its education system from one providing a high-quality conventional education for people who largely played supporting roles in foreign-invested firms into one providing a world-class education for people who would be called on to lead global firms to a future they would have to invent. Education and training were the keys to the national economic strategy, and Singapore's leaders knew it.

## EDUCATION STRATEGIES TO MEET EVOLVING ECONOMIC NEEDS

When the newly independent government took over in 1959, there was no school system in Singapore. Each ethnic and language community ran its own schools, while the families of the colonial government and others were served by Christian mission schools and a few government schools. When the British left, the loyalties of each ethnic group ran not to Singapore but to nations outside the infant country. The survival of Singapore depended on creating a national school system that could somehow serve to integrate these rival groups, produce a feeling of loyalty to the new nation, and provide a workforce for a new kind of economy.

### Education Development Phase I: To Match the Low-Cost, Low-Skill Export Economic Strategy (ca. 1945 to mid-1970s)

In 1961, the government drafted its first Five-Year Plan, which laid out the basic blueprint for what would turn out to be the first stage of its economic growth. But the government knew that none of this would work unless it addressed the skills problem. Low-wage manufacturing did not require high-level skills, but it did absolutely require basic literacy and a large number of people with strong vocational skills in areas like machining, electrical work, carpentry, welding, and simple accounting. Developing these basic skills would require a monumental effort.

At the start, the government required only a few schools to teach in English, but increasing pressure from parents to provide instruction in English led the government to make a fateful decision to make English the primary language of instruction in the schools. Contributing to that decision was the realization that Singapore's economic plan would have the greatest chance of success if its workforce could speak English. The government was also aware that choosing any of the rival languages of the Chinese, Malaysian, Indian, and Indonesian people among their citizens as the national language of Singapore could provoke conflict from which the new country might never recover. All students were to be bilingual, proficient in their home language and in English. The plan also determined that the curriculum would be the same for all languages and that it would emphasize mathematics, science, and technical subjects. There would be common national examinations for all primary school students. And all schools were to be public, common schools.

This must have seemed like an impossible dream to those responsible for carrying out these ambitious policies. Much of the adult population was illiterate. There were only a thousand college graduates in a population of 2.5 million people. The new nation lacked teachers, school buildings, school books, examinations, and money. In undertaking this plan, finding somewhere to begin, it was recognized that teachers were by far the most important component.

In the beginning, and for a long time to follow, teachers were trained in the new curriculum for three years while they served as teachers. There were not enough teachers to pull them out of the classroom for training. And because there were not enough teachers or buildings, the schools were run on double shifts, with teachers working both shifts and students attending only one each day. Singapore managed to keep up with the exploding demand for primary teachers in this period but fell behind for secondary teachers, mainly because the expanding industrial economy was competing for the very small number of people with the skills needed by secondary school teachers. The government could not compete with the private sector. The problem was exacerbated by the requirement that the teachers be able to speak English. It was not until the Institute of Education was established in 1973 that teacher training in Singapore, for both primary and secondary teachers, was put on a firm footing.

### Education Development Phase II: To Match the Capital-Intensive, High-Tech, High-Skill Export Economic Strategy (mid-1970s to 1990s)

In 1979 the government released a landmark report prepared by Minister of Education Goh Keng Swee, referred to ever since as the Goh Report. In this rather candid report, Goh pointed to the low rate of literacy among graduates, often in both English and their native languages; the high rate of student attrition, which he characterized as wasteful and inefficient; and the generally low level of quality produced by the system to that point. He proposed what came to be called the New Education System: students would be assessed on their language proficiency at the end of grade 4 and assigned on the basis of the assessment to one of four streams. The purpose, he said, was to provide more to those students who could race ahead and to give those at the other end of the ability spectrum the extra time they needed to attain high standards. A new standardized curriculum was introduced, set to much higher standards, especially in English, mathematics, and science, along with an appropriate examination structure. Paths through the system were rationalized. And the commitment to English was greatly strengthened.

None of this would have worked without much better teachers and more money for everything that had to be done to upgrade the system. The plan was given a powerful push by Minister for Trade and Industry Goh Chok Tong in his 1981 Budget Statement, in which he announced Singapore's "Second Industrial Revolution" and plans to "develop Singapore into a modern industrial economy based on science, technology, skills, and knowledge."[3] The revolution in education policy and structure needed to support the Second Industrial Revolution was already under way. Public expenditures on education rose from US$21.4 million in 1978–79 to US$245.38 million in 1982–83, a stunning increase.

Equally important to the outcome of such a plan was the needed improvement in the quality of teachers. Work in that direction began in 1971 when the School of Education in the University of Singapore was closed and Ruth Wong H. K., who had trained under the renowned cognitive psychologist Jerome Bruner at Harvard University, was appointed to run the Teachers' Training College (TTC). The TTC, founded in 1950, then took over all responsibility for teacher training in Singapore, at both the primary and secondary school levels. Wong immediately began a substantial upgrade of the quality of teacher training. She took a very traditional, third-world teacher training system and turned it into an internationally competitive, modern one. As early as the early 1980s, Singapore was recruiting the teachers in their two-year training programs only among high school graduates who had completed their A-level exams, Singapore's top students. This was true for the primary schools as well as the secondary schools. Beginning in 1980, all teachers were trained full time, not part time. By 1986, Singapore was recruiting trained engineers to teach a new program in design and technology in their secondary schools. Graduate programs were added for school administrators and secondary school teachers.

Increasingly, the teacher training program was informed by the research going on at the world's leading teacher training colleges and graduate schools of education. The standards around what teachers had to know about the subjects they were going to teach and the craft of teaching were raised substantially. Anticipating the work of Stanford professor Lee Shulman by many years, Wong introduced the idea of training teachers in the pedagogy specific to the subjects they would be teaching. In the mid-1980s, with help from England and Australia, the Institute of Education introduced the Practicum Curriculum, intended to greatly improve the connection between theory and practice by carefully structuring the various roles a teacher must play during practice teaching. Wong also made it clear that teachers, like their students, and like professionals everywhere, were meant to continue their own professional development throughout their career, and she began to put in place the tools and resources they would need to do that. Singapore made aggressive use of continuing education programs to upgrade their experienced teaching force even as they radically upgraded the quality of the new teachers coming into the system.

Payday came when the results from the 1995 Third International Mathematics and Science Study were released. Singapore students scored right at the top of the distribution worldwide. Singapore had joined the ranks of the nations with the world's best education systems, a remarkable achievement for a nation that had hardly any education system at all when Singapore became an independent country only thirty years earlier.

### Education Development Phase III: To Match the Creativity and Entrepreneurship Economic Strategy (1990s to Present)

The Singapore education system did not rest on its laurels. It had played an important role in making the city-state a world leader in high-tech, high-value-added manufacturing, and it would play an equally vital role in taking the next step toward making Singapore an international nerve center for an economy based on creativity, innovation, and research and development. But doing so meant moving way beyond the system it had developed to meet the needs of the second phase of the Singaporean economic development program.

In 1991, the government abolished the Institute of Education, merged it into the National Institute of Education (NIE), and made it part of the Nanyang Technological University (NTU). In doing so, it moved teacher education back into the formal university structure—and into an institution that was already getting high marks in international rankings of universities. NIE faculty would provide both the content and the pedagogy; these two aspects of teacher education, usually very separate, would in Singapore be highly integrated. Teachers at both the primary and secondary levels would learn at the same time what to teach and how to teach it.

Singapore continued to recruit its teachers from the top echelons of high school graduates (and to pay the beginning teachers at levels comparable to the compensation of beginning engineers), but the new home for teacher training made it easier to raise the standards of teacher preparation even further, to enable the training of classroom teachers in research methods and to develop postgraduate programs for teachers and school leaders. The new emphasis on problem-solving skills, creative and critical thinking skills, and collaborative and communication skills required the NIE to make major changes in the instruction designed to prepare teachers to teach this new curriculum. Under the leadership of Gloria Lim, Leo Tan, and Lee Sing Kong, the NIE has become a world-renowned teacher education and educational research institution.

On June 2, 1997, Prime Minister Goh Chok Tong delivered a speech on education that would set the tone for everything to come. In that speech he said that "a nation's wealth in the 21st Century will depend on the capacity of its people to learn." He then engaged in a shrewd analysis of the strengths and weaknesses of the education systems of the United States, England, and Japan. He pointed out that Japan had long had one of the world's most successful education systems but had become deeply worried that it would not be able to produce "the individual creativity, the originality of thought and inventiveness . . . they need to retain their competitiveness."[4] The prime minister promised a fundamental review of Singapore's curriculum and assessment system to develop creative thinking skills and the ability and desire for lifelong learning. The Ministry of Education, he said, was studying how to reduce the expanse of the required curriculum to introduce more choice and more projects that would enable students to develop new skills without lowering their standards. He made it clear that it was very important to create a kind of education that would "fire a passion for learning" instead of studying for the sake of getting good grades. In the future, he said, excellence will be defined by the eagerness and capacity to learn, not by how much one learned in school, because it will be impossible while anyone is in school to know what that person will need to know in the future. He noted that there were enormous implications in this for teachers, who would themselves have to become lifelong learners. Schools would have to become model learning organizations. Teachers would have to have the time to reflect, learn, and keep current. Schools would have to have more autonomy to define their own direction. And the Ministry of Education would have to improve communication to make sure that policy was adjusting to the needs and learning in the schools. Singapore, he said, would have to "get away from the idea that it is only the people at the top who should be thinking."

The prime minister was announcing a revolution. Thinking Schools, Learning Nation became the driving vision. The first step was the Innovation and Enterprise initiative, which was summed up by a list of core life skills and attitudes that the Ministry of Education declared it wanted developed in students:

- a spirit of inquiry and thinking originally;
- a willingness to do something differently, even if there is risk of failure;
- a ruggedness of character, the ability to bounce back and try again;
- a willingness to stand in a team, lead a team, and fight as a team; and
- a sense of "giving back" to the community.

That was followed in 2004 by the Teach Less, Learn More initiative. Perhaps the best commentary on the spirit of Teach Less, Learn More was a speech delivered by Minister of Education Tharman Shanmugaratnam in 2005 in which he talked about "developing a spirit of inquiry . . . helping our young develop the strength of character that will help them ride out difficulties and live life to the fullest . . . and injecting fluidity through the system—recognizing more talents besides academic achievements, providing more flexibility in the school curriculum and streaming system and introducing new pathways—all to help our students discover their interests and talents, and know that through our education system they can go as far they can." He also described the centralized, exam-focused Asian education systems as first-rate at producing adults who can focus on a task and get the job done but said that was not enough in a world in which "the future would be driven by innovation, by doing things differently with verve and imagination, not by replicating what has been done before." Newly returned from a trip to Japan with Ministry of Education officials, Shanmugaratnam said the Japanese understood the need for the kinds of changes called for in Thinking Schools, Learning Nation and in Teach Less, Learn More, but they had imposed these changes from the top down, and there was no buy-in from the schools. That would not happen in Singapore, he said. The goal would be reached with leadership from the schools and support from the top, or, as he put it, "top-down support for bottom-up initiatives."[5] Since June 1997, the Ministry of Education has been working hard to implement the vision Prime Minister Tong laid out in his speech.

## VOCATIONAL AND TECHNICAL EDUCATION: THE BACKBONE OF SINGAPORE'S ECONOMIC DEVELOPMENT STRATEGY

### VET Development Phase I: To Match the Low-Cost, Low-Skill Export Economic Strategy (ca. 1945 to mid-1970s)

The first government trade school in Singapore was established by the British in 1930. Then, not much happened until they built two secondary Technical Schools in 1956. The 1959 election of the political party that continues to run Singapore marked an explosion of vocational and technical education in Singapore. From a standing start of 1,379 students in 1961, there was a fourteen-fold increase in the number of vocational students in the system by 1967.

The difference was simple. The British were running Singapore as a trade center backed up by their own navy, and they had no interest in raising the standard of living of the natives. The new government, made up of Singaporeans, saw education and training in vocational and technical subjects as the key to their very ambitious economic development plans to improve the lives of their own people. That is just as true today as it was then.

The new government knew that their plan to carve a new industrial development zone out of the jungle in Jurong would come to nothing if they could not provide thousands more carpenters, mechanics, metal workers, machinists, plumbers, shipyard workers, and electricians than they had available, both for the construction of the industrial zone and port and for their operation. And they knew that Jurong, if successful, would have to be followed by other similar developments if they were to reach their goals for reducing unemployment in Singapore and increasing the standard of living. Singapore's new leaders had discovered that other former colonies that had tried to implement foreign-direct-investment development strategies had failed because they had not attended to the need to develop indigenous workers with the necessary technical skills, and they did not intend to make that mistake themselves.

Between 1962 and 1966, Singapore, with a population then of less than 2.5 million, built forty new secondary schools, of which nineteen were secondary technical and secondary vocational schools. In the program at Balestier Trade School, the original colonial trade school, students were studying the "crafts" in such courses as Mechanical Engineering Practice, Electrical Fitting, Electrical Installation, Radio Servicing, Motor Vehicle Mechanics, Refrigeration and Air-Conditioning, Plumbing, Woodcraft and Construction, Building Drawing, Shipbuilding, and Sheet Metal and Welding. So even as the new schools were being built at breakneck speed, the old ones were being refitted to meet the needs of Singapore's economic development plan.

Singapore's unemployment rate in 1968 was 9 percent. But these new graduates were offered jobs as soon as they graduated. The plan, evidently, was working. The problem was finding enough teachers for the rapidly expanding vocational and technical schools. In 1961, two years after the grant of autonomy and four years before independence, the TTC started offering a two-year certificate program for people who wanted to teach technical education. But demand for semi-skilled and skilled labor was so great that, in 1963, the two-year full-time training program was changed into a one-year program followed by two years of workshop practice, to get the new teachers into service one year faster. Just like the new programs to train primary school teachers, the idea was to press new teachers into service before they were fully trained and to continue their training after they started work. Yet, that still did not produce enough teachers. Even as it was working overtime to increase the number of people available to expand the primary schools and the regular academic secondary schools, the government pressed many of the teachers it was preparing for the regular academic classrooms into service as vocational and technical teachers, sending them into the new certificate program. Since the TTC did not have enough capacity to train everyone who needed training, the government sent others to the United Kingdom and other Commonwealth countries, such as Australia, Canada, and New Zealand, to get their vocational training. Clearly, Singapore was again pulling out all the stops, working as hard as it possibly could, to produce the trained technicians required to substantially lower unemployment and kick-start the economy.

In 1968, the year the British announced they would close their naval base, the government consolidated responsibility for technical education in a new Technical Education Department (TED) of the Ministry of Education, complementing the ministry's General Education Department. One year later, its first director, Lim Ho Hup, finding that the efforts to prepare a technical workforce adequate to meet Singapore's needs had still not produced enough trained technicians, took an extraordinary step. He announced that all male and half of the female students would be required to take classes in metalwork, woodwork, technical drawing, and basic electricity during their first two years in secondary school. There were not enough teachers to staff these courses in the high schools, so the ministry set up centralized workshops for this purpose and transported the high school students to these classes. A whole generation of students had their first taste of technical education.

The new program was not very popular at first, but it turned out that many students who had a strong academic record really liked these classes and chose to pursue a technical career. This greatly strengthened the quality of students opting for the polytechnics and undoubtedly contributed to their subsequent success. And because girls were required to participate in this program, the taboo against women in technical careers was broken, another important reason for Singapore's later success. By 1997, half of the applicants to the polytechnics were young women.

But the number of well-trained technicians, though much greater than before, was still small. In 1968, 84 percent of students were enrolled in the academic stream, 8 percent in the technical stream, 7 percent in the vocational stream, and 1 percent in the commercial stream.[6] That was why an introduction to vocational education had been made a required subject for all males and half the females in lower secondary education. The full-on vocational program was a separate stream for the lowest-ability secondary students. That had made sense at the time when a large portion of students left school when they finished primary school, when unemployment rates were very high, and when these dropouts faced a bleak future. But as the demand for labor skyrocketed, those who left school at the end of primary found jobs, though those with more education found much better jobs. Schooling was expanding to meet the demand, the dropout rate was plummeting, the vast majority of students stayed in school beyond the compulsory age, and the policy of using lower secondary vocational education to keep kids in school no longer made sense. In 1969, the TED abolished the separate stream for vocational education in the lower secondary schools.

The TED had done a very good job, and its location within the Ministry of Education made sense when success depended on very close cooperation with the regular schools. But as the initial needs for technicians with the minimum level of competence was satisfied, it became more important to make sure that there was very close collaboration between the vocational education system and private industry. That led to the end of the Technical Education Department and the creation, in its place, of the Industrial Training Board (ITB) in 1973. This new independent agency, constructed outside of the Ministry of Education, had a legislative mandate to focus on Singapore's industrial training needs. However, though the leadership for this whole area had passed to the ITB, the Ministry of Education was still responsible for the technical schools.

Among its other responsibilities, the ITB was tasked with establishing a new occupational skill standards system that would drive skills training at every level. Training advisory councils worked closely with industry to create a rigorous process to develop curriculum matched to the standards. Not least important, the ITB developed new structures to produce very close collaboration between the training system and the employers to give trainees access to the state-of-the-art equipment and personnel in industrial plants that were necessary to train candidates in the industry standards. The ITB devised a whole range of schemes to make this possible for various groups of full-time students and employed workers, including apprenticeships and on-the-job training programs. It developed memoranda of agreement between government and key employers like Bosch, Mitsubishi, Siemens, IBM, Cisco Systems, and Sun Microsystems to enable the teaching staff to stay up-to-date in leading-edge developments in industry so they could pass on what they were learning to their students.

Toward the end of this initial phase in the development of Singapore's technical education system, the ITB created a new system of skills certification, the National Trade Certificate (NTC), that would drive vocational and technical training. The same standards were used for full-time training of new workers in the vocational school system as for the part-time training of employed adults in the adult and continuing education system. The ITB set up a Public Trade Test System that enabled experienced workers to get credentialed under the new skills certification system at the semi-skilled (NTC-3), skilled (NTC-2), and master craftsman (NTC-1) levels by taking the appropriate tests without having to take the related courses. Because the standards for this system had been set by the employers, the employers recognized the certificates offered by the trainees. Because the certificates were recognized by the employers and the candidates demanded them, the training institutions designed their courses around the skill standards.

By the early 1970s, the ITB had benchmarked the world's leading apprenticeship programs and concluded that they should be the basis for conveying skills to the craftsman level in the NTC system. Yet, apprenticeship training was only available to men who were already out of school and finished with their compulsory National Service, and, at the time, there were very few men who wanted to do it. Good jobs were readily available to them without having to go through an apprenticeship, so the incentive to become an apprentice was not great. So the ITB bribed them with the offer of an allowance over and above the stipend they would get from their employer. That worked pretty well, but not well enough. The government then offered to defer the compulsory National Service for young men who signed up for apprenticeships and cancel it altogether for those apprentices who stayed with the same employer for six years. That worked.

The ITB had designed an apprenticeship program that consisted of full-time training in a vocational institute in the first year, followed by two years of on-the-job training in an approved program. Employers participated because the apprentice was bonded to stay in that company for a specified period of years following the award of a certificate. The first year the ITB training system was offered, enrollment in the first-year full-time courses went up more than 15 percent, and the number of working adults enrolled in the part-time programs increased by 90 percent. ITB was a great success right out of the box.

But ITB was not the only player on the vocational education scene. As Singapore's new government was getting started, it concluded that it needed a strong, independent government agency to focus on the critical task of attracting foreign multinational corporations to Singapore. Established in 1961, the EDBoard moved to set up offices in most of the highly-developed countries to actively promote investment by firms in Singapore. At the same time, the new EDB was charged with designing and managing what proved to be the hugely successful development of the industrial park on Jurong Island, with its ready-to-move-in factories and wraparound services. It sold Singapore partly on its low-cost labor, but mainly on the basis of its lack of corruption, great facilities, and strong support services for industry. But the idea was to offer a complete package, everything a multinational company might need to succeed, and that had to include trained labor. So by virtue of its charter, the EDB also came to be centrally involved in the development of Singapore's VET system.

Singapore was being advised at that time by the UN Development Program, which worked with the EDB to help Singapore get assistance from Japan, Britain, and France, each of which helped Singapore establish industrial training centers in the metal, electro-mechanical, electro-chemical, woodworking, or precision engineering industries. From the beginning, training was built in part around the actual production of components needed by the companies with operations in Singapore, ensuring that the training would be grounded in up-to-date requirements and techniques. These training centers were modest in size, producing in four years only eighty-six graduates (though many were hired by the firms before they could graduate, so great was the demand for skilled technicians). But the successful effort to engage these other countries' governments in providing direct assistance to Singapore in the creation of state-of-the-art vocational education would have far reaching effects on the further development of the Singaporean vocational education system.

However, because this system produced relatively few technicians, and the government wanted to find a way to induce foreign-invested firms to train Singaporean youth for high-value-added, high-pay technician work, another approach was needed. So the EDB established a new program for industrial training. It did not have the money to set up its own schools, which required expensive specialty equipment and specialized instructors; but they knew that the very type of companies they were looking to attract did have both the up-to-date equipment and the highly trained instructors. So it made a deal with the first companies willing to locate in Singapore. The EDB offered the company land and buildings expense for a training center in Singapore, a sum of money needed to cover some of the costs of equipping the training center, and an amount of money sufficient to cover 70 percent of its operating costs. In exchange, the company would train not only the Singaporeans it needed for its own operations but an equal number who would be available, on graduation, to other firms coming to Singapore. In this way, the EDB managed to create a system that was attractive to the firms—their own training to meet their own needs would be heavily subsidized, and they would get to do it in their own way—but was also a good fit for the Singaporean government, which could be sure the training would be world class and done with state-of-the-art equipment and highly trained instruction—and it would cost far less than if Singapore had set up its own such training facility.

The training program lasted two years, including one year of basic training and another of production training. Students got a stipend while in the program, and those who successfully completed it were awarded an Apprenticeship Certificate. On completion of the program and earning the certificate, participants were bonded to serve any company to which the EDB sent them for five years. The program quickly expanded beyond the Tata Group of India, the first company to sign on, to Rollei and Phillips. It is very unlikely that Singapore would have become a major world center for precision engineering had it not been for this program.

To get a complete picture of the early development of Singapore's technical education system, though, we have to retrace the development of the polytechnics, the part of the system that sits between the vocational education system and the university system. The former is responsible for training the semi-skilled and skilled workers in the economy, while the latter educates the engineers, scientists, and managers at the top of the system. The polytechnics train those in between, the people who provide much of the technology know-how and leadership that has enabled Singapore to enter and then dominate one new high-tech industry after another. The polytechnics have been described as the "backbone" of Singapore's industrial development system.

Singapore Polytechnic, the first of the line, was opened by the Prince Regent in 1959, just before Singapore gained autonomy from the Crown. Most of its original thirty full-time and 130 part-time faculty came from Great Britain and other parts of the Empire and were augmented by the British who staffed the naval base. One wonders if the British had somehow peered into the future when they established this institution, as they designed it to train people for industry at a time when there was virtually no industry. Since Singapore's founding more than a century earlier, the heart of the Singaporean economy had been trade. But industry was to be its future, the British recognized, and Singapore Polytechnic would prove to be a very important investment in that future. It would offer an injection of highly trained teachers who could then train their successors, the acorn from which the proverbial oak tree would grow.

A few months after the Prince Regent's departure, the first Singaporean government was sworn in. One of its first actions was to appoint Toh Chin Chye, the new deputy prime minister and chairman of the majority party, as the chairman of the board of Singapore Polytechnic. Nothing could have more clearly signaled the intention of the new government to make technical education the linchpin of its economic development strategy. Toh canceled all the classes in typing and stenography and instituted instead a program of technical courses designed to provide the skills needed by the kind of industries Singapore wanted to attract. Then he announced that Singapore would create its own unique skill standards system. He wanted to be sure that Singapore would not depend on skill standards systems devised by other countries but would instead be free to develop standards particularly appropriate for the leading-edge industries and firms that Singapore would be going after. This was a remarkably courageous and far-sighted decision. Had Singapore continued to use the British occupational skill standards system, employers everywhere would have known what the qualifications presented by Singaporean vocational education students meant. Abandoning that system meant that Singaporean skill standards and the qualifications based on them would not be recognized outside Singapore and, in fact, global employers in Singapore might refuse to recognize them. But neither of these possibilities became reality, and the decision to develop a uniquely Singaporean skill standards system turned out to confer enormous advantages on Singaporean workers.

### VET Development Phase II: To Match the Capital-Intensive, High-Tech, High-Skill Export Strategy (mid-1970s to 1990s)

The next phase of development of Singapore's vocational education training system was driven by the Council on Professional and Technical Education, chaired by the Minister for Trade and Industry. The EDB also played a very important role.

By the time the first phase of Singapore's development was coming to an end, the EDB had concluded that the development of a highly-skilled technician class would prove crucial to the strategy for the second phase: attracting the kind of high-technology, high-value-added firms that could serve as the foundation for a high-wage economy. The EDB realized that neither the Ministry of Education nor the ITB would be able to produce by themselves enough of the highly skilled technicians fast enough to meet the demand that the EDB intended to create, so it decided to develop a new system for training highly skilled technicians that would draw on what it had learned from the training centers and the industry-operated apprenticeship program.

In the early 1980s, the EDB went back to the three countries it had worked with on the training centers and asked them to collaborate once again, through renewable five-year agreements, to create a new form of postsecondary school. These new schools were to be known as the German-Singapore Institute of Production Technology, the Japan-Singapore Institute of Software Technology, the Japan-Singapore Technical Institute, and the French-Singapore Institute for Electro-Technology. The German-Singapore Institute was designed to train the core of the technical workforce for the production of advanced factory automation systems. The French-Singapore Institute produced technologists for the electronics industry. One of the Japan institutes focused on IT and the other on "mechatronics." (One of the secrets of Japan's stunning success in manufacturing in the 1980s was its marriage of the previously separate disciplines of mechanical engineering and electronics.) In 1988, Japan set up a Precision Engineering Institute in Singapore based on this new discipline. The seminal idea animating the design of all the new institutes—the idea of a "teaching factory"—came from EDB official Lin Cheng Ton.

I visited the German-Singapore Institute in 1989. My memory of that visit is quite vivid, for it struck me as being the best vocational school I had ever seen. The features that made the deepest impression on me were the characteristics of the teaching factory. On entering the school, I had the impression that I was in a modern factory. The students wore white lab coats and punched a time clock. Everything possible was done to create an environment as much like a factory as possible in terms of both the physical environment and the way the students were treated. It was a two-year program of study. Students coming directly from high school had to have completed their A levels, but the school also admitted recent graduates who had experience working in high-tech companies who were nominated by their companies and who had only their O levels.

The first-year program was devoted to basic studies designed to provide a foundation for the applied work to follow in the second year. This included a CAD/CAM course, a course in electronics, another in pneumatics and hydraulics, and so on. In the second year, the students worked on factory automation projects. These were not mock-ups. Rather, the faculty was responsible for getting contracts from the global firms with facilities in Singapore to build new factory automation systems for them, which they would use and for which they would pay the school. The school had to charge market prices for these systems in order to avoid being charged with undercutting companies in business to provide such systems, so the customers expected a product that would be competitive with the best such systems in the world and would be delivered on time.

The faculty supervised the design, construction, and testing of these systems, but it was the students who produced them. They worked in teams. Some would work on the mechanical systems, others on the electronic subsystems, still others on the pneumatic and hydraulic subsystems, and so on. Most projects were completed within the year, but some took longer. Many of the faculty members were engineers who had degrees from the engineering program at the National University of Singapore. Every five years they were expected to take a year away from the German-Singapore Institute to work at one of the world's top manufacturers of automation systems. On their return, they were assigned to revise the relevant parts of the school's curriculum in light of what they had learned.

The élan of both teachers and students was indescribable. The students felt very lucky to be there, as did the faculty. Both worked very hard. The standards were very high. I had the sense that everyone knew that Singapore's future depended on their success, as indeed it did.

In time, the demands on these training institutes grew to the point that no single company or nation could provide the needed resources. The EDB then reconfigured them to draw on all the major industry players in their respective fields. In the case of the German-Singapore Institute and factory automation, Hewlett-Packard, ASEA, Seiko Instruments, Sankyo Seiki, Siemens-Nixdorf, and others agreed to join the consortium, loaning experts, training EDB lecturers at the firms' worldwide locations, assisting with curriculum and program development, and donating and loaning equipment and software and upgrading it when necessary.

This phase of Singapore's development was to prove explosive for the polytechnics. At the beginning of this period, there was only Singapore Polytechnic, established in 1954. In 1982, Ngee Ann Technical College was renamed Ngee Ann Polytechnic, and Temasek Polytechnic was established in 1990. Nanyang Polytechnic followed soon after in 1992. What is hard to convey is the urgency with which all this was done, and the determination to reach not only large numbers but also high standards very quickly.

Ngee Ann had a rocky start as a private college in the mid-1960s and did not really get off the ground until it was taken over by the government and turned into a technical college in the late 1960s with programs in industrial chemistry, industrial electronics, management studies, and institutional management. By the mid-1970s, its enrollment had grown to three thousand students, and a major building program was financed in part by the Asian Development Bank. It forged a close collaboration with the Polytechnic of Central London, with three of its faculty members transferred to key positions at Ngee Ann. By that time it had an Electrical and Electronic Engineering Department and a Commerce Department, and, very importantly, all of its diplomas were jointly awarded by Ngee Ann and the Polytechnic of Central London.

In the mid-1970s, Ngee Ann added the Building Services Department and the Shipbuilding and Repair Department. Singapore had taken over the naval shipyards and expanded its port facilities to accommodate the needs of the businesses it was recruiting. Also, the brief closing of the Suez Canal, which followed President Nasser's takeover of the canal from Britain, was forcing ships to reroute through the straits and right by Singapore. The extra stress placed on the ships from going around Cape Horn meant that the Singaporean shipyards kept very busy. At this time, too, Singapore was beginning to develop its offshore oil business, which also required the kind of technically trained staff that Ngee Ann was ready to provide.

By 1980, surveys showed that Ngee Ann's graduates were in as much demand as those of Singapore Polytechnic. Its student population rose from three thousand in 1980 to nine thousand in 1986. Its second five-year plan, scheduled to begin in 1986, was projected to cost $200 million. Built into that cost was the construction of a new Center for Computer Studies, with the director of the center recruited from Huddersfield Polytechnic in England. All this took place under the watchful eye of the Council on Professional and Technical Education, which was arranging for the creation of the Japan-Singapore Institute of Software Technology under the auspices of the EDB, thus putting in place all the required elements of a strong core of professionals and technicians to support this critical new industry in Singapore.

Just as Ngee Ann arranged for its graduates to earn diplomas from the Polytechnic of Central London in other fields, it also arranged for its graduates in Computer Studies to get the National Higher Diploma authorized by the British government and recognized around the world. The engagement of its new computer center director from England was not a one-off; Ngee Ann was also recruiting its faculty and administration from leading institutions from all over the world. Singapore was determined to show that the graduates of its home-grown institutions could compete with the very best in the world.

By the end of the 1990s, Ngee Ann had programs in environmental engineering, public health engineering, building services engineering, microprocessor technology, robotics, computer numerical control machines, digital communication, plant engineering, air conditioning and refrigeration, fabrication technology, manufacturing technology, flexible manufacturing systems, business data processing, mechatronics, quality assurance engineering, and much more. And it was busy creating a whole new program in mass communications, which would, among other things, complement EDB's plan to create a new film industry in Singapore.

Ngee Ann was a major achievement for Singapore. But it was only one step in the development of a solid group of very high-quality polytechnics in this period under the leadership of the Senior Minister of State for Education Tay Eng Soon, who was in charge of the polytechnics and chairman of the

Vocation and Industrial Training Board. In 1989, N. Varaprasad, the deputy principal of Singapore Polytechnic, headed a team to study the feasibility of creating another polytechnic. Varaprasad submitted his team's report to the government in November, and in December the government asked him to be the first employee and principal of the new institution, named Temasek Polytechnic. He was given six months to open its doors for to the first students. Five years later, it occupied a new, fifty-hectare campus comprised of architecturally stunning, world-class buildings that offered almost two million square feet of space. By that point, Temasek had become one of the world's leading polytechnics. It had created many new diploma programs, perhaps the most interesting of which was its Apparel Design and Merchandising program, which has allowed Singapore's home-grown designers to take their place among the world's leading clothing designers. This is one more example of Singapore's determination to create a VET system at lightning speed and, at the same time, to be world class in every arena it took on.

For Nanyang Polytechnic, the government chose Lin Cheng Ton, the director of the Manpower Development Division at the EDB, to head the planning work and then the new institution itself. Ton had led the development of the new postsecondary institutions and been the one to insist on the use of the teaching factory model as the core design element in the German-Singapore Institute and its sister institutions, which the EDB had hoped might serve as models for a new round of polytechnics that would prepare the highly skilled technicians who would continue to drive the Singapore economy. Ton convened the planning committee in August 1991. By April 1992, the new Nanyang Polytechnic was up and running. Ton was able to put together his first operational team, five colleagues from the EDB, only ten days before the annual announcement of the fall program for all the polytechnics had to go out. Half that time was taken up by the printer. They had no program and no one to teach it, let alone a description of it, but failing to meet that deadline would have meant that they would have lost a whole year in opening the new polytechnic. They met their deadline and were able to use the announcement to recruit enough students to open the new institution in temporary quarters the next fall.[7]

Nanyang Polytechnic started that fall with programs in occupational therapy, nursing, physiotherapy, and radiography. The following year, all the EDB institutes were transferred to Nanyang. With that move, Nanyang instantly acquired world-class offerings in factory automation, mechatronic systems, industrial electronics, software engineering, servo-mechanisms and motion control, and a score of other key technologies. But it also acquired all the disciplines of the "factory school," which included not only the design of its heavily applied curriculum and pedagogy but also the whole schema of methods for closely intertwining the work of the most advanced firms in the world with the work of these schools. This virtually guaranteed that Singapore would continue to have some of the most efficient methods ever developed for making sure that its curriculum for the training of top-level technicians would reflect the most advanced technologies, forms of work organization, and training systems. In transferring the EDB institutes to the new polytechnic, the government was not just lodging them in that one institution but, rather, finding a way to take what they had learned and spread it through the whole mainline career education and training system.

The move certainly included the vocational education system supervised by the Industrial Training Board. The ITB had worked hard in the first phase of Singapore's industrial development to provide the carpenters, electricians, and other semi-skilled and skilled workers required by the low-skill, low-pay, low-value-added employers first attracted to Singapore when the goal was to reduce unemployment to acceptable levels. They were doing this at a time when a large portion of the Singapore workforce was illiterate and when most of those who were literate had not completed a primary school education.

In 1960, the government had set up the Adult Education Board (AEB) to provide continuing academic education and enrichment programs for the adult population. In 1973, the government greatly expanded its vocational education program and formalized it as a pre-employment training system organized outside the school system for those who had left primary school. In 1979, the ITB was merged with the AEB to form the Vocational and Industrial Training Board (VITB), formed in 1992. The aim was to create a single consistent framework for the training of both youth and adults using a common occupational skill standards framework and matching course structure. The VITB consisted of five highly placed and well-connected representatives from the government, four from labor, three from employer associations, and seven senior business executives. Each area of the VITB's curriculum had an advisory committee composed of experts in the relevant fields, including, but not limited to, automotive, commercial, construction, electrical, electronics, fashion arts, hotel management, mechanical engineering, precision engineering, shipbuilding and repair, printing, and wood-based trades.

Between 1973 and 1991, the ITB, and then the VITB, trained and certified 150,000 skilled workers. But by the late 1980s, it was clear that the model was no longer working. Employers were less and less interested in hiring certificate holders who had only a primary school education followed by the VITB skill training. They wanted workers who had a full primary and secondary education followed by postsecondary vocational training. (In the Singapore context, that meant ten years of schooling through lower secondary school followed by vocational education.) Another problem was that 60 percent of the students coming from primary school into the vocational education program could not successfully complete their vocational courses because the level of their academic achievement was so low. So Singapore had to find a way to make vocational education a postsecondary program and, at the same time, help the students falling through the cracks to successfully complete both the primary and secondary programs.

This was the point at which the government engineered a major redesign of the school system by postponing vocational education until the postsecondary years, making it one option available to students after they had completed their O-level exams. The designers of this reform believed that all or nearly all of the students who had been struggling could succeed against high standards, but they would need more time and more help to do so.

When I was in Singapore in 1989, I was astonished to find that the primary schools we visited were assigning their most capable teachers to the students in the lowest track. Those students typically had a longer school day than their peers and often came to school on the weekends, when other students did not. Though the students in the lowest track scored lower on the international tests than did their peers in Singapore, we discovered that they were scoring higher than the average for all students in many of the world's leading industrial nations. The curriculum these students studied was not as demanding or as rich as the curriculum in the upper streams, but, by global standards, it was demanding enough to enable these students to achieve at very respectable levels and, most important in the Singapore context, to give these students a very good chance of success in the redesigned—now post-secondary—vocational system. It was a remarkable achievement. In effect, all streams were performing above the average for the industrial nations. With this accomplishment, Singapore could run a vocational education system that attracted the lowest quarter of its graduates and still produce technicians who would hold their own with the world's best.

And that is just what they set out to do. Singapore's vocational education system was completely revamped. The New Apprenticeship Program was launched in 1990. Like the old apprenticeship training program, it was designed to accommodate both students who wanted to "earn as they learn" and companies that wanted students trained by their own staff. It would not compete with the system for full-time vocational education but, instead, complement it. One of the new features was the requirement that firms offering the training use instructors from their own staff who had been certified after taking a standard course in vocational pedagogy offered by the government.

Under the new scheme, the government provided higher subsidies than before, which allowed firms to pay the apprentices more, as well as more support for students who needed basic skills instruction to meet the skills threshold that would enable them to profit from the apprenticeship training. The government provided guidelines for the compensation of apprentices, and that compensation was quite attractive. The apprentices could choose among 650 companies sponsoring a total of seventy programs. The government tested the candidates at the end of their apprenticeship and certified those who met the standards. Courses in the apprenticeship program could be offered in government-approved training centers, which had to meet requirements around curricula and facilities, and the staff had to have completed the necessary training and been certified for the program. A major part of the companies' expenses could be paid through the Skills Development Fund, which was initially run by the EDB and later transferred to the Standards, Productivity, and Innovation Board, a part of the Ministry of Trade and Industry that aims to help Singapore businesses grow.

For the apprentices, this was very attractive because they could not only make good money while getting their training, but they could also have the inside track to good jobs and the prospect of a career with some of the world's leading companies. It worked for the companies because their training costs were heavily subsidized by the government, they could train the apprentices in their own way, and they got a chance to look over the candidates without having to commit before they saw the candidate under real working conditions.

But the really big development came in 1992, when the Ministry of Education, under the charge of Tay Eng Soon disbanded the VITB and created the postsecondary Institute of Technical Education (ITE) in its place. Not just a name change, this was a whole new commitment to vocational and technical education at the level below the polytechnic. It was launched with a capital budget of $300 million, enough to build campuses for ten technical institutes with quarters that would be equal in architectural excellence to the best universities in Asia and many in the rest of the world, and with equipment and staff to match.

The Singapore government would spend whatever was necessary to provide its vocational education students with world-class training for the world-class jobs that would await them, and it mounted a relentless and sophisticated public relations campaign to make its point. Top government officials made speeches describing skilled technicians as the driving force of Singapore's economic success and encouraged young people leaving school to attend the technical institutions. They built first-rate facilities and equipped them with the latest machines and staffed them with a highly trained faculty, and they worked hard to build a strong web of connections to business.

But two other things the government did may have had the greater impact on the attractiveness of these new institutions. The first was the sheer size of the investment made in building the magnificent campuses for the new vocational education system. The second was the fact that the program that awaited the new students at these reborn institutions was far more like what one would expect to find in a university than in the old-style vocational schools. There were beautiful dining halls, extensive libraries, sports programs, arts and music classes. In all these ways, the government conveyed the message that Singapore really valued the students who chose to go to these institutions and that it intended to place these young people in the center of the new economy, not on its periphery.

The new ITE facilities were situated close to both Singapore's industrial parks and the residences of the workers in an attempt to foster close connections between the schools and the businesses they served and also to make it as easy as possible for the young people and those needing adult education to access the programs. The New Apprenticeship Program was brought under the control of the ITE because the government wanted the apprenticeship program to complement the full-time training program and to make sure that both were developed as integral parts of one coherent system. The ITE was responsible for, among other things, the common occupational skills system, the standards for trainers and instructors, the criteria for award of occupational certificates, the testing of candidates, and the award of certificates, whether the candidate was a full-time student on its ITE campuses, the product of the apprenticeship program, or simply taking courses in the adult education system at any of these locations.

Most of the ITE programs, however, were intended for recent high school graduates who would come to one of the ITE campuses for a full-time program of training. These programs did not take the form of a European-style "sandwich," or "dual," program, combining on-the-job training with school-based teaching. Rather, the ITE adopted some features of the factory school pioneered in the EDB institutes and also created its own Authentic Learning Approach. For instance, programs for hairdressers have working salons, and young people training for work in retail train in a real coffee shop that has real customers. Auto mechanics train on new Mercedes and Nissan vehicles and on special cutaway engines provided by those firms, and they use the specialized tools the mechanics in training need to work on those cars. Similarly, draftsmen in training are using state-of-the-art CAD/CAM software and other computer-aided design software. Classroom instruction takes place in the same buildings in which these shops and workshops have a home, so the theoretical and the applied work are closely integrated.

ITE's orientation toward learning is heavily applied. The idea was to create an environment in which young people whose academic skills were not very strong could still flourish, an environment that would appeal to young people who are much more likely to learn by doing than by studying theory in a textbook. The ITE became one of the world's great laboratories for experiential learning, a hands-on, sleeves-rolled-up approach to instruction. About 70 percent of the typical program core is taken up with practical training, the rest with theory.

The three new mega ITE colleges—completed in 2005, 2010, and 2013 under a ten-year master plan to upgrade vocational education—share a common curricular core. There are some programs that are offered on all three campuses, but each also has additional unique programs. The system motto "Hands-On, Minds-On, Hearts-On" conveyed the idea that it engages head and hand equally and is about the whole person, which includes not just cognitive development and a very applied approach to the development of technical skills but also twenty-first-century employability skills, such as motivation, personal and team effectiveness, independent thinking, flexibility, agility, a passion for vocation, confidence, cross-culturalism, and a sense of responsibility for the community.

About 85 percent of the curriculum is offered in the form of modules in career-related skills, and 15 percent is in life skills, which are mixed and matched to assemble complete programs. The ITE does this to make it easier for individuals to add additional modules to adapt to changes in career direction, new technologies, and new forms of work organization. Modularizing the curriculum in this way not only makes it easier for graduates to adjust as their career progresses, but it also makes for a much more efficient institution. Employability skills are covered under a Life Skills module, mandatory for all students, that includes communication skills, teamwork, thinking and problem solving, sports and wellness, career development, and planning and customer service. The ITE aims to produce "thinking doers." It has developed a process-oriented pedagogic model for this purpose: the Plan, Explore, Practice, and Perform Model. The idea is for the student to learn how to focus on a goal, gather the information required, practice what has been learned, and then perform the task to demonstrate competence.

A story Chan Chin Bock tells in *Heart Work* captures nicely the spirit of the times and the way the Singapore system fits together.[8] It was the beginning of the 1980s. The EDB was working hard to bring leading global computer firms to Singapore. It had struck out with Wang and Digital Equipment Company (DEC) and then went after Apple Computer. Apple was very interested in the Asian market, but it was uncertain about manufacturing in third-world countries. It sent a top manufacturing engineer, John Sanders, to Singapore to take a look. He first arrived in Singapore at 3:00 in the morning to be greeted planeside by the senior EDB official assigned to him. He never forgot that gesture. Still skeptical, Sanders agreed to set up a small plant in Singapore to make motherboards to be sent abroad to assembly plants in developed countries. The company had designed the plant to be very unsophisticated, capable of being operated with the kind of relatively unskilled labor they expected to get, with automation to be slowly implemented over a period of years. The aim was just to get some production experience in Asia. Nonetheless, it was very important to Apple that the plant be delivered on time, with high-quality output.

Sanders was stunned by the speed with which the facility was built. His next surprise was the quality of construction and services. But the big surprise was the quality of the staff that EDB had trained and provisionally hired for him. Apple had expected it to take nine months to ramp the plant up to the point at which it was ready to accept the components from California for assembly into motherboards. EDB had enabled him to get that job done in three months.

This experience with Singapore changed Apple's mind about producing in

Asia. Instead of just assembling motherboards, they decided that the Singapore plant would be responsible for producing the entire Apple II computer. It would save the company a lot of money, buying and making everything needed for the computer in Singapore rather than shipping it from Silicon Valley. This meant, though, that much higher manufacturing skills would be required, as well as a greater degree of automation. But this was what the EDB had hoped for from the beginning. This was their dream for Singapore.

Over the next five years, Apple's Singapore plant became "the most modern and efficient PC plant in the Apple world." EDB-trained technicians not only ensured that the plant was productive, but they introduced process innovations that were later adopted by other Apple computer manufacturing plants elsewhere in the world. To continuously upgrade its highly skilled workforce, Apple encouraged its workers to sign up for evening classes at EDB's technology institutes. In addition, it also sent especially bright technicians to the polytechnics, as well as to its plants in the US.

> [John Sanders] had come [to Singapore] expecting a Third World operation but, in the end, he had a plant that any production engineer in the world would be proud of. Singapore went beyond just being a great plant itself; it introduced world-class manufacturing innovation to Apple plants elsewhere in the world. For many years, Apple's plant in Singapore became a model and eye-opener for executives of new companies considering investing in Singapore. They were all impressed, especially those from Japanese companies . . . It encouraged them in their own plans to design more automated plants for Singapore.

### VET Development Phase III: Infusing VET with Creativity and Entrepreneurship (mid-1990s to 2014)

The whole structure of the Singaporean VET system was put in place by the middle of the 1990s. Since that time, within that structure, the institutions and their programs have continued to adapt to changing industrial needs as the Singaporean economy has evolved.

Certain trends stand out. Just as Hong Kong had, over time, become the drive wheel for the whole Pearl River Basin South China economy, the

Singapore government was developing a plan to create a "triangle" economy with Malaysia and Indonesia. Those countries would relate to Singapore in much the same way that Guangdong and the rest of the Pearl River Delta economy related to Hong Kong. Singapore became the financial center for the whole region, and manufacturers based in Singapore developed supply chains in Malaysia and Indonesia. Much of the relatively low-skill work, especially manufacturing, that used to be done in Singapore moved to the other triangle countries.

The results were much the same as those in South China. The standard of living in Singapore continued to rise, but, at the same time, the standard of living in the two neighboring countries was rising too, in tandem with Singapore but at a lower level. For those countries to play that role well, however, they needed to do what Singapore had done many years before: they needed to greatly raise the education and skill level of their own populations. Singapore was ready to help. Education and training has been added to the list of major Singaporean export industries. The ITE and the polytechnics work with countries in East Asia and Southeast Asia, including China, consulting with them to help them develop their training policies capacity, providing technical assistance as they redesign their systems, and providing training for their people in Singapore and on-site in their countries. And increasing numbers of the nationals in those countries began coming to Singapore for their education and training.

As this process evolved, and as more of the lower-value-added manufacturing work either became automated or went offshore to other members of the triangle, where it could be done more cheaply, Singapore's economy began to shift toward services, beginning with finance but then embracing many other kinds of services as well. And in this time Singapore has turned into a major tourist destination, which has entailed, among other things, building up its hospitality and gambling industries. The vocational education system recognized this shift in the economy and reduced its emphasis on manufacturing and increased its focus on services.

Although the institutional structure of Singapore's vocational and technical education system has remained remarkably stable over the last two decades, the institutions themselves have adapted to evolving changes rapidly. One of the most important drivers of the changes in the training system has been the government's commitment to increasing the creativity and innovative capacity of its workforce. Part of this has been accomplished by saturating Singapore education and training institutions with information technology.

A good example of the system's approach to the development of the creativity and innovative capacity of students in the VET arena is the Innovation Modules offered by Ngee Ann Polytechnic's School of Interdisciplinary Studies. The modules are named Idea Jumpstart, Idea Blueprint, and Idea Launchpad. Idea Jumpstart is given to all year-one students and offers a series of highly engaging activities that culminate in a full-day session in which they compete with others in a Jumpstart Challenge. Modeled after the television shows *The Apprentice* and *Project Runway*, the Jumpstart Challenge gives students eight hours to solve a real problem and pitch their proposals to the facilitator.

Students get Idea Blueprint and Idea Launchpad in sequence in their second year at Ngee Ann. They are taught to understand user needs, come up with ideas and concepts to address them, and put those ideas into action by creating a prototype of the product. They are encouraged to take risks and are given exercises that build their confidence. Idea Blueprint gives them a chance to work in groups, exploiting each other's strengths and compensating for each other's weaknesses. Idea Launchpad then gives them an opportunity to turn their idea into a real product or service and try it out on customers and stakeholders.

Some of Ngee Ann's students come out of the junior colleges with A levels that could have gotten them into university. Most come out of the secondary schools with relatively strong grades on their O levels. Yet another group comes out of the ITE. These students were in the bottom quarter of their high school class and therefore usually did not have as strong an academic record as those coming directly from the secondary schools. For these students, Ngee Ann has a suite of special courses designed to strengthen their skills in English and mathematics. The students coming into Ngee Ann can be expected to have passed algebra, trigonometry, and calculus. The curriculum is both textbook based and project based. Final exams are paper-and-pencil, but teachers assign both small and large projects that are also graded and count in the final course grade. These are authentic projects, like a diagnostic device for a biomedical company, a software application for a bank, or a piece of market research for a commercial firm.

Ngee Ann also offers a wide range of support services for student entrepreneurs, connecting them with people in industry who can provide assistance, helping them participate in international entrepreneurship competitions, assisting them in getting funding for their ventures, and mentoring them through the process. Also, Ideawerkz, Ngee Ann's student innovation incubation center, runs events designed to get students involved in innovative projects and provides them with funding as they get started.

Yet, providing opportunities for students to develop their creative, innovative, and entrepreneurial capacities is not the only way Ngee Ann is adapting to a changing world. The school pioneered the use of mobile e-learning as an integral part of its instructional system as early as 1999. The whole campus is covered by wireless internet access, and all students are required to own laptops so that instructors can count on students being able to fully utilize a wide range of information technology resources, including courseware.

The development of strategies to promote creativity and entrepreneurship were not the government's only focus in this period. Again, Ngee Ann provides an apt example. The government is convinced that Singapore will have a competitive edge because its students are at ease in a truly global world. Every student is required to participate in at least one overseas-based program before graduating. Though most last just five days, 30 percent of the students have overseas assignments lasting between six weeks and six months. Every year, one thousand students head for China for six weeks, and there they focus on both Chinese culture and their own discipline. Students have to pay for these experiences, but Ngee Ann has a fund that enables them to subsidize the expenses for students with limited resources.

Ngee Ann is no less interested in making sure that its students have experience in industry while they are in school. Every student has to do an internship of two to six months, usually in the third year of the program. Someone from the receiving company is assigned to each student, and that person, with input from a supervisor, is responsible for grading the student during the work experience period. The firm is responsible for coming up with a clear plan for the internship, including defining a project the student must do as well as the deliverable the student will be responsible for producing and the nature of the training. The student must keep a journal of the whole experience. Ninety-three percent of Ngee Ann's graduates who look for jobs on graduating find them within three months. Almost 30 percent go on to university directly; more than 50 percent go on to university eventually.

The creation of the ITE in 1992 proved to be a major turning point for VET in Singapore. The government committed to reconceiving the technical curriculum to make it an important driver of the new Singaporean economy and reconceiving the whole program of the institution to address all the needs of the young people it was primarily intended to serve, not just their need for technical skills.

In 2007, Bruce Poh, who had been with the EDB, was brought in to further build an institution that would train not only electricians and enrolled nurses but also skilled professionals to meet high-value-added niche industry needs, such as biotech laboratory technicians, digital animators, digital media designers, games software engineers, marine offshore technicians, avionics technicians, performing arts technicians, and a host of other people whose jobs did not exist until very recently. Also, and far more important, by the time Poh took over, Singapore was on the verge of becoming one of the world's leading centers of VET. ITE had already begun consolidating its smaller campuses into new, very modern, sophisticated postsecondary college campuses and had completely revamped and upgraded the curricula and services of the institution. The first of the new ITE mega-campuses had been completed under the leadership of Law Song Seng. Under Poh's leadership, two more were developed so that all regions of Singapore could be served by ITE. Though these institutions are different from one another and have somewhat different program emphases, they are not independent from each other. As the motto states, "One ITE System, Three Colleges." The first, opened in 2005, was ITE College East. ITE College West opened in 2010, and ITE College Central opened in December 2012. The model of close industry partnership first pioneered by the EDB has continued unabated under Poh. ITE counts among its almost one hundred industry partners global players like ABB, Cisco, Conrad Centennial, Hewlett Packard, IBM, Microsoft, Rolls Royce, Siemens, Singapore Airlines Engineering, and Yokogawa. And just as it was the case in the original EDB institutes, and then in the polytechnics that were modeled on them, ITE requires its staff to return to industry for a relevant assignment for a minimum of three months. Poh put in place the Total System Capability Scheme when he assumed leadership, charging ITE faculty to remain up-to-date by demonstrating their ability to "Do or Lead" in consultancy or on industry projects. Those who don't do this cannot get promoted. About one hundred (6–8 percent) go overseas for this purpose; the rest are trained locally.

ITE thinks of its development trajectory as consisting of four phases of transformation. In the first phase, ITE 2000 (1995–99), ITE concentrated on developing the first class it aspired to and building the infrastructure and systems it would need to develop further. The blueprint was a very ambitious physical development plan. ITE called its second phase ITE Breakthrough (2000–04), signifying the passage to world-class status, and relying mainly on its global partnerships to get there. In this period that ITE created and implemented its Key Competencies Model, addressing Technical Competency (the technical skills and knowledge pertaining to the occupation being trained for), Methodological Competency (the ability to learn and work independently, with capabilities to plan, solve problems, and make decisions), and Social Competency (the ability to cooperate with others, share responsibility, and communicate effectively). It also created the Curriculum and Pedagogic Model, relating these three key competencies to the means for achieving them and putting a plan in motion to create a rich information technology environment to support the teaching and learning process, including especially the new eStudent Services and eTutor Systems.

ITE's third phase, ITE Advantage (2005–09), was when the first mega-campus, ITE College East, was opened. ITE was turning into a global force in VET. The fourth phase, ITE Innovate (2010–14), parallels the efforts in the schools, the economic development agencies, and the polytechnics to create the conditions under which Singapore will become known not just for its high competence but its creativity and innovative capacity as well. As in the polytechnics, this drive for creativity and innovation is making itself felt in both the content and the processes of education and training at ITE.

The evidence suggests that these ambitious plans and the enormous investment made in their implementation have paid off. In 1997, an independent survey of Singaporeans found that only 34 percent viewed ITE favorably. That figure had shot up to 69 percent by 2010. In 1995, ITE was capturing 18 percent of the secondary school cohort. In 2010, one-quarter of the cohort chose ITE as their postsecondary education option. In 1995, 61 percent of ITE's students graduated. By 2010, 83 percent of them graduated, and, on average, nearly 90 percent of ITE's graduates received job offers within six months of graduating. ITE had doubled the number of full-time students enrolled between 1995 and 2006. Not least important, over the last several years Singapore has registered some of the world's lowest youth unemployment rates.[9] The government succeeded in transforming the ugly duckling of its education system into an institution that many Singaporean youngsters are proud to go to, a place producing graduates businesses want to hire.

But Singapore aimed even higher. It wanted a world-class VET system, a system that would be admired by the world's leading industrial powers. And it got it. By 2010, the Organisation for Economic Co-operation and Development (OECD) was hailing it as "perhaps the best in the world."[10] *The Economist* said that, in ITE, "Singapore has created yet another centre of excellence."[11] But the recognition ITE is most proud of came from the United States. In September 2007, the Ash Center for Democratic Governance and Innovation at Harvard University's John F. Kennedy School of Government announced that ITE was the winner of the IBM Innovation Award in Transforming Government. ITE was recognized as a model program in improving vocational and technical education. The panel for the worldwide competition found that ITE had had a "profound impact on the social progress and economic growth of Singapore" and had "created a highly sustainable model for transforming poorly-performing educational institutions worldwide."[12]

In March 2011, in an article about Singapore, *The Economist* noted that "ITE—originally dubbed 'It's the End' by ambitious middle-class parents—was the dark side of Singaporean education . . . Since the 1990s, the government has worked hard to change ITE's image. It has not only spent a lot of money on new facilities and better teachers, but also put a great deal of thought into it . . . This attention to detail has paid off. Most of [the new graduates] are snapped up quickly . . . Singapore has created yet another centre of excellence."[13]

### VET Development Phase IV: SkillsFuture (2014 to Present)

In typical Singaporean fashion, the country's leaders did not rest on these laurels. Instead, they immediately set out to examine their systems, develop solutions for them, and look toward the kind of workforce development system they would need for the emerging economy. The government created a high-level commission called ASPIRE (Applied Study in Polytechnics and ITE Review) in late 2013 to develop recommendations for strengthening VET in Singapore. The commission was led by Deputy Prime Minister and Minister of Finance Tharman Shanmugaratnam and included several other cabinet ministers, CEOs of major corporations, and leaders of trades unions, among others. The commission's report was issued in August 2014 and set the country on a course to substantially upgrade its already-world-class VET system. The SkillsFuture Council, led by Shanmugaratnam and including leaders from business, labor, and government, was charged with overseeing the system.

The plan envisioned a coherent workforce-development system that would build on the existing system, beginning in middle school and extending throughout adulthood. For young people, it would include strengthened education and career guidance, "enhanced" internships, more overseas market immersion opportunities, and the development of individual learning portfolios. For those starting work, it would include apprenticeships, or "learn and earn" programs, and credits toward course fees for work skills–related instruction. And for adults, it would include monetary awards for skills courses, subsidies for midcareer professionals pursuing additional coursework, and fellowships. In designing their plan, the ASPIRE commission benchmarked world-class VET systems, such as those of Switzerland, Germany, and Denmark. And while they did not adopt those systems wholesale, the principles behind them informed their thinking—exactly what benchmarking should do. The new system's commitment to guidance is significant. Singapore has had a career guidance curriculum for primary grades students since 2012 and added one for secondary students in 2014. Under the new plan, the Ministry of Education created a web portal that allows students to examine their own strengths and interests and find careers that might appeal to them. In addition, the ministry deployed education and career guidance counselors in schools to help advise students about their options. For students in ITE and polytechnic courses, a minimum of forty to sixty hours across two years (for ITE students) and three years (for polytechnic students) are set aside for education and career guidance. Counselors are also available in those institutions. According to Bruce Poh, the ASPIRE recommendations reflected both a recognition of the shortcomings of the existing system and the needs of the changing economy. The existing system produced "leakage": although students are trained for particular skills, they often left that field or took jobs in other areas.[14] At the same time, industry was changing, and it was no longer sufficient to prepare young people in a single set of skills. People needed lifelong learning so that they could adapt to a changing workforce. This recognition also reflected a growing maturity in the Singaporean economy. As Poh noted, "Our government believes that companies could do better in terms of productivity and innovation. In the past, many companies in Singapore employed cheap foreign and semi-skilled labor, which yield low productivity. The government has put a limit on the influx of foreign labor, so that companies will employ more local trained manpower, and with these, work towards improving productivity."[15]

Implementing the ASPIRE recommendations has posed some challenges. Unlike European countries, Singapore has no tradition of apprenticeship, so putting in place the enhanced internships has required convincing both young people and employers that they are worthwhile. The country has elected to do so in two ways. First, they elected to craft it as an extension of the training program, rather than as a stand-alone apprenticeship, to reassure parents who might worry that students are not getting a full education. Second, they agreed to provide hefty subsidies to students and to employers: S$5,000 to students to sign on to the program and S$15,000 to companies to offset costs of training. The plan for lifelong learning faces challenges as well. In other countries, efforts to encourage adults to pursue skills development have often run aground because many adults are reluctant to shift into a new field.

Yet, Poh believes the country is in a good position to succeed, and Singapore's track record suggests he might be right: "The government's approach to solving problems starts by putting ourselves in a position of strength, and then makes a long-term strategic plan. Don't wait until you have a weak economy to fix things because then it will be harder to fix. Although the ruling party lost a few seats, they are still a big majority in the government. Because of this stability in government, they can make tough choices."[16]

## A SNAPSHOT OF THE WHOLE SYSTEM TODAY

Because it is easy to get lost in the detail of this portrait of the development of the Singaporean VET system, it's important to look at the structure of the system as it is experienced by students flowing through it. Singaporean children start their formal education at age six. They generally spend six years in primary school and then another four or five in secondary school. Then, at age sixteen or seventeen, they sit for their General Certificate of Education (GCE) exams, after which they have three options (see figure 1.2). (The reference to the GCEs is not a reference to the standard GCEs offered to countries outside the United Kingdom by the University of Cambridge but, rather, to customized GCEs that Singapore contracted with the University of Cambridge to produce to standards higher than those of the regular GCEs.)

About 25 percent of the cohort leaving compulsory education enrolls in two-year junior colleges, the primary route to university. About 40 percent enroll in one of the five polytechnics (Singapore Polytechnic, Ngee Ann Polytechnic, Temasek Polytechnic, Nanyang Polytechnic, and Republic Polytechnic); another 25 percent go to the ITE. Thus, a total of about 65 percent pursue some form of VET. But, within ten years of leaving ITE, about half of the graduates go back to school, most of them to the polytechnics for a diploma. And a significant fraction of polytechnic graduates go on to university, either right after they get their diploma or at some later time.

In the polytechnics, full-time students typically pursue a diploma, normally a three-year program of study. In the ITE, students are seeking a Nitec (National ITE Certificate) qualification, a Higher Nitec qualification, a Master Nitec qualification, or a diploma. The Nitec and Higher Nitec are regular two-year programs for full-time students. The newer Master Nitec is given to students with a regular Nitec plus three years of relevant work experience in a program that is run in collaboration with participating employers (roughly equivalent to Germany's Meister qualification). There are three new Technical Diplomas offered by the ITE: Machine Technology, in collaboration with the German Ministry of Education, Youth, and Sports, in Baden-Württemburg; Automotive Engineering, also in collaboration with the Ministry of Education, Youth, and Sports; and Culinary Arts, in collaboration with the Institut Paul Bocuse of France. Most of these diploma programs take two years to complete.

This is a relentlessly meritocratic system. The options available to a student at any given point in their progression through the system are a function of how well that student has performed thus far. A student who is admitted to ITE or one of the polytechnics on the basis of their prior performance cannot choose any program they wish when they are admitted. Some programs within these institutions are much more difficult to get into than others. The number of slots available in each sector is not a function of consumer demand, as is the case in many other countries. The National Manpower Council, chaired by the Minister for Manpower and including participants from many key government agencies, such as the Ministry of Education, the

## FIGURE 1.2 The Singapore education system

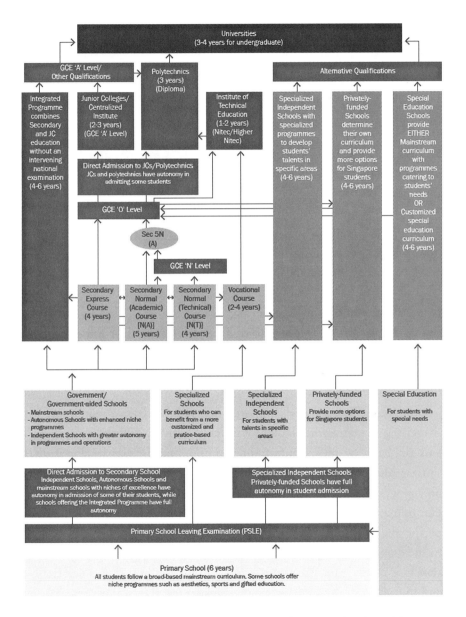

Source: Center on International Education Benchmarking, National Center on Education and the Economy.

Ministry of Trade and Industry, the EDB, the Public Service Commission, and others, analyzes and projects Singapore's manpower requirements into the future and serves as the arena in which all the relevant agencies will align their strategies to meet those projected needs. The allocation of slots to the various education and training institutions and to sectors within these institutions is a function of this process.

In January 2013, there were 102 ITE programs, which the National Manpower Council divided into eleven sectors. It allocated slots to the sectors and ITE and then decided how to allocate these sectoral slots to the programs. This process has produced a kind of market within the education and training institutions in which highly desired slots can command a high price in terms of the qualifications required to qualify for entrance into a program. Thus, the government does not tell anyone what occupation they can or must pursue; but the process aligns the number of slots available to train in any given occupation with projections of the number of positions that will be available in that occupation, and it sets the level of qualification required to get training in that occupation.

It is important to point out that the government does not simply ask employers what they think they will need in the future. Singapore's government is trying to shape the pattern of that need by being able to offer highly qualified candidates in areas in which it would like Singapore to have a strong industrial presence. Projected demand will have a role, but it will shape that demand with supply in order to provide Singapore as a whole with the best possible economic opportunities. In this way, the allocation of slots within the Singaporean education and training system is a vital part of Singapore's economic development system, and it plays an equally important role in that system as the provision of education and training itself.

The SkillsFuture plan builds on this system by helping link young people to the employment opportunities that are available. First, enhanced education and career guidance, from primary schools through the polytechnic and ITE, provide young people with information about career options and counseling to help them understand their options and what they need to do to pursue them. Second, the web portal enables young people to assess their own strengths and interests and match them to careers and then to develop an individual portfolio to show potential employers the skills they can demonstrate.

Performance on exams is the basis for selection for three-quarters of the ITE programs, with aptitude tests and interviews playing an additional role in the other quarter. Yet, the government has worked hard not simply to run a sorting system ("Too bad. You did not do well on your exams, so you're out") but to provide support for young people in school and for adults who have been in the workforce for many years to enable them to succeed ("You don't seem to be doing too well. Let's see if we can help you do better, much better"). Recently, in this vein, the Ministry of Education created specialized schools for the least capable of the graduates who will attend the ITE to give them extra help and attention for the four years of their secondary education, making available additional resources and support intended to increase their chances of success. Taken as a whole, ITE can be viewed as a very large effort to provide for the children in the bottom quarter of the distribution options, to give them the kind of support they need to become strong contributors to the economy and proud members of their society. The way the government looks at it, these people need the economic opportunity, and the economy needs their participation. The same is true of the myriad forms of support available to adults in the workforce who want to go back to school to improve their basic literacy and technical skills, namely the Basic Education for Skills Training, the Worker Improvement through Secondary Education programs, and the Workforce Skills Qualification System.

Under the SkillsFuture system, the learning and support does not end when young people enter the workforce. The individual learning portfolio will enable those midcareer to determine whether they have gaps in skills they need to fill to advance to another level or move to a different career. And the government will provide everyone twenty-five and older with a credit of S$500 to pursue additional learning—along with additional awards of S$5,000 for up to two thousand people annually thereafter. The government will provide additional financial support for skills development for older workers as well. The strong insistence on meritocratic selection combined with an equally strong determination to help everyone succeed at some level makes the system seem almost schizophrenic at times, at odds with itself. But it works in practice as a mechanism that continues to drive achievement up for every major group of Singaporean citizens.

The 2012 study trip ended with a round table conversation with a group of Singaporean business executives. They described Singapore as a great place to do business and had strong words of praise for the government— "Singapore is number one for bright people who think ahead, plan, and then orchestrate development. This is unique in Asia." The government, they said, has provided first-rate infrastructures of the kind business needs. "It's a well-oiled machine." They noted that the mining industry is considering coming to Singapore, even though there is nothing to mine; it will be a hub for buyers and sellers. Global companies, they said, "don't think of Singapore as a big market, but they come anyway for the talent and the tax benefits." According to these business leaders, Singaporeans are "good at operating with discipline, rigor, depth, and follow through." They have strong project management skills, multitask with efficiency, and work hard. Creativity in the Singaporean workforce "was weak up until 10 years ago, compared to the West," they said. At that time, the Japanese were more creative in design, but creativity is now up in Singapore. They noted, too, that while drive is up in China, in Singapore it is easier to find competent managers. The talent they have access to in Singapore, they told us, is as high quality as any they can find anywhere else in the world.

This kind of praise from leaders of some of the world's leading firms is, of course, what Lee Kaun Yew and the Economic Development Board were shooting for when Singapore began its long journey. But the workforce development system in Singapore is not without challenges. Nearly 20 percent of the population are not citizens. Many are highly educated and very talented people from other countries who are assigned to Singapore by their companies or come to Singapore looking for professional work. But a substantial portion are people who come from China, India, Malaysia, and Indonesia with very little education or skills looking for the low-wage work, or shift work, that Singaporeans no longer need or want to do. As in other parts of the world, in Singapore this new underclass is growing. Many people worry that as the middle class has grown in Singapore, and as the people in that middle class learn how to make sure that their children are positioned to get the best that society has to offer, there will be less and less mobility for those Singaporean citizens who are now at the bottom of the economic and social hierarchy. Others worry that Singapore has been remarkably successful at building an education and training system with very high average performance but not enough peak performance in global terms. They wonder whether Singapore will ever produce Nobel Prize winners or others who make truly remarkable contributions. In the same vein, they are concerned that Singapore has not yet produced any global companies or major new products.

Still, Singapore's accomplishments are truly remarkable. By the testimony of people in global firms with global brands whose job is to source the best people in the world for their firms, Singapore has accomplished what it set out to do all those years ago. It is producing world-class talent to meet the needs of every level and every sector of its now very diversified and very high-tech economy.

## WHAT CAN WE LEARN FROM THE SINGAPOREAN VET SYSTEM?

*A fierce determination to match the performance of the best in the world while constantly learning from the best in the world.* The relentless quality of the story of the development of Singapore's VET system is impressive. In part, the system is as good as it is because the Singaporeans would not settle for less than being the best. And they got there in no small measure because they are relentless benchmarkers. They drew heavily, for example, on Germany's Key Competencies Model and Dual System apprenticeship model. Their curriculum development process for VET was adapted from the DACUM model from the United States. The US was also an inspiration for the design of their health-care simulation center and design-thinking programs. The design of their diploma-level culinary arts program came from the Institut Paul Bocuse in France. The apprenticeship program followed the model of Switzerland. The Singaporeans systematically and continuously look the world over for the best examples they can find anywhere of successful policies and practices, and then they meld them with their own ideas in a unique configuration that fits their own circumstances, values, and aims.

*Good government.* One of the most important reasons Singapore was able to develop such a successful VET system was the quality of its government, which made smart decisions, one after another, for a long time. This is not an accident. Prime Minister Lee Kuan Yew decided early in the nation's independence that he could not succeed in his ambitious aims unless his government consisted of the best and brightest Singapore had to offer. He identified the most promising high school students and sent them, at government expense, to the finest universities in the world *if* they promised to return to help run his government. The top ministers in that government today make about S$2 million a year, which provides a strong incentive for those who could be top corporate executives to stay in government and also reduces the incentives for corruption. They are moved from ministry to ministry as they ascend the ladder, which eliminates the "postholes" that are usually present in the government workforce and creates a team that shares a common vision and is able to work closely with one another—not for their ministry, but for Singapore.

*Stability.* The People's Action Party (PAP) is the only party that has ever held office in Singapore. I am certainly no advocate of one-party government, but there can be little doubt that the government's ability to both lay and implement long-term plans is due in part to a confidence that it will be around to take credit for its accomplishments. When I asked the head of Singapore's teacher union why he chose to work with the PAP instead of playing one party against another, he said that he had no need to do that, that the door of the prime minister's office was always open to him, and the ministers, knowing that, were generally eager to solicit his views and pay attention to them. The PAP now gets about 60 percent of the vote. As long as this government continues to avoid corruption and to be reasonably responsive to the needs of its people, it is likely to remain in power, and the Singaporean people will likely continute to enjoy the benefits of a government that has a long-term outlook for education as well as other arenas.

*Step-by-step, aligned, coherent planning.* The current Singaporean VET system did not spring all at once from the head of Zeus. It proceeded in stages. At each stage, the system was coherent and aligned both internally and with the contemporary needs of the evolving Singaporean economy. The government did not try to make every major component of the system state-of-the-art at the same time but instead invested in cycles. In one five-year period, it was the vocational education system, in another the compulsory system, in another the polytechnics, and so on. But at every stage, everyone was at the table who needed to be at the table to make sure that the system was coherent, efficient, and pointed in the right direction. Around the metaphorical table were the Ministry of Education, Ministry of Trade and Industry, Ministry of Manpower, the EDB, and the Workforce Development Agency, as well as the people responsible for setting manpower targets, for setting qualification standards, for deciding on curriculum, for ensuring the quality of the system's human resources, for designing economic strategy, and so on. This created a culture in government that, at one and the same time, provided for an unusual degree of coordination and action at lightning speed.

*A strong link to the national economic development strategy.* Any VET program must be linked to national economic strategy to be successful. Singapore is a textbook case for how to do just that. First of all, Singapore has had, from day one, a sound long-range strategy of which the human resources component has been a very important part, and the government has laid out detailed plans for achieving it. Because the most senior officials have been deeply involved in creating and revising the strategy, including the human resources components, they have provided strong support for the nation's VET program whenever it was needed. But that was also because the VET program delivered. It delivered in part because the policy makers and top managers for the VET program had been deeply involved in making the economic development strategy and knew what they had to do to deliver what the government needed. The primary links between economic development policy and VET policy were formed by the EDB, the Ministry of Education, the Ministry of Trade and Industry, the Ministry of Manpower, and other manpower development systems. Countries interested in learning from the Singaporean system for linking VET to economic development would do well to look at the roles played by these institutions in relation to one another as the system evolved.

*A strong compulsory education system.* A senior officer in the Danish government once told me that "you cannot build a world-class VET system on a bed of sand." He meant, of course, that a VET system can be no better than the compulsory education system on which it is built. In this case, Singapore built a world-class compulsory education system, so the skills and knowledge of those in the lowest quarter of graduates, the students entering the ITE, measured above the median of the skills in the whole OECD student population. This gave Singapore's VET system a big leg up on success.

*The factory school model.* Though the ideas that underlie the VET system in Singapore came from all over the world, the factory school model came from Singapore. And it is a very powerful idea. Within the scope of one de facto policy, it enables Singapore to train its workforce to truly state-of-the-art standards, to engage industry as a close partner in training, and to allow students to train in an environment that is designed for training but, at the same time, is similar enough to the real thing to present challenges for the students very much like those they will face in the workplace. In many respects, it combines most of the advantages of a first-rate apprenticeship system with the advantages of a first-rate school-based VET system.

*A strong link to business.* Throughout the Singaporean VET system, it is clear that a great effort has been made to forge close links to business. The design of the apprenticeship system, the requirement for faculty members in the school-based system to work periodically in a firm in the same field in which that person teaches, the requirement for students to spend time working in firms, and the deep involvement of employers in advising the various VET institutions and programs and in setting occupational standards, assessing candidates for diplomas, providing state-of-the-art equipment for instruction, and advising on broad program direction all attest to the close ties with business that are a hallmark of Singapore's VET program.

*A determination to "rebrand" VET.* All advanced industrial economies, in varying degrees, are challenged by the low status of VET relative to other forms of education and training that provide access to high-status professional and managerial occupations. This may be especially true in Asian countries, where educational credentials are more closely tied to social status than is typically true elsewhere. In Singapore, in particular, where vocational education was for a very long time viewed as a dumping ground, the effort that government made to rebrand vocational education as a valued and respected option was desperately needed and remarkably successful. This was the result of both a very large investment of financial resources and a very carefully planned and well-executed rebranding campaign. Nations that have a similar problem would do well to study that campaign.

*A combination of meritocracy and support.* Singapore's system is fiercely meritocratic, but, at the same time, it strives very hard to provide extra support to students of all ages to succeed, to make the fullest possible use of whatever talents they have. This is not just a slogan. It is a persistent feature of their system. Expecting a lot, even from the young people who have shown the least academic ability, and then relentlessly providing both the financial and nonfinancial help they need to live up to those expectations, may be the secret weapon of the Singaporean VET system.

*A commitment to implementation.* The attention Singapore's government pays not just to making the right policies but to making sure that those policies are carefully and completely implemented is impressive. That holds for the VET system. The Singaporeans, it would seem, leave nothing to chance.

They have systems for everything. They have plans and timetables for everything. They think the work is just beginning—not ending—when the policies are approved. The hard work, they believe, is turning policy into action, and they work very hard at it. Studying how Singapore does this is important for any system hoping to match its results.

# CHAPTER 2

# GOLD STANDARD

### The Swiss Vocational Education and Training System

*Nancy Hoffman and Robert B. Schwartz*

Switzerland is a small country, with its roughly eight million inhabitants divided into twenty-six cantons (states). It has four distinct language groups—German (67 percent), French (23 percent), Italian (8 percent), and Romanish (1 percent)—and a handful of other spoken languages.[1] It is diverse linguistically and ethnically; nearly a quarter of Swiss students are born outside of Switzerland. In the world's oldest direct democracy, the presidency rotates among seven elected secretaries, and the Swiss vote on every imaginable type of public policy, far beyond anything we know in the United States. The Swiss maintain a very high standard of living while also having the lowest income inequality among the Organisation for Economic Co-operation and Development (OECD) countries, along with the four Nordic countries.[2] And while Switzerland was a founding member of the OECD, and in 1992 joined the World Bank, it is not a member of the European Union. Nor does it use the Euro. It has hosted the UN headquarters in Europe since 1966 but did not join until 2002. Most important for our purposes, Switzerland has, over the past twenty years, modernized its VET system in ways that have made it an international leader in educating youth and in maintaining its position as a world economic leader. And the two are connected.

In Switzerland, small and large companies, state-of-the-art factories, insurance agencies, banks, hospitals, retail stores, and child-care centers host sixteen-to-nineteen-year-old apprentices who serve customers, work on complex machines, carry out basic medical procedures, and advise investors—in short, they do everything an entry-level employee would do, albeit under the wings of credentialed trainers within the company. About 30 percent of Swiss companies, participants in the Swiss vocational education system, host this sort of "educational" employee. They rotate among three learning sites—workplace, intercompany courses, and school—over the three- or four-year period of their apprenticeship. Their learning is highly personalized; their interests and talents are at the core of their training, and options for further study and changes of course are encouraged. They get paid an average monthly starting wage that ranges from the Swiss equivalent of $400 to $700 in the first year, rising to around $1,100 to $1,200 by the time they are in their third year.[3] And they do productive work that returns the cost of training and a bit more to their employers, according to the studies of Stefan Wolter, managing director of the Swiss Coordination Centre for Research in Education and a professor of economics at the University of Bern.[4] In return, the Swiss have a talent pipeline of young professionals, youth unemployment in the single digits, and the highly skilled workforce needed to produce high-quality goods and services that sell well at high prices.

## THE STRUCTURE OF THE SWISS VET SYSTEM

To appreciate the role of VET in Switzerland, it is important to understand some basics about the structure of the larger Swiss education system (see figure 2.1). The first important feature is that compulsory education ends at grade 9, which marks the end of lower secondary school. While lower secondary schools are tracked in Switzerland, the curriculum is common for all students; the pace of delivery is what varies. Compulsory education in Switzerland gets strong results, as evidenced by performance on the 2015 Programme for International Student Assessment (PISA), especially in math, where Swiss scores were the highest in Europe. The compulsory education system is focused on the goal that all children get a solid foundation of core academic skills for whatever path they choose.

Another feature of Swiss education is its university system. As in most other countries in Europe, but unlike in the US, universities in Switzerland do not offer a broad general or liberal arts education. Rather, they provide a much more specialized education focused on preparing young people for a relatively narrow band of professions. A young person who wants to be a lawyer, a doctor, or a professor or who wants to conduct scientific or mathematical research attends a university. Students receive a strong enough general education in upper secondary school to enable them to proceed directly to professional studies. So for those studying to be doctors, for example, their medical studies begin immediately on entry to the university.

This means that as young students near the end of compulsory education and begin to think about their futures, their choice between two broad upper secondary options—academic and vocational—is influenced by their goals beyond high school. If they know they want to head toward one of the handful of occupations for which a traditional university education is required, and if their academic performance in lower secondary school was strong, then academic upper secondary school is the obvious choice. They need to be comfortable with the idea of spending the next six or seven years learning mostly in a classroom setting. If, however, they want the opportunity to choose from among 240 different occupations, running the gamut from the traditional trades and crafts to banking, insurance, IT, health and social care, dance, and pre-engineering, upper secondary vocational education is a very attractive option. Four features in particular make it especially attractive to many young people:

- it immediately puts young people in a setting with adults where they are treated differently than they are in a school setting or at home and are given significant responsibility coupled with lots of coaching and support;
- the learning is much more hands-on, contextualized, and applied so that academic concepts are made real;
- it pays students while they are learning a salary substantially below the Swiss minimum wage but very attractive for a teenager living at home; and

**FIGURE 2.1   The Swiss education system**

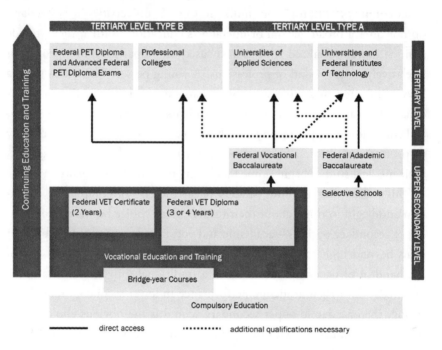

Source: SERI, "Vocational and Professional Education and Training in Switzerland 2018: Facts and Figures," https://www.sbfi.admin.ch/sbfi/en/home/services/publications/vocational-education-and-training.html.

- it provides students, on completion, with a nationally recognized qualification that is portable, which means they have the opportunity to move directly into full-time employment or continue on to get more education.

Given these two choices, it's not surprising that over 70 percent of Swiss students take the vocational route and only about 25 percent the academic course (about 5 percent go to work at the end of compulsory schooling or are supported in programs for youth with special issues).

Yet, to characterize this solely as a matter of student choice is not entirely accurate. As the rector of the Swiss Federal Institute of Technology in Zurich (ETHZ) told us, Swiss leaders are justifiably proud of the high quality of their universities and believe that enrolling more than 25 percent of students in that system might lead to a diminution in quality. There are three points at which access to the system is controlled: entrance to academic upper secondary, exit from upper secondary, and entrance into the second year of university study. Anyone with an academic diploma (*matura*) can enroll in a university; there is no entrance exam. But at the end of the first year, there is a rigorous exam; only about half of the entrants continue on to completion. This may be one more explanation for why so many students opt for the vocational route.

For those who do choose vocational education, the vast majority succeed in lining up a three- or four-year apprenticeship contract (which they sign with their parents) that leads to a Federal VET Diploma. Vocational students can get help finding apprenticeships from a local career guidance center, but all students learn in grades 8 and up about the labor market and how the availability of openings in the apprenticeship market signals which careers are growing and which are stagnant or declining. For those who don't succeed in signing an apprenticeship contract, either because of weak academic preparation (especially language skills) or an inability to make a choice, there are two options. One is the so-called tenth-year program, a transitional year in which students are given additional training and support in finding placement. Before the year is out, most of these students are counseled into starting a two-year apprenticeship. The second option is to go directly into a two-year apprenticeship. These opportunities, typically in less-demanding fields that are better suited for young people with a more practical inclination, lead to a Federal VET Certificate. But, in keeping with the systemic goal of permeability, a set of modules is available to qualify certificate holders to move on to a regular VET Diploma.

For students who are identified in lower secondary school as being at risk of dropping out or not making a successful transition into the VET system, the Swiss have put in place a case management system to provide individualized attention and support. There is a case management team at the cantonal level that includes staff from social service agencies, migration offices, and career centers, as well as from the education and training systems, who oversee the case management system, assign an appropriate lead staff person for each case, and track the progress of each young person. This strategy is designed to prevent any young person from falling through the cracks at the point of transition and throughout the next year. While these career centers are organized outside the education system, they do outreach in the schools as well as offer individual consultations to students and their families.

During a visit to a Zurich career guidance center, we saw how these centers are used by students and parents. The services they offer range from providing interest inventories, help with resumé-writing and portfolio development, and assistance in lining up "sniffing" opportunities, or short pre-apprenticeships to sample prospective sites. It is the student's responsibility to write the application for apprenticeship, and it is not uncommon for students to send out ten or more applications before landing an apprenticeship, since many are very competitive. The career counselors support students through this process, helping them persevere until they have found the right match.

Although the basic divide in the system is between the academic and vocational sides, one of the most impressive features is the number of crosswalks and points of transfer between the two sides (see figure 2.1). A growing number of students who start a three- or four-year apprenticeship decide to pursue, either simultaneously or with an additional year of study, a more applied version of the academic baccalaureate (the Federal Vocational Baccalaureate, often referred to as the Professional Bac). This diploma entitles students to admission to a university of applied sciences (UAS). These institutions, created in the 1990s, offer a wide variety of practical university-level education and training for students interested in becoming an architect, a psychologist, an engineer, a social worker, or a linguist, among other professions.[5] Students with the Professional Bac can also sit for an additional exam, the University Aptitude Test, which qualifies them to enroll in the more traditional university system if they choose. Students from the academic side can also transfer to a UAS, but only after they complete at least one year of full-time work; otherwise they are at a significant disadvantage as compared with other UAS students, all of whom have had at least a three- or four-year apprenticeship that gave them work experience.

Another impressive feature of the system is that there are two major options for students on the vocational side to get continuing professional education, even if they do not choose to pursue the path leading to a UAS. By far the most popular option is a competency-based set of exams in virtually all occupations that students can study for while they work. This option is pursued mostly by people with many years of work experience; the only requirement is that a candidate needs to be working at least part time. These exams lead to a Federal Professional Education and Training (PET) Diploma, which not only qualifies the holder for advancement in their chosen field but is considered a postsecondary degree (comparable to an associate degree in the US). For those seeking management positions in their sector, there is also an Advanced Federal PET Examination. In 2016, roughly 27,000 Swiss workers earned a PET degree, about half via the competency-based exam route.[6] For those who prefer to take courses rather than study on their own for a PET degree, there is a web of PET colleges overseen by the cantons— some private, some public—that offer preparation help, although this can be a more expensive option.

Yet another interesting feature of the Swiss education system, and where it differs from Germany's and Austria's, is that between half and two-thirds of apprentices leave the company where they were trained upon completion of their apprenticeship.[7] In fact, many companies encourage apprentices to move to new businesses; in exchange, they get an apprentice with equivalent general qualifications but also with knowledge from another firm that can benefit a new employer.

## ONE MISSION, THREE PARTNERS

"One Mission, Three Partners" sums up the political and structural under-pinnings of the Swiss system that, central to its strength, are encoded in law.[8] There is a clear division of responsibilities among the partners, all of which share a vision of what is best for the future of the Swiss economy and, most importantly, the healthy development of its young people.

The first partner is the federal government, generally referred to as the Confederation, whose role is to regulate and steer the system. There is a whole series of specific functions under that broad heading that are carried out through two governmental units: State Secretariat for Education, Research, and Innovation (SERI), the closest thing Switzerland has to a Ministry of Education, and the Swiss Federal Institute for Vocational Education and Training (SFIVET), a small, highly focused institute responsible for the basic and continuing training of all teachers in the VET and PET systems, including those based in firms and in interfirm training centers. SERI plays an especially important role in ensuring transparency and comparability of programs across the cantons, especially in its role overseeing the examination systems for both VET and PET. Both SERI and SFIVET play a key role in quality assurance across the system, and both ensure that the skills and knowledge of apprentices are not company specific but broad enough to enable students to "own" what they learn and transfer out of their apprenticeship company to another company in their sector. While the cantons are responsible for providing three-quarters of the public funding for the system, the Confederation is responsible for the other quarter.

The second critical partner is the employer organizations and associations. In an important sense, they are the drivers of the system. Not only do they decide the training content of VET and PET programs, since it is their industry standards that must be met, but they also take the lead in determining when new occupational programs need to be developed and when existing programs need to be closed down or radically revised, taking into account projected changes in the economy. This is a fundamentally different model than what is used in the United States, where it is the responsibility of schools, colleges, and other providers to take the lead in developing vocational program content, ideally with advice from industry. In Switzerland, both the government and the education community understand that their system works because it is designed to meet the needs of industry. One outcome of this decision is the enormous support the VET system gets from the employer community—the associations and the member companies that employ apprentices—which contributes about 60 percent of the total cost.

With member employers representing some 317,000 employees, Swiss-MEM, the association of mechanical and electrical engineering industries, is a useful example of an employer association that plays a key role in training the next generation of workers. The MEM industries represent the largest subsector of the manufacturing sector in Switzerland, accounting for more than 52 percent of manufacturing positions and 48 percent of industrial added-value jobs. They employ 11 percent of the nation's total workforce, including more than eight thousand apprentices. Furthermore, alongside the chemical-pharmaceutical industry, the MEM industries represent Switzerland's key export sector and account for 35 percent of its exports, totaling $51.264 billion in 2018.[9] SwissMEM represents the interests of the MEM industries to the Swiss government, national and international organizations, employee representative bodies, and the public and, as such, is an important economic and political player. It also acts as the MEM industries' service center. In its capacity as employer representative, SwissMEM negotiates the terms of the collective bargaining agreement for the MEM industries with the unions and sets the standards and training curriculum for members, 98 percent of which are small and medium-sized firms. Today, Swiss manufacturing is highly demanding, and much of the routine work is done outside of the country, so SwissMEM's mission to recruit and train the best technicians and engineers in the world is a top-priority challenge for the MEM industries.[10]

SERI and SFIVET work closely with industry associations in the development of the "ordinances" that define the curriculum frameworks, or "training plans," for entry into each of the 230 occupations for which there are apprenticeships. Each occupation has a qualification certificate that is attained through a final assessment and standardized across the country. As in other VET systems, key skills are categorized as knowledge, abilities or competencies, and attitudes or behaviors. The Swiss tripartite system has slightly different names for these skills and defines them in detail for each occupation:

- *technical or professional skills.* The content of the work and its application
- *methodological skills.* The ability to organize work efficiently, solve problems systematically, and improve how work is carried out
- *social skills.* Team work and conflict management; the abilities to acquire new knowledge independently and to interact professionally

The training plan breaks down each skill and specifies which are learned in the workplace, in interfirm training centers, or in the VET school, as well as how they are integrated, sequenced, and demonstrated. For example, while presentation skills are introduced in school, they are applied both in interfirm training centers and at the worksite, while principles of quality for an occupation are introduced in school but only applied in the interfirm training centers.

The employer associations also play a crucial role in working with their members to ensure that there are adequate numbers of apprenticeships offered each year to match the numbers of students seeking contracts. Because Swiss employers view the VET system as one that is designed to meet their long-term workforce needs, they neither expect nor receive any direct governmental subsidy for taking on an apprentice. They are aware that in addition to the benefit of having three or four years to support the development of a young person in their own work setting before having to make a longer-term hiring decision, the likelihood of hiring a worker who will be productive from day one is much greater than if they hire someone off the street. They also know, based on careful cost-benefit economic analysis, that for most employers the costs in apprentice wages and associated training expenses over three or four years are more than offset by the bottom-line increases in productivity provided by the apprentice. Participating Swiss employers tell visitors over and over that this is a classic win-win situation—it's good for both the firm and the young person.

The third partner in the Swiss VET system is the canton. The cantons—and, within them, the municipalities—are the decision makers: taxes are set locally, not by the federal government, and cantons have the primary responsibility for most services, including education. Consequently, the school component of the VET system is organized and run by the cantons. Each canton has a VET office that has broad responsibility for overseeing the implementation of VET programs. The cantons are also responsible for funding and operating the PET colleges and for funding and operating the network of career centers. They play an important role in marketing apprenticeship to the employer community and ensuring that firms which offer apprenticeships meet a national set of quality standards. Yet, because the employer associations are national, and because the federal government is responsible for standardization of processes for developing, revising, and supporting VET, there is sufficient counterbalance even with such a strong tradition of local, cantonal control.

## HOW STUDENTS EXPERIENCE VET

The Center for Young Professionals (CYP) is a short tram ride from Zurich's old city in a second-floor, handsome, light-filled refurbished foundry with restaurants and stores below.[11] Sixteen-to-nineteen-year-old vocational education students come here for initial orientation to the banking profession and then return periodically during their apprenticeship years for short courses as part of their upper secondary program. Founded in 2003 by five large banks (Julius Baer, Credit Suisse, UBS, Raiffeisen Switzerland, Surcher Kantonalbank) and funded by the Association of the Swiss Banking Industry, with twenty-seven member banks, CYP orients apprentices to the standards and practices of the entire banking industry.

Banking is one of twenty-one areas of specialization within the commercial sector. In the early 2000s, commercial training was restructured in response to a call for reform from employers based on the changes under way in an increasingly globalized market. Consequently, commercial training today promotes worker autonomy and "business process thinking" among its teen apprentices, who must learn to be reflective and to self-assess using a required "course journal." CYP introduces this approach in the banking industry while students go to regular school (for such topics as languages, math, specialized theory, and history) and work at a bank, where, in six-month rotations, they learn by doing, by testing theory in practice.[12] It defines itself as taking a "connected learning" approach, whereby the process of training is in the hands of the learner, not the teacher. Its pedagogic tenets replicate the requirements of the workplace and include learner autonomy, blended learning, problem solving, and teamwork in which learning is co-constructed among peers.

During a 2014 study trip to better understand the apprenticeship system, we visited CYP and saw these principles in action. The students all had tablets from which they could download course materials, and, throughout the building, small groups of students gathered to solve problems together. When we pulled aside at random two first-year apprentices, they were unequivocal in their belief that they were much better off participating in CYP than spending more time sitting in classrooms at an academic high school. Now that they had seen what they would be doing in the industry, they said, they planned to earn the Professional Bac and, after working for a while, earn an advanced degree at a UAS.

There is a slightly different routine for teenagers who start their training at the Lernzentrum Industrielle Berufslehren Schweiz (LIBS), a VET center for the manufacturing industry that is conveniently located just across the parking lot from ABB Turbocharger and next to the VET school where students complete the academic and theoretical requirements for upper secondary. Just as CYP partners work with the Swiss Bankers Association to design competence standards, curriculum, and assessments and keep up with member needs, LIBS is one of several training partners of SwissMEM. LIBS is technically a nonprofit club to which member companies belong. Under contract to train for 90 companies, LIBS works with about 1,100 of the more than 8,200 young people under training in MEM industries at a cost per student for four years of over $105,000. This cost is on the very high end because of the state-of-the-art equipment required for training.

LIBS trains in the fields of manufacturing, automation, and electronics and prepares students to be computer technicians, commercial employees, engineering designers, and logisticians. During our visit, we found the students working at LIBS and in the ABB factory next door to have high levels of professionalism. Standing at their machines, they could readily present an account of the work they did, why it was important to the company, and why they chose LIBS. One student told us how he had started learning to work on CNC machines but showed an interest in CAD and was now working a floor above the machines and using his talent for design.

Swiss students entering the popular social care sector also work as apprentices. Bildungszentrum Interlaken (BZI) is an impressive vocational school training for occupations as diverse as electronics, elder care, hospitality, and construction. BZI students begin their elder care training, for instance, in a nursing home, where they attend to Alzheimer residents and other elderly people with serious health conditions. While young people in the United States might volunteer in such a place, they would not be entrusted with drawing blood to test a diabetic's blood sugar, taking blood pressure, identifying and distributing medications, and helping a severely impaired resident get their daily exercise. The facility's staff took pride in the apprentices; managers talked about the competence and joy the young people brought to their practice.

## HOW DID THE SYSTEM EVOLVE?

Understanding how the Swiss devised such a unique education system, one so responsive to the developmental needs of adolescents and that serves the needs of employers and the Swiss economy, requires undoing one of the persistent myths about the Swiss vocational education system—that its current structures were inherited from the guilds of medieval times and have existed ever since. This faulty "history" has led to the unfortunate conclusion that these structures are so deeply embedded in Swiss culture and tradition that their characteristics cannot possibly be adapted or their features replicated elsewhere.

A form of vocational training was practiced in medieval times and up through the eighteenth century throughout most European countries. Guilds controlled entry into the trades, and skilled masters passed on their knowledge to apprentices or journeymen who gained entrance. But by the end of the eighteenth century, as capitalism developed, guilds became a target rather than a supporting structure for industrialization because they restricted entry into professions and were often seen as conservative rather than innovative forces, impediments to the freedom to practice a trade of one's choosing. Whether guilds are seen as outmoded institutions left over from feudalism or regarded as the foundation for modern trade unions and employer associations, their presence in medieval Europe does not explain the success and particular design of the Swiss vocational system of the twentieth and twenty-first centuries.[13] The more appropriate context for Switzerland's current VET system lies in paths taken and decisions made over the last century.

Several characteristics, namely the heterogeneity of its population, its neutrality in foreign policy, and its grassroots democracy, set a context for the development of its VET system in the twentieth century. A very small country with no natural resources but water, Switzerland sits at the center of the European continent. Despite being landlocked, merchants, travelers, and merchandise have always had to pass through its mountains to move from one European market to another, making it both a stopping place for foreigners and a home to immigrants and refugees. And with a very small domestic market, it has had to sell its goods abroad. In his study of the great Swiss industrialist families and companies, R. James Breiding makes the point that "most prominent entrepreneurs were not Swiss at all," and some arrived as impoverished immigrants.[14] Henri Nestlé was a German political refugee; Charles Brown of Brown Boveri was from the UK; Nicolas Hayek of Swatch is Lebanese; and Zino Davidoff, of cigar fame, was a Russian Jew. And so on. The point is that Switzerland has had to accommodate multiple cultures and languages over centuries, and in so doing it has created a diverse culture that works, particularly on the business side. As Breiding points out, in corporate mergers, Swiss entrepreneurs have a reputation for melding diverse corporate cultures more successfully than most other nationals.

A second distinctive feature of Switzerland is its neutral foreign policy, which has allowed it both to avoid the devastation of war and function as the supplier of goods and services to other countries when their markets were disrupted by conflict, a lucrative though not always palatable endeavor. (The Nazis were controversial consumers of Swiss goods during World War II.[15]) Nor did it ever have colonial pretensions. It profited from the great wars of the twentieth century and avoided devastation. The Swiss also seem to have made a bargain about the minimalist role of a central government and the benefit of making most decisions locally; they have opted for maximum individual freedom, but the trade-off is active engagement in governing themselves responsibly.

The transition from the nineteenth-century guild system to a national apprenticeship system began with a vote in 1908 by the Swiss electorate in favor of a proposal that the federal government be empowered to regulate the trades. This ultimately led to the passage of the first federal law on VET in 1930. This law drew heavily on cantonal legislation already in place and regulated the duration of vocational programs in industry, the hotel and restaurant sector, commercial training, and the crafts, as well as the assessment of vocational students and master craftsmen. It was also the first VET law that responded to the early-twentieth-century's suffrage movement, opening vocational training to women (though it took until 1970 for Swiss women to get the vote).[16]

The 1930s law that marked the nationalization of VET in Switzerland did not immediately lead to a substantial increase in VET enrollment. In 1935, only about 40 percent of male graduates and 20 percent of female graduates went beyond compulsory school to enter vocational education. But after World War II, in the 1950s, Switzerland experienced a phase of continuous economic growth that lasted, with few minor interruptions, until the early 1990s.

The second phase of legislation on vocational education and training was developed in the 1960s to cope with a rising number of VET students. The new law determined that vocational education should prepare young people not only for a profession but for a more comprehensive education, including general education, and it should enable the apprentices to become entrepreneurs and managers, one of the distinguishing characteristics of today's VET system. The vocational education sector expanded rapidly over the next two decades, and today there are more than 60,000 apprentices in VET programs.

A third phase, enacted on January 1, 1980, introduced several innovations to improve the VET system. One was a third learning site, the interfirm training company, where practical skills and orientation to an occupation could be learned in a setting outside of the shop floor to alleviate the burden of foundational training falling on employers. The law obligated VET teachers and trainers to attend a specific preparatory course, an important step toward professionalizing the VET system. Several options for weak students were created out of an increasing awareness of the importance of providing every young person with a minimum education that would enable them to perform in an increasingly complex labor market.

While VET development in the early twentieth century was not out of keeping with what was going on in education and training across Europe, beginning in the 1960s and 1970s the Swiss made a series of decisions that did not reflect trends elsewhere. As other countries were expanding academic upper secondary and access to higher education (especially bachelor's degree programs), the Swiss stayed on course and continued development of VET. Switzerland suffered a lengthy recession in the 1990s in large part due to the high value of the Swiss franc, and while the economy recovered in the late 1990s, there were substantial layoffs, and companies were forced to restructure. Unemployment rose from virtually zero to just above 5 percent, a number that would be positive in other countries but was a warning to the Swiss, who were accustomed to almost full employment and hadn't seen a number like 5 percent since the 1930s.[17]

The decisions made by Swiss leaders during this period shaped the VET system as it stands today. Instead of expanding academic programs in the 1990s, the Swiss enhanced the general education component of VET and planned and launched the Federal Vocational Baccalaureate and the UAS system. It is also important to note that the "modern" apprenticeships of today—in health, the social sector, agriculture, forestry, and arts—were only added in the most recent revision of the VET law in the early twenty-first century.[18] These decisions reflected a knowledge of the kind of labor force needed to fuel the Swiss economy: highly skilled, proud, professionally trained technicians who would come out of the VET system and go on to hone even greater applied skills in the UAS and then on to partner with the small number of researchers, entrepreneurs, and inventors who graduated from universities, making for a culture of collaboration and innovation.

## CEOS' VIEWS OF THE VET SYSTEM

During our 2014 study tour of the Swiss VET system, we visited with Lino Guzzella, then the rector of the Swiss Federal Institute of Technology and now its president. We also met with a group of CEOs of major companies at the 2014 Swiss Economic Forum in Interlaken. Their views of the factors underlying Switzerland's economic success and the role VET has played in it generally confirm the historical analysis. But the CEOs' unique voices add a dimension of special interest, since they are participants in and the end users of the VET system, and several of them are products of it. These distinguished CEOs from such companies as Price Waterhouse, UBS, the Swiss postal service, and Alpiq (an electrical power producer) see the VET system as one among four or five interconnected factors that have resulted in Swiss business success.

Perhaps the most striking theme from ETHZ rector Guzzella and the CEOs is that because Switzerland is a very small country with no mineral resources to extract, process, and sell, it can only flourish economically by being number one, two, or three in everything it produces. It *must* produce the highest-quality services (including education) and material goods. While the VET system doesn't guarantee such an outcome, it makes a major contribution to it. As Guzzella remarked, "In the United States you have the same brilliant innovators in research and development as we have here in Switzerland, but here the lab technician can make prototypes to specification that are higher quality than anywhere in the world. PhD students have highly trained and respected technicians who can do what's asked right, better, and faster than anyone else." Swiss leaders across the sectors have decided that the only way for Switzerland to maintain its high standard of living is to compete with other countries not on the basis of costs but on the basis of skills. At all levels of the system, the focus is on investing in the skills of its current and future workforce.

In 2013, INSEAD and the Adecco Group published the results of the first-ever analysis across 103 countries of how nations approached the challenge of human talent development. To conduct this analysis, the researchers constructed a comprehensive Global Talent Competitiveness Index. With forty-eight indicators, Switzerland ranked first across all levels of the talent pipeline, including initial vocational education and training. It has remained first every year.[19] The CEOs made similar points about the Swiss commitment to quality, efficiency, and competitiveness. Speaking to its small domestic market and its lack of natural resources, and thus having to focus on customers outside of Switzerland, Hans Hess, president of SwissMEM, noted that "over and over we Swiss have had to prove we can be competitive, and we are." Jasmin Staiblin, the CEO of Alpiq Holding AG, and one of the few women CEOs in Switzerland, added, "When I worked in manufacturing, I thought it was best to work in the highest cost country because you know you are the most competitive . . . The highest cost puts so much pressure to be better than the rest . . . It's also about the efficiency. The country is very, very efficient because they can get the right skills."

The CEOs had a list of factors they felt contributed to the Swiss economic success, among them: political stability; democracy; a governmental guiding economic framework that provides industry with great flexibility; a good mix of small, medium, and large companies and a wide mix of services and products; its own currency (not the Euro); a free flow of people, including immigrants; and close cooperation between industry and universities. But they all agreed that the vocational education system was among the very top factors. Valentin Vogt, chairman of Burckhardt Compression and president of the Confederation of Swiss Employer Associations, said:

The academic and the VET system *is* the education system—not one, but both. Unlike some other countries, Switzerland isn't moving to increase the numbers in academics. You would have the wrong mix, and it would lower standards for both types. The Swiss economy is based on the VET system; two-thirds of students go to apprenticeships after compulsory school, while 20 percent to 30 percent go to academic upper secondary schools.[20] It is a public-private partnership: companies pay for apprentices and government pays for school and associations provide the profiles of the jobs and provide mentors. If any of the three is missing, the system wouldn't work. It is at scale.

He then he added a refrain that we heard from almost all the adults involved in the VET system: "It is hard for fifteen-year-olds to grow up. But in the Swiss system, young people work with adults that they respect, and it helps them become good Swiss citizens and efficient, productive employees."

To confirm the centrality of VET, these major global players provided data about their own routes to the corner office, as well as about the educational attainment mix among their employees. They demonstrated that, in contrast to similarly successful US companies, the bachelor's degree is not the screen to get an interview at one of these firms. Among the SwissMEM companies, for example, according to an interviewee, in 2014 about 10 percent had a research university degree; another 15 percent started as apprentices and then, after working for a while, completed a degree at a UAS; 55 percent had an apprenticeship as a base but may have gone on for further VET; 5 percent had only the apprenticeship; and about 15 percent had not completed the full apprenticeship or had just finished compulsory school. At the postal service, for instance, about 10 percent had academic degrees, but most of these employees started as apprentices, as did the 80 percent who went on to get UAS degrees.

Lukas Gaehwiler, president of UBS Switzerland, told us that he started as an apprentice and then went on to get a UAS degree. He reported that of UBS's 22,000 employees in Switzerland, only 10 percent had "a straight academic degree"; another 20 percent had degrees from a UAS; and 8 percent finished only compulsory school. In 2014 about 1,800 employees were in training, of whom about two-thirds were apprentices; the rest were either getting graduate degrees or in company-designed training to help drop-outs from upper secondary or UAS to complete their degrees. Gaehwiler explained the bank's training philosophy regarding dropouts:

> It's not easy to find good people. All of the dropouts, or at least 95 percent, get a diploma or degree while they are training with the bank. This is our safety net for dropouts—to make sure they finish and get a degree. The best 20 per-cent get an additional year of training that includes a three-month assignment abroad. If you give those incentives to apprentices, it is ten times more likely that they will stay with the bank as university grads. We understand that 65 percent don't drop out because of bad grades; they are just sick of school and want to be more independent.

There is additional pressure on the Swiss VET system today to educate all young people to a high enough level so all can contribute to the economy. Like other OECD countries, Switzerland is an aging society. The proportion of young people (under age 20) fell from 40.7 percent in 1900 to 26 percent in 2017, while the proportion of older people (age 64 and over) rose from 5.8 percent to 18 percent during that same period. And it's estimated that in the coming years the proportion of people aged 65 and older will grow steadily and by 2050 will represent 28 percent of the entire population. This means that there will be 51 people at retirement age for every 100 people at working age.[21] So, providing every young person with skills and experiences that are relevant to the labor market is key to the future of Switzerland.

## LOOKING AHEAD: STRENGTHS AND CHALLENGES

The Swiss VET system is well supported by employers, who see it as their obligation to help prepare young people for productive and meaningful employment. The system also makes economic sense for employers, pro-viding them with further incentive to participate. Apprenticeships provide hands-on and applied learning opportunities that give students real work responsibilities with plenty of coaching and adult support. This is an attrac-tive learning option and why so many Swiss students choose a vocational route. The Swiss system also intentionally provides a number of "crosswalks" and points of transfer to allow students to move seamlessly between academic and vocational studies, as well as from VET on to higher education at a UAS. This feature helps motivate students to keep pursuing further education and advanced qualifications.

At the end of our discussion with Swiss employers, we asked them about potential threats to the continuing strength of the economy and to the VET system, which they all saw as an essential contributor to that strength. The changing demographics are one threat, they noted, as are shifts in the interests of young people. Today, there are more apprenticeships offered than there are young people to fill them, with as many as ten thousand vacancies. There are some patterns that require attention. Occupations such as architecture, construction, crafts, health and social services, IT, agriculture, and manufacturing have more applicants than places, while some branches of the commercial sector are lacking applicants.[22]

Another potential threat they cited is the growth of an anti-immigration faction coming from both the far Right and the environmentalist party, Ecopop, which is committed to combating overpopulation and preserving natural resources. While the Swiss surprised themselves by passing legislation (barely) in early 2014 to limit immigration to sixteen thousand admittances a year, in a subsequent referendum nearly three-quarters of voters rejected this quota, leaving the matter open to further debate. After three years of negotiations with the EU, Switzerland resolved the issue in 2017 by giving preference in certain employment situations to workers already residing in Switzerland. But other anti-immigrant plebiscites are in the offing. In this nation of immigrant industrialists and entrepreneurs, for the business leaders we spoke with, this is a major concern. They feared that if the doors to immigration were closed, they would not have the workforce they need in the coming decades. This may yet come to pass.[23]

But perhaps the greatest fear expressed by employers as well as VET educators is that, over time, Swiss parents will succumb to the view that their children, whatever their talents and interests, will be better served by pursuing an upper secondary academic pathway leading to a traditional university degree than by taking the VET pathway. Germany, with perhaps the best known and most admired apprenticeship system, now has fewer than 50 percent of young people choosing that option. There is currently no sign that this fear will be realized in Switzerland. For while the number of young people has declined, the percent choosing the apprenticeship system remains stable.

 The Swiss system represents the gold standard in vocational education and training. A major source of its strength is derived from being the mainstream system, the way most young people make the transition from school to working life. It offers proof that it is possible to design a system that can simultaneously meet the needs of a highly developed, innovative economy and the vast majority of young people. The public- and private-sector partners that drive the system aggressively communicate its successes to successive generations of Swiss parents. And, undoubtedly, the status and value of the apprenticeships have been helped by increasing attention from a multitude of countries wanting to adapt or replicate the Swiss vocational education system.

## CHAPTER 3

# MADE IN CHINA

## Challenge and Innovation in China's Vocational Education and Training System

*Vivien Stewart*

Since Premier Deng Xiaoping opened up the People's Republic of China to the outside world in 1978, China has leapt from being a poverty-stricken rural society to the second-largest economy in the world. And it is only a matter of time, and the subject of intense speculation, as to when it will become the largest. The "Made in China" label has become ubiquitous as China has become the de facto manufacturing workshop of the whole world, fueling three decades of high rates of economic growth. China also has some of the world's most modern infrastructure, from the spectacular skyscrapers of Pudong, to high-speed Maglev trains, to modern airports, to thousands of miles of new highways. More than five hundred million Chinese have moved into the middle class over the past twenty-five years, with all the accoutrements of middle-class life—homes, televisions, computers, and cars. Yet, just ten years before Deng Xiaoping's momentous move, China had utterly destroyed its education system during Mao's Cultural Revolution. But from a standing start after the Cultural Revolution, China has powered more than three decades of spectacular economic growth. So where did the skills come from to build this economic juggernaut?

The Chinese economy is now at another inflection point. Its astounding growth over the past thirty-plus years has been substantially based on low-cost, low-skill manufacturing for export. But the US banking crisis of 2008, which shook the whole world, revealed the dangers of China's over-reliance on an export-dependent growth model, and the rising cost of labor in the great eastern cities has made this model increasingly unviable. The frenetic pace of development has come at great cost in terms of economic imbalances, regional and social inequalities, and environmental destruction. China needs to transform its economic model and the government has, in fact, announced that it wants to move from an economy based on low-cost, low-skill exports to one based on services, consumer demand, agricultural modernization, higher-value-added products, and innovation. But does China have the skills necessary to build this new economy?

China has the largest population and largest labor force in the world. It has been highly successful in rapidly expanding both secondary and higher education to a significant portion of the youth cohort. Indeed, Shanghai topped the world in reading, math, and science achievement of fifteen-year-olds on the Programme for International Student Assessment (PISA) in 2009 and 2012. But the success of fifteen-year-olds in Shanghai masks the fact that the overall level of knowledge and skills in the Chinese labor force is extremely low. In 2010, only 4 percent of the adult labor force was considered highly skilled, and only half of the 140 million workers in urban enterprises was classified as skilled.[1] Moreover, educational opportunities and standards across China are highly uneven. China has abundant labor power, but it will need a far more skilled and productive labor force to meet its goals of developing an advanced, high-income economy and society. It is therefore designing a new approach to human capital, including a major focus on developing a modern vocational education and training (VET) system.

Generalizing about China writ large is dangerous. It is a vast country of 1.35 billion people.[2] It is both an advanced industrial society and a third world economy. It is a country of enormous contrasts, with prosperous rapidly growing mega cities abuzz with new cars and high-end department stores and also with vast poor rural areas from which millions of people seek escape by moving to the cities. Based on a series of visits in 2013 and 2014 to schools, vocational colleges, Chinese and foreign-invested firms I made with the research team of Marc Tucker, Nancy Hoffmann, and Betsy Brown-Ruzzi, and subsequent exchanges with Chinese researchers and government officials, this study focuses on the most advanced provinces, where the future of China's skill development and innovations in technical education can most easily be seen. But away from the advanced coastal cities, much of China's vast rural hinterland is still primarily devoted to low-productivity agriculture. The study examines the success of China's unique dual-track, export-led economy from 1978 until 2009 and explains where the skills came from to build this economic powerhouse. It also describes the turning point China now faces and the reasons why its economic model going forward will require far higher levels of skill and productivity. This is the context in which China is trying to develop a modern VET system.

While China's VET system is lacking in many respects, its recent history has shown that when China decides to tackle an education problem, it has the determination and drive to accomplish it. China faces some unique circumstances, but many of the problems it faces are similar to those of other countries trying to create new economies for the twenty-first century. I compare China's current VET system to the best practices of the world's most advanced systems to which it aspires. Therefore, this study will be of broad-ranging interest to any country interested in creating a twenty-first-century VET system.

## CHINA'S ECONOMIC DEVELOPMENT

For much of recorded history, China was one of the most advanced countries in the world. Economic historians have estimated that in the early nineteenth century the Chinese Empire may have accounted for as much as one-third of the global GDP.[3] It was responsible for several breakthrough inventions, such as gunpowder, the compass, and paper and printing, and the accounts of European visitors in the seventeenth and eighteenth centuries marveled at its large and prosperous cities. But the discovery of the New World and the Industrial Revolution led Europe to far outpace China, and by the mid–nineteenth century it was seen as a backward, agrarian society. In fact, from the mid-1800s on, due to the Qing dynasty's internal weaknesses and inability to adapt to modern times and invasions by European powers (starting with the Opium Wars of 1840), China suffered a century and a half of economic decline, humiliation, and exploitation by foreign powers. China was forced to sign what it regarded as unequal treaties with twenty other countries and was reduced to a quasi-colony.

During this period, generations of Chinese thinkers and leaders dreamed of and wrestled with different ideas about how to overcome China's backwardness and poverty, to catch up with the West, and to restore prosperity and strength (*fuqiang*) to China.[4] In 1911, Sun Yat-sen overthrew the imperial Qing dynasty, and the next forty years were marked by political instability, civil war between the Nationalists and the Communists, and invasion and occupation by Japan. Eventually, in 1949, Mao Zedong defeated the Nationalists and established the People's Republic of China. He threw out the occupying foreign powers and united the country. However, Mao's economic policies of prioritizing heavy industry and collectivizing agriculture were disastrous. It's estimated that more than forty-five million people died during the Great Leap Forward in the 1950s, and during the Cultural Revolution (1966–76) schools and universities were closed and millions of educated people were sent to the countryside. At that point, China's share of global GDP had dropped to less than 5 percent.[5] But since 1978, after more than a century of decline, civil war, occupation, socialist revolution, and isolation, China has experienced thirty-plus years of extraordinary economic growth. How did this come about?

### The Thirty-Year Miracle, 1978–2010

In 1978, Mao's successor, Deng Xiaoping, initiated a period of "reform and opening up"—the Open Door Policy—hoping to lift China out of its poverty and backwardness by learning from more advanced countries such as Japan, the United States, and European nations. Realizing that China was at least forty years behind the world's most advanced countries in economic and education terms, he called on China's leaders to "emancipate their minds" and "seek truth from facts."[6] The more pragmatic approach to economic development embraced by Deng had no master strategic blueprint. Instead, over a period of three decades, China slowly shifted from a solely state- and centrally controlled economy to a dual-track economy with an increasing role for the market.

The first developments were in agriculture, where the control was gradually returned to households from the collectives that had been created under Mao. The result was a big increase in agricultural production and the availability of food. Inspired by the success of the rural reforms, the government began to introduce market-oriented reforms in other areas. Managers of the state-owned enterprises were given more autonomy to make decisions and to keep a part of the profit from the successful running of their businesses.

In the early 1980s, Special Economic Zones were piloted in Shenzhen (near Hong Kong), Zhuhai, Shantou, and Xiamen (across the Straits from Taiwan). These opened up China to foreign direct investment through the vehicle of joint enterprises that benefited from special legal regulations and tax incentives. For example, to encourage processing of goods for export, joint enterprises were allowed to import raw materials duty free. These initial zones were so successful that the concept was expanded. In 1984, fourteen cities had Special Economic Zones; by 1993 there were two thousand of them. Hong Kong, Taiwan, Korea, and Japan were particularly important investors and managerial partners in the early zones.

In 1994, fiscal reforms decentralized much greater responsibility to local governments, with provincial and local governments given incentives and resources to compete with each other in developing infrastructure and businesses suited to their local circumstances. Local officials were rewarded for their performance in delivering key goals: growth, foreign direct investment, employment and social stability. Also in the 1990s, the government, which owned most of the urban housing stock, sold it to its residents at a discount. Homeownership in cities shot up from 9.7 percent in 1963 to 80 percent in 1998.[7] In 1998 the market expanded again with the reform of many of the state-owned enterprises. While these reforms led to large-scale unemployment, workers were quickly absorbed by the growing export-oriented industries and by government-financed major infrastructure developments. Roads gradually connected the coast to the interior and allowed a huge integrated domestic market to develop. Firms were able to expand and achieve economies of scale.

In 2000, China's accession into the World Trade Organization was critical, further expanding its economic integration into the world economy (see figure 3.1). The move brought large and rapidly increasing foreign investment, advanced technologies, and international management expertise. It also further opened international markets to Chinese goods, which were low cost and highly competitive because of the country's low-wage structure and government support for infrastructure, energy, capital, etc. (Compare China's growth with India, for example, which also had low wages but lacked these other advantages.) China's low-cost foreign trade strategy was so successful that foreign trade rose from 9.9 percent of the GDP in 1978 to 44 percent in 2008.[8]

However, the 2008–09 global financial crisis hit Chinese exports hard. Exports fell by about 17 percent, and twenty million jobs were lost.[9] But China weathered the global recession more successfully than the West due to the government's early and large stimulus measures that, among other things, accelerated the development of the high-speed rail network and electricity grid. In fact, China's continued strong growth during this period helped the world economy recover. Although China's growth rate recovered to 10.4 percent in 2010, it has declined every year since then and in 2018 it hit a low of 6.5 percent, the lowest growth rate since the financial crisis.[10] Chinese leaders and economic advisers learned that its high dependence on exports made it very vulnerable to global economic recessions. Further growth of the export strategy was also limited by the weak recovery of global demand in Europe and the United States.

Throughout the period 1978–2009, China adopted a strategy of what Deng Xiaoping called "crossing the river by feeling the stones."[11] Local areas were encouraged to undertake pilot projects, and, if they were successful, the ideas were spread to other areas and tried on a larger scale. This trial-by-error evolution allowed for workable and localized transitions from one stage of economic development to the next. This gradualist approach also enabled the best use of limited skills. When Deng took power, China had a

**FIGURE 3.1** China's economic growth

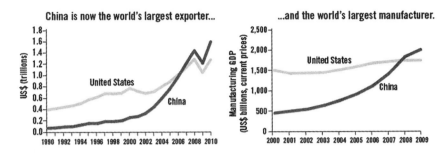

*Source:* Reprinted from *China 2030: Building a Modern, Harmonious, and Creative Society.* Washington, DC: World Bank, 2013. © World Bank. https://openknowledge.worldbank.org/handle/10986/12925. Creative Commons Attribution License: (CC BY 3.0 IGO).

vast supply of unskilled and hard-working labor but a very limited supply of people with education. Formal education had only reached a small fraction of the population in the early years of the People's Republic, and most educational institutions had been closed during the Cultural Revolution. In the early days of developing the Special Economic Zone in Shenzhen (Guangdong Province), for instance, the only people with the skills for infrastructure development came from the army. Foreign firms brought managers from their home countries and also invested significantly in training for their Chinese workers. China's limited pool of university graduates was also concentrated in the newly developing enterprises, especially in the coastal cities. Gradually education did expand as government resources grew, but the economic model was substantially built on low-wage, low-skill workers.

Despite the dire predictions of conventional economic theory, China's unique dual-track development model—a socialist market economy in which the government allowed state-owned enterprises continued to operate in old priority areas while encouraging development of private enterprise in others—has been spectacularly successful for three decades. Annual growth rates have averaged 9.9 percent, and China's foreign trade has grown annually by 16.3 percent.[12] China is now second to the United States as a destination for foreign direct investment, and it has amassed gigantic foreign reserves. Over this period, more than 500 million people were raised out of poverty, the largest antipoverty program in world history. State-owned enterprises, which accounted for three-quarters of output in 1978, now account for one-quarter, and China has the world's second-largest highway network, and six of the ten busiest container ports.[13] In 2018, China had thirteen of the world's top fifty banks and 120 companies on the Fortune Global 500 list.[14]

In 1978, China was one of the world's poorest countries. Today it is considered a middle-income country. In 2010, it overtook Japan as the world's second-largest economy and overtook Germany as the world's largest exporter. If such growth continues at this rate, China is projected to become the world's largest economy before 2030.[15]

### A New Economic Strategy, 2010–30

No economic strategy can last forever. Deng Xiaoping created a fundamental turning point in the Chinese economy. Now China is at the point when another significant transformation is needed. Three decades of extraordinary economic growth averaging nearly 10 percent per year brought significant benefits to China's people, but this achievement came with tremendous costs and has produced significant imbalances. And the growth rate has slowed and is projected to slow further.

The costs include appalling environmental damage. A pall of health-damaging pollution hangs over Beijing and many other Chinese cities, and there is substantial water and soil pollution, much as there was during the Industrial Revolution in Europe and North America in the nineteenth century. There is also substantial pressure on resources. Supplies of energy, food, raw materials, and water are all being depleted. Social strains are equally strong. There is a three-to-one disparity between urban and rural wages. According to the World Bank, China is home to more than a million millionaires, while 170 million people live on less than $2 per day.[16] The cities have rising wages and better public services in education, health, and social security, and hundreds of millions of Chinese have migrated to the cities. But because of the internal barrier of the household registration system (*houkou*), many live in cities but do not have access to urban services, while millions more farm families, unable to move, are trapped in low-wage, low-productivity agricultural work.[17]

China's economy is also significantly imbalanced in a number of ways, especially around manufacturing. Encouraged by low wages, an undervalued currency, and state subsidies of land and energy, manufacturing climbed to 48 percent of the GDP after 2003 while agriculture declined to 10 percent. Farming is conducted on small plots by individual farmers who have no buying power in the market; and with food prices kept low and a shortage of arable land, agriculture is a low-productivity and low-income sector. Meanwhile, the services sector, which is more labor intensive and less energy absorbing than manufacturing, is small relative to other countries at China's stage of development.

China's growth has been driven primarily by manufacturing and by huge national and local government investments in construction and infrastructure. By contrast, private consumption makes a relatively small contribution to GDP growth. Until recently, Chinese families have saved heavily because of the lack of health care and social security systems. And because bank interest rates are kept very low, families have invested heavily in property, causing a housing boom (some say bubble). Because of its enormous exports, China has also amassed large foreign exchange reserves that are invested in low-yield US Treasuries.[18] There is a lot of debate among economists as to the meaning of these imbalances. Pessimists argue that the economy is likely to crash, while optimists argue that the imbalances are being dealt with. Cai Hongbin, dean of Guanghua School of Management at Peking University, argues that Chinese services and consumption are undercounted in national statistics and that while China's services sector, calculated at about 42 percent, is low compared with developed countries' 70 percent, China's services are closer to 55 percent, which is comparable to Japan and South Korea in the 1960s.[19]

Overall, however, economists seem to agree that the Chinese economy at this point is dangerously imbalanced with low private consumption, an outsized manufacturing sector, a small services sector, too much foreign exchange, a property boom, and too much reliance on government investment and manufacturing to drive growth. Reducing these imbalances will require significant reforms, especially in the currency exchange rate, financial sector, and pricing of energy, land, and water.

China also faces a potential middle-income trap. Over the past fifty years, a number of countries, such as in Latin America and the Middle East, have entered the middle-income category, as China has, but then experienced a sharp deceleration in growth, which has made them unable to grow into high-income countries. In this so-called middle-income trap, the strategy that enabled these countries to grow fast initially—labor-intensive, low-cost products using technology developed abroad—is lost when they reach middle-income status. Rising wages and the limits of what can be achieved through imported technology make them less competitive.

In urban China, real wages in the formal sector have been rising steadily. In 2010, nominal annual wages for formal sector workers were almost seven times those of 1995. Taking all sectors into account (formal employment, migrant workers, and self-employment), the average real wage in urban areas rose 10 percent per year from 2000 to 2010.[20] Some of this, according to the International Monetary Fund, was offset by increases in productivity of 9.3 percent between 2000 and 2008 in the tradeable goods portion of the Chinese economy. Although the lower wages in China's western provinces will make the country competitive globally on wages for many years to come, and while China's global competitiveness is also a function of its government-induced lower costs of capital and energy and its artificially low currency, it is clear that the "China price" phase of low-wage, export-led growth is nearing its end. An export-led strategy can also no longer rely on nearly insatiable demand from the United States, as the Asian Tigers did at the end of the twentieth century. Stagnant economies in Europe and Japan limit global demand even further. Moving from a middle-income to a high-income economy requires more complex economic policy, whereby nations gradually move up the value ladder by producing more complex industrial goods and services. Accomplishing this requires an effective strategy for producing highly skilled talent across a range of advanced industrial and service sectors.

China's leaders have recognized that the current economic model is unsustainable. In 2007 Premier Wen Jiaobao said, "China's growth is unsteady, imbalanced, uncoordinated, and unsustainable." Under President Hu Jintao and Premier Wen Jiabao and now under President Xi Jiping and Premier Li Keqiang, the Chinese government has enunciated the dream of becoming a "modern, harmonious, and creative high-income society" with more inclusive growth, reduced inequality and economic insecurity, higher priority to develop in west and central China, and an emphasis on innovation. The ideas include being *modern* (industrialized, urbanized, having a quality of life on par with developed countries), *harmonious* (inclusive, having a common stake, following a rule of law, being in harmony with nature, being an equal and accepted partner among nations), *creative* (innovative, high-value-added, competitive with advanced nations), and *high-income* (on par with advanced countries, eliminating poverty, having a large middle class, reducing inequality).

The government's Twelfth Five-Year Plan (2011–15) embraced the theme of rebalancing. It called for scaling back the government role in production by further shrinking the state-owned enterprises and in resource allocation through financial reforms that allow for the market and society to drive economic growth. The government is also changing the incentives for local leaders to a broader mix of social and environmental goals (the "green index") in addition to economic growth. It also calls for modernizing agriculture, for increasing expenditures on scientific research and development, and for promoting innovation.

China has many opportunities as it seeks to move from being a middle-income to a high-income country. It has a high savings rate and a large and growing middle class that will want consumer goods and better health and education. China is also urbanizing rapidly; it is estimated that it will grow from one-half to two-thirds urban by 2030 (the equivalent of adding a Tokyo or Buenos Aires every year).[21] Cities tend to be engines of growth, allowing economies of scale in production and distribution and encouraging technology spillover. The emerging global middle class, two-thirds of which is in Asia, also provides a large market for China's goods and services. So the economic model is moving from "Made in China" to "Made and Sold in China and Asia." Some of its firms such as Alibaba, Huawei, Tencent, Haier, Baidu, and the Shanghai Construction Company are already going global. And China's new focus on services coincides with the fact that, thanks to information technology, services previously considered untradeable, like health and education, are being provided across national borders, and trade in services is now the fastest-growing component in world trade.

But China also faces significant challenges. Because of its one-child policy, beginning in 2015 China's labor force will have more retirees than workforce entrants, making for a concomitant need to boost labor productivity. Rising labor costs in the eastern cities and the increasing enforcement of environmental standards will erode China's global competitiveness in low-cost manufacturing. There is a general consensus that the growth rate will slow. While China's economy has been booming for thirty years, its average per capita income is only $6,807.[22] Since this is only a fraction of that of developed countries, it needs to keep growing faster than developed countries. And any sudden slowdown in the economy could precipitate a financial crisis.

Many of the important changes proposed in the Twelfth Five-Year Plan also face significant constraints and domestic opposition. For example, coastal provinces benefit from an undervalued currency, and local officials everywhere derive income from land sales and pirated goods (hence the lack of local enforcement of China's intellectual property laws). Also, China's strained relationship with some of its international trading partners, particularly the US, over market access, intellectual property protection, and forced technology transfer are also slowing its growth.[23]

Perhaps China's most ambitious goal is to become an innovation-oriented society by 2020 and a world leader in science and technology by 2050.[24] China is already investing significant funds in research and development and plans to increase expenditures to 2.5 percent of GDP annually. The country's pool of scientists and engineers devoted to R&D is now second only to the US.[25] The government has designated twenty pilot cities as "knowledge centers" and incubators for innovation: for example, opto-electronics in Wuhan, aviation in Chengdu, and financial and engineering services in

Shanghai. It has also designated twenty strategic research areas and is already an emerging global innovator in fields such as green tech.

Yet, while China has some top-ranked universities in global terms, the quality of tertiary education more broadly is problematic, and despite an increasing number of patents, the government research institutes are not well connected to industry and their work has not yet translated into new products.[26] Innovation conferences are being held around the country to identify barriers to innovation that include lack of enforcement of intellectual property laws, the lack of large private-sector firms that account for a lot of innovation in advanced economies, and a critical shortage of the right skills at all levels.

### Does China Have the Skills to Become an Innovation Society?

There are many different perspectives on the current human resource situation in China, depending on the region of the country, the type of industry, and the level of skill required. There are huge skill gaps but, at the same time, rapidly increasing skills.

Overall, the current adult workforce reflects the lower educational provision of a previous era and is substantially unskilled. For those businesses that rely on low-skill manufacturing, there is a plentiful supply of unskilled but highly motivated workers. But as costs in the eastern cities rise, businesses will increasingly automate their processes or move inland, and the more than 285 million migrant workers who make up one-third of the entire labor force will either have to move inland or face massive structural unemployment.[27]

For industries needing higher skills, there are substantial shortages. According to National Industry Development Plans, in the electronics and information industry, of the 8.5 million employees, only 50 percent are classified as skilled; in equipment manufacturing, 60 percent of the 16 million workers are classified as skilled; in the steel industry, more than 25 percent of workers are junior high school leavers without additional training.[28] The lack of qualified workers affects the economy in many ways. It is estimated that 30 percent of Chinese products cannot pass quality tests. Many advanced equipment lines can't operate at full capacity due to lack of qualified technicians or maintenance workers. In fact, "Made in China" has become mostly synonymous with low quality, compared with "Made in Japan, Korea, or Germany." Cities lack skilled technicians and service providers, such as mechanics to repair the rapidly increasing number of automobiles. And in the service industry, workers in hotels and restaurants, except those at the very highest end, by and large do not meet common international standards.

At the management level, the American Chamber of Commerce in China (AMCHAM), in its 2014 Business Climate Survey, said that human resources are the second biggest challenge to American businesses operating in China. Thirty-six percent of their members said that the shortage of qualified Chinese managers is a risk to their Chinese operations. Young skilled workers are at a premium and, because they're in demand, move around a lot, so high employee turnover is an additional problem for companies of all sizes.

Over the last thirty years, Chinese public authorities at the national, provincial, and local levels have been investing increasingly in education. How far has the Chinese education system come toward meeting the needs of a modern and increasingly skill-intensive economy?

## CHINA'S EDUCATIONAL DEVELOPMENT

While the current adult workforce in China may not be very well-educated, the next generation will be much more so. China's economic rise is the stuff of countless newspaper articles. What is much less well-known is that its educational growth has been equally spectacular. At the founding of the People's Republic of China in 1949, more than 80 percent of the population was illiterate.[29] But with the Open Door Policy, education has been a major focus. In discussing the importance of education to China's modernization, Deng Xiaoping famously said that "education should be oriented towards modernization, the world and the future."[30]

With the world's largest population and yet extremely limited resources at the beginning of the People's Republic, it was a significant challenge to expand China's education system. But decade by decade, China has done just that. In the 1950s, primary education first expanded but then declined during the economic crisis caused by the Great Leap Forward (1958–62), and then most schools were shuttered during the Cultural Revolution (1966–76). As late as the mid-1970s, only one in four students actually graduated from primary school.

The most rapid development in education in China has come in the decades since the 1980s. In the 1980s, schools reopened and both primary and junior secondary enrollments began rising gradually. In 1986, a new law guaranteed children nine years of compulsory education, six years of primary, and three years of junior secondary, with the target of achieving this by 2000. By 2004, primary schooling had become a universal system and 74.4 percent of students were enrolled in junior secondary. Today, more than 94 percent of students graduate from junior secondary school.[31]

Beginning in the 1990s, senior secondary education, which follows compulsory education, also expanded significantly, rising from a gross enrollment rate of 42.8 percent in 2002 to 84 percent in 2011.[32] Access to senior secondary schools is by examination, and senior secondary schools are primarily academic in orientation, aimed at university entrance. To increase participation at the senior secondary level, senior vocational schools were also developed. Unlike academic secondary schools, vocational secondary schools are primarily terminal institutions, leading directly into the workforce. About 50 percent of senior secondary students in China are now in vocational schools.

In higher education, there was little enrollment from 1949 up through the Cultural Revolution. After the Open Door Policy began in 1978, demand for placement grew. Because of limited available places, access to higher education was highly competitive, and the government controlled admissions through a unified national university entrance examination system, the *gaokao*, which had been restored in 1977.[33] The late 1990s saw an enormous and rapid expansion of higher education, with gross enrollment going from less than 10 percent in the late 1990s to 26.9 percent in 2011.[34] The number of students enrolled in higher education rose from under a million to 30 million. The number of tertiary institutions grew from 442 in 2000 to 1,147 in

2006.[35] China has moved swiftly from the phase of elite higher education to mass higher education.

Another important aspect of China's education development strategy has been sending its students abroad for graduate and undergraduate education. Deng began to send students abroad in 1978 as part of his modernization drive, and since then nearly 2.25 million Chinese students have studied outside of China. Today China is the largest supplier of students to universities in many countries, with approximately 363,341 students on US campuses in 2017–18.[36]

After three decades of effort and many milestones, China reached its goal of allocating 4 percent of its GDP to education.[37] Education has evolved organically from the expansion of primary education, then secondary, then higher education. Access has expanded enormously, and China now runs the biggest educational system in the world. Looking to the future, the 2010–20 National Medium and Long-Term Educational Reform and Development Plan calls for senior secondary education graduation rates to reach 90 percent; if achieved, this would put China ahead of the US high school graduation rate—but with millions more students. The plan also calls for the development of world-class universities. There can be no doubt about China's ambition for and commitment to education.

As might be expected from such a huge and rapid expansion, it has not been without its problems. In China's higher education system, there has been a widely recognized decline in teaching standards and a high unemployment rate among college graduates. As the number of new graduates rose from one million per year in 2000 to over eight million per year in 2017, the unemployment rate among graduates rose as well, with only 27 percent of graduates having signed employment contracts on graduation.[38] Although the employment rate of college graduates rose to 90 percent in 2012, according to the Chinese College Graduates Employment Annual Report of the Chinese Academy of Social Sciences and MyCOS Research Institute, and has remained at that level throughout the decade, half of all graduates reported that their jobs did not make use of their degrees.[39]

Large-scale educational expansion has produced significant quality and equity problems in elementary and secondary education as well. One of the reasons education was able to expand so rapidly initially is that responsibility for basic education was devolved to the local level (within a national framework of standards and curriculum). But because of the uneven economic development of China, this led to great regional disparities in educational funding, quality of facilities and teachers, availability of technology, and access to higher education. The quality of education is significantly lower in western and central China than in the highly developed cities on the east coast. There are also quality gaps in urban areas between schools for middle-class families and those for disadvantaged social groups, such as migrant children.

Over time and as resources have expanded, the central government has devoted significant resources to trying to remedy these regional disparities, for example, through funding additional teacher positions in rural areas, establishing boarding schools to replace one-room rural schoolhouses, subsidizing fees for compulsory education and eventually abolishing them, and providing scholarships and loans to students from rural areas for upper secondary and higher education. Also, in many cities high-achieving schools are expected to pair with lower-achieving schools to improve teaching and management. And as part of the professional learning system of Chinese schools, the lead or master teachers in each school in a district work together to share best practices and make standards more consistent across all the schools in the district.

From the 1990s on, there has been increasing attention to the quality of Chinese schools, rather than just their quantitative expansion. In particular, a major curriculum reform tried to modernize the curriculum and teaching methods of schools. The goals of the reform were to encourage more inquiry-based methods and practical hands-on experiences; to put more focus on applied skills; to offer students more choices and optional modules beyond the core curriculum in math, science, and languages; and to leave room for more local and school-based additions to the curriculum.

Implementation of this curriculum has been difficult for teachers trained in traditional pedagogy, and the reform has also been hampered by the gaokao, which is seen as a guarantor of fairness but which restricts curriculum innovation and turns much of upper secondary education into an extended and intensive exam preparation period to the exclusion of other learning. Recent reforms of the gaokao in some provinces are intended to try to address some of these challenges.[40]

Overall, the expansion of China's general education system over the past three decades has been breathtaking by historical standards. And the world-beating results in Shanghai show that China is aiming toward very high standards. But students and parents increasingly complain about the examination pressure and the rigidity and lack of choice in subject matter. Employers view the system as unable to produce students who can apply their knowledge. And the huge regional inequalities mean that students from poor rural backgrounds have relatively low chances of getting to university.

Vocational education has also grown, although it has lagged behind general education. Vocational secondary schools were introduced in the 1960s, but this policy was reversed in the 1970s because of the view that these structures promoted social differentiation and elitism. During the 1980s, the emphasis on vocational education was renewed, and since then VET has expanded substantially. In China, vocational education is provided through separate secondary schools and tertiary institutions rather than through vocational programs within a general secondary school or community-type college.

Junior secondary vocational schools are found primarily in rural areas where the economy is less developed. Graduates of junior secondary vocational schools become farmers and lower-skilled workers. Students in junior secondary vocational schools can take the examination to move on to upper secondary schools, but most students who enter upper secondary school come from the junior secondary general school.

At the upper secondary level, there are four types of vocational schools: *specialized high schools*, which provide three-year certificate courses and allow students to enter the labor market directly (the most popular type of VET); *vocational high schools*, which have been transformed recently from general senior high schools to allow students to either enter the labor market directly or go on to tertiary vocational colleges; *skilled worker schools*, which provide three-year certificate courses for state occupational licenses; and *adult specialized high schools*, which provide full- and part-time and short-form courses that can be either academic or technical. For the country as a whole, in 2009–10, about twenty-two million students, roughly 47 percent of all secondary students, were in vocational institutions. Currently, manufacturing, information technology, finance, and services are the top specialties.[41]

Tertiary vocational education mainly enrolls graduates from general high schools and secondary vocational schools. It started in the 1980s but developed mainly from the mid-1990s on. There are four types of VET institutions at the tertiary level: vocational-technical colleges or polytechnic colleges provide two- or three-year diploma courses; specialized junior colleges provide two- or three-year diploma courses, mainly for capacity building rather than technical training; technician colleges provide two- or three-year certificate courses for state technician licenses; and adult higher educational institutions provide full-time and part-time certificate courses for knowledge enrichment and self-improvement.[42] The proportion of students in tertiary education enrolled in vocational institutions varies enormously across China. In Beijing, fewer than 25 percent of students in postsecondary education are in vocational institutions, whereas in provinces like Guangxi, Fujian, and Sichuan it is more like 40 percent to 50 percent.

Beyond the diploma programs of the formal VET education system, there is a range of nondiploma programs provided by secondary and tertiary vocational schools and colleges and other providers. Since 1978 industry has played and continues to play an important role in vocational training, although it is hard to find data on the extent of this training. Chinese state-owned enterprises (SOEs), for example, ran their own schools and provided training to their workers in a way that provided an automatic connection between training and jobs. This sector of VET is now being phased down with responsibility shifted to the Ministry of Education as the role of SOEs in the economy is being reduced. Foreign employers in joint enterprises also played an important role in the early years in bringing training and expertise to China while its education system was developing. The army also provides a lot of technical training, as do some industry associations, labor bureaus, and nongovernmental organizations. In some fields, such as opera, medicine, and martial arts, traditional apprenticeships continue the tradition of passing the craft on from one generation to the next. And in recent years there has been a significant growth of commercial VET providers. There were 21,811 such providers in 2008.[43]

Vocational education and training in China is administratively complex. It is divided primarily between the Ministry of Education, which focuses on occupational and technical education, and the Ministry of Human Resources and Social Security, which focuses on skills training. But there are other government entities involved as well. Within the Ministry of Education, VET is divided between the Department of Higher Education and the Department of Vocational and Adult Education. The Central Institute for Vocational and Technical Education, attached to the Ministry of Education, provides policy advice. The Ministry of Human Resources and Social Security's Department of Occupational Capacity Building is responsible for administration of VET programs in technician colleges and skilled worker schools and for developing occupational skills standards, assessing skill qualifications, and issuing occupational licenses. It also partners with the Department of Employment Promotion to run short-term skills training programs in job centers around the country. In 2004 the Chinese government established an interministry mechanism to try to better coordinate the activities of the seven ministries around VET: the Ministry of Education, the National Development and Reform Commission, the Ministry of Finance, the Ministry of Labor, the Ministry of Personnel, the Ministry of Agriculture, and the Poverty Alleviation Office. Each of these administrative entities is mirrored at the province and local level (see figure 3.2). It is said that the administrative structure is so complex that nobody understands it![44]

China now runs the largest VET system in the world. There are more than 15,000 vocational institutions at the secondary and tertiary levels, more than 22 million students in secondary VET, and almost 10 million students in postsecondary VET. This equals 47.6 percent of total tertiary

**FIGURE 3.2**   The contemporary structure of education in China

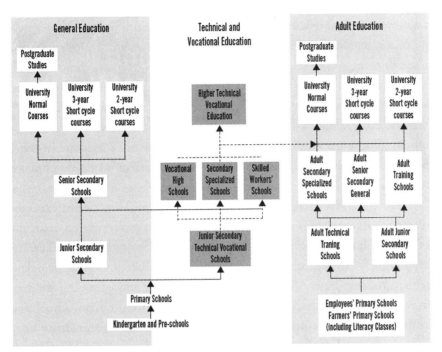

*Source:* Reprinted by permission from Springer Nature Customer Service Centre GmbH: *Education and Training in China* (Springer Nature) by Zhenyi Guo and Stephen Lamb © 2010.

and 47.6 percent of secondary education enrollments.[45] The VET system has developed enormously in a relatively short period of time, providing skills for the economy and opportunities for millions of students, especially those from lower income or rural backgrounds. But, as this study shows, the system has significant problems.

## CHALLENGES IN CHINA'S SKILL DEVELOPMENT

China is at a turning point. All of the interrelated challenges it faces—the need for an alternative to the low-wage and low-skill export economy, the need to address its environmental challenges, the need to improve its agricultural productivity, the need to raise living standards for poorer Chinese, and the declining size of its labor force and growing size of its elderly population—require dramatic changes in the skills of its workforce.

To assess how well China's VET system addresses these challenges, the research team visited secondary vocational schools, tertiary vocational colleges, Chinese and foreign employers, and Chinese government officials and academic experts in four cities: Shenzhen, Tianjin, Shanghai, and Beijing.[46] We saw both relatively strong and relatively weak examples of VET institutions, but when compared with top-performing VET systems in other parts of the world, it was clear that China's VET system is in need of major restructuring.

There are many strengths in China's VET system. Historically, expenditures on VET have been substantially lower than expenditures on academic education. But this is changing, and expenditures have grown significantly, enabling VET to expand to the point where about half of China's secondary school students are in VET schools. It is absorbing and educating children from lower-income backgrounds who previously were not in school and enabling a far higher proportion of younger age cohorts to graduate from secondary school. Increased resources have also been poured into handsome modern buildings and, sometimes, equipment. Many of the schools we visited had developed connections to firms, albeit with the caveats discussed below. In places, like Shanghai, that have high educational standards, the mathematics scores of VET students far exceed those of academic students in many other countries, thus creating a strong foundation for advanced technical training.

But VET in China has even more challenges.

*The curriculum design of school-based VET programs is narrow.* Many of the programs we observed seemed to be focused primarily on the entry-level skills students need for their first job and did not provide the depth and breadth of skills that needed to move up in a career. This partly reflects the manpower planning model that underpinned the development of some of the schools. But as the lifetime of work skills gets shorter and shorter, and as China's economy changes, VET will need to include more general education so that workers can be more adaptable and able to learn new skills. Although there have been efforts to broaden VET curricula, the skills are generally not high enough for a rapidly changing economy or to enable individuals to move up in the economy. Further, curriculum development does not seem to be designed with the most advanced companies or leading edges of the economy in mind. Nor was there the strong focus on innovation and entrepreneurship, features that are increasingly prevalent in the world's strongest systems.

*Connections to industry are weak.* Although there are connections between VET schools/tertiary institutions and industries, they are weak compared with those in the world's best systems. For example, some VET institutions have modern buildings but not modern equipment, so graduates are not being prepared adequately for the current job market. Organized work experiences typically consist of only a few weeks of working at the end of a course. They rarely incorporate the kind of sequenced and supervised interplay of learning and work that characterize the world's best systems. VET institutions do not seem to be connected to foreign-owned companies that often incorporate the most advanced industries and international standards. And many employers do not even pay attention to the certifications provided by VET institutions in their hiring. There are some exceptions, though. Shanghai is working to develop majors in vocational schools according to industry demands and has set up fifteen training bases jointly run by vocational schools and qualified enterprises. One of the strongest examples of integrated work and learning experiences we saw was in a state-owned company, the Shanghai Construction Company, which ran both a secondary vocational school and a college that trained students on the most modern equipment, offered significant supervised work experience in the second and third years, and provided opportunities for upward mobility through the company, accompanied by more advanced training. But since many SOEs are out of date and unproductive, and their role is being significantly reduced in the economy, this tradition of industry-run schools is being phased out. Overall, there is a huge disconnect between the VET system and employers, and there are few incentives for employers to cooperate with VET institutions. Given the high rates of labor mobility in eastern cities, there is indeed little reason for employers to invest in helping to train someone who won't stay with a company for very long.

*VET has a low status in the public mind.* Beyond the weak connections to industry lies a cultural problem. In China, the idea that "those who do mental labor can govern those who do manual labor" extends back to the *Analects of Confucius* and has influenced the Chinese view of knowledge and education. These status distinctions between academic and vocational education exist in most countries but are deeply rooted in China. Whereas John Dewey, for example, advocated for an education that worked both the hands and the brain, in China education has come to mean "academic reading." Consequently, vocational education is perceived by the public as low status.

*There are structural barriers.* Compounding this cultural problem are structural ones. Until recently, there has been no real pathway between vocational education and academic education. While the gaokao can theoretically be taken by any student, only students in the general academic curriculum are well enough prepared to be successful. For most students in vocational education schools, education finishes at the end of secondary school. Vocational education is literally an educational dead end. Add to this the fact that blue-collar salaries are far lower than white-collar ones. Cultural, structural, and economic reasons therefore suggest that there is no good reason why Chinese parents should encourage their one child to go into vocational education if they have the option of taking the general (academic) path. This is beginning to change, though, as specialized technical postsecondary institutions are expanding and as pilot efforts begin to create pathways between vocational and academic education.

*There is a mismatch between employers' needs and graduates' capabilities.* Employers we interviewed, both in foreign-owned and Chinese firms, complained of new employees' inability to apply their knowledge. "Students know bookwork and nothing else" was a widespread complaint. Graduates were also seen as lacking the kind of general employability skills needed in modern settings—the ability to work in teams, think critically, and solve problems without having to be told what to do. Childhood in China is for studying; there is little of the formal or informal work experience through which students in other countries acquire some of these general skills. With respect to engineers, for example, managers at Boeing and Walmart said that after hiring Chinese tertiary graduates from engineering programs, it takes another two years to get them up to a US bachelor's-level standard in engineering primarily because of their lack of applied experience and their reluctance to undertake hands-on work. The annual AMCHAM surveys of US employers reveal similar concerns about Chinese graduates at all levels.[47]

*Faculty have limited experience in industry.* Another aspect of the disconnect between the VET system and industry is the background of most VET faculty. The main role of teachers in China is to provide academic content and guidance on students' moral or character development. Consistent with this, most VET faculty do not come from industry, have industry experience, or keep current with technical and scientific advances in industry. There is an urgent need to upgrade the industry knowledge of VET teachers and to find ways to hire more faculty with industry backgrounds.

*Standards and qualifications systems need to be developed.* Occupational standards and qualifications systems are essential to the functioning of VET systems because they help establish quality and consistency across institutions and allow worker mobility. Vocational colleges in China have certificates and diplomas, but the existing five levels of skills standards are only for some of the highest-demand, lower-skill occupations. The world's best occupational standards are broad, are linked to the leading edges of industries so that they are constantly updated, and integrate academic and vocational skills within an overall qualifications framework. Such a standards and qualifications system does not yet exist in China.

*Adult education is undeveloped.* The VET system is designed primarily to provide initial training for young people to enter employment. But as the life cycle of skills gets shorter and as China transitions from a low-skill to a higher-skill economy, the need for skills training of adults will greatly expand. There are some mechanisms for upskilling the current workforce (e.g., adult schools and contract training with employers), but lifelong learning is relatively undeveloped in China. It exists, but there is not an overall system with a comprehensive policy and legal framework. The role of technology in training adults, such as through online courses, also appears to be relatively undeveloped.

*The governance structure of VET hampers innovation.* Split among two ministries, other national entities, and a host of provincial and local levels of government, the complex and bureaucratic administration of vocational and educational training makes it hard for VET institutions to adapt to the changes in the economy quickly. The Chinese economy is becoming more market driven, yet VET remains government planned. It will be important to create mechanisms, such as local industry associations, to swiftly communicate the changing needs of business to VET institutions and different governance mechanisms to enable local institutions to respond.

These problems are pervasive in China's VET system. The immense diversity in levels of development between different parts of the country—such as between the coastal cities of Shanghai, Tianjin, Shenzhen, and Beijing and poorer provinces like Yunan—need to be taken into account in fashioning solutions. But as China seeks to modernize agriculture, move up the value-added chain in manufacturing, and expand its service and science- and innovation-based industries, it will need to address these major deficiencies in the design and functioning of its current VET system if it is to succeed.

## REFORM AND INNOVATION

### New Government Policy Directions

All this may be about to change as China enters a period of intensifying focus on and experimentation in VET. In the 1980s and 1990s, VET schools and colleges expanded enormously in scale but had major problems of quality.

But beginning in the mid-1990s the government adopted a series of policies and measures to further expand VET and try to improve its quality, though these have met with mixed results. In 1996, at a time when Chinese universities were expanding, the first national vocational education law expanded tertiary vocational education. However, while expenditures increased, they never matched the levels of general or academic education, which meant that the infrastructure and equipment of most VET schools was very old.[48]

Then, in 2005, after three national conferences on VET, the State Council, China's cabinet, issued a new policy document titled "Decision on Accelerating the Growth of VET."[49] Students in rural areas were exempted from upper secondary school fees and one hundred key, or model, secondary and tertiary vocational schools and colleges were established to pilot new approaches. The government began to encourage dual certifications for VET teachers to attract those with both industry expertise and academic qualifications into VET programs in schools. In 2006, the Tertiary VET 211 Initiative also focused on upgrading one hundred tertiary vocational colleges. In addition to these national models, there are several thousand key vocational education institutions designated by local governments.

The global recession of 2008–09 caused massive unemployment in China and created a renewed sense of urgency about both the social and economic purposes of VET. Premier Wen Jiabao's 2009 annual report to the National People's Congress designated VET as "the next key target of education promotion."[50] Compared with the successful development of nine years of compulsory education and the huge expansion of higher education, VET was seen as a weak link in the education system. Critical shortages of qualified technicians and skilled workers, mass unemployment in the economic downturn, and the higher employability of VET graduates compared with university graduates all led to a greater focus on the role of technical training in meeting the country's economic and social goals. A series of measures was taken to strengthen the quality of VET, including the creation of the interministerial coordination mechanism for formulating overall strategies and policies at the national level, with provincial governments responsible for planning, resource allocation, and supervision of VET institutions at the local level. Many of the measures undertaken at this time were focused on increasing rural participation in education and reducing unemployment, with various promotion targets spelled out.

In November 2013 the new president of China, Xi Jinping, at the Third Plenum of the Eighteenth Central Committee of the Communist Party, committed the country to further economic reforms, calling for "comprehensively deepening economic reform by centering on the decisive role of the market in allocating resources."[51] As part of this, the Central Committee went on to discuss the need to narrow gaps in education and modernize vocational education. The State Council also confirmed the centrality of VET in China's national strategic and talent development and called for: more innovation in VET models, especially with respect to stronger cooperation/integration between VET institutions and companies; a strengthening of the quality of VET to include more "comprehensive competencies," including soft skills; and a reduction in the national government's role from managing the VET system to providing significant financial support but decentralizing more authority in the actual operation of institutions to the provinces, the schools themselves, and the market.

## Experiments and Pilots

One of the characteristics of China's development has been its pattern of piloting or modeling at the local level, allowing for testing out what works or does not work before scaling-up the most successful aspects to a whole region or even the whole country. Pilots are seen as useful learning tools— "Small steps can produce big things."[52]

In the general education system, key schools are being downplayed because of concerns about the inequities they created, yet these strong model schools are important to China's strategy for improving the quality and relevance of VET. We visited a number of these key schools and colleges. Though they were all different based on the circumstances and period in which they were founded, the nature of the local economy, and their technical fields of focus, all were trying to address some of the most significant vocational educational problems, including updating the curriculum, creating connections to industry, attracting teachers with more experience in industry, and developing some pathways to higher education.

Beyond these experiments in individual institutions, there are broader developments in some cities and provinces. In Shanghai, for example, a leading province in both economic development and education, several consortia exist to promote cooperation between companies and education institutions in particular sectors, such as nursing, IT, transportation, tourism, and finance. The goal of having teaching staff with dual capabilities is also being achieved by requiring traditional VET teachers to spend one year out of every five years in an enterprise and by recruiting part-time teachers from industry. In addition, a more applied version of the university entrance exam is being piloted to help students from vocational education attain higher education. Shanghai is implementing a new academic test and a comprehensive quality evaluation for students in secondary vocational education and allowing tertiary vocational schools or colleges to recruit students separately through their own assessment and evaluation scheme that measures general competence and vocational skills, rather than basing admission solely on a student's gaokao, which measures academic achievement alone. And to promote greater equity, the province has opened its VET schools to the children of migrant workers and ensured that 90 percent of students in secondary vocational education receive fee subsidies. It has also paired some of its VET institutions with their counterparts in more rural provinces, such as Yunan and Xinjiang, to strengthen curriculum and teacher training and to develop cooperative enrollment schemes through which students can begin in one institution and finish in another institution with higher-level courses.[53] Under the Shanghai pilot, after completing upper secondary vocational studies, students can apply for either a three-year higher vocational education program to work toward a technical degree or for placement in a four-year University of Applied Technology to work toward a bachelor's degree (see figure 3.3). Based on the success of this pilot, these options will eventually roll out across China.

**Innovations in VET**

Included in the following sketches of some of these key secondary and tertiary institutions in four different Chinese cities are the VET reforms and developments they are pursuing.

*Shanghai Institute of Health Sciences*

The Shanghai Institute of Health Sciences is a model for China in allied health fields. It educates four thousand students on a large new campus in the Pudong area of Shanghai, and its physical infrastructure includes simulation environments for many health fields. It receives half its funding from the national government and half from the Shanghai Municipal Education Commission, and it offers both upper secondary and tertiary (diploma and associate) programs. Students pay tuition, but poorer students and those from rural areas receive their education free. After training, rural students are encouraged to go back to their home communities and provide much-needed health care.

The training of nurses is particularly important. Nursing practices in China have long been below international standards. Nurses are closely supervised by doctors and, traditionally, have not been expected to exercise much independent judgment. The psychiatric aspects of nursing are also less developed. The college's goal is to raise the status and quality of nursing by changing the curriculum, the amount of clinical experience, and the standards. Now, students work for eight months in a hospital after they finish their course of study. And, to learn current practices, every three years college faculty members must spend three months in a hospital; also, some part-time faculty work at a hospital and are jointly paid. This has resulted in 100 percent of the students passing the Chinese nursing exam, and some also take the US nursing exam (in English), since there is a need for international nurses in Shanghai and potentially abroad as well.

Internationalization is key to the college's reform strategy. It seeks faculty from many countries in an attempt to introduce modern curricula and teaching methods. It also sends many of its own faculty and some students abroad for periods of time. The long-term goal is to develop an associate

**FIGURE 3.3   Administration of vocational education and training in China**

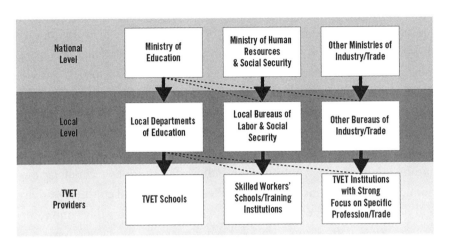

Source: Reprinted by permission from Springer Nature Customer Service Centre GmbH: *Education and Training in China* (Springer Nature) by Zhenyi Guo and Stephen Lamb © 2010.

degree that is comparable to international levels (only 25 percent have an associate degree; most have a diploma). The dean of nursing is also chair of the National Nursing Education Committee, so the college provides a model for how China as a whole can gradually move toward international standards for all nurses. The school is visited by delegations from all over China.

*Tianjin Sino-German Vocational and Technical College*

The Tianjin Sino-German Vocational and Technical College is part of an enormous educational park in Tianjin that includes several other universities and technical colleges. Tianjin is an area of extremely rapid economic growth because of its proximity both to Beijing and to a very large port. The college's programs have developed as the local economy has changed.

The institution was founded as a training center in the mid-1980s, shortly after the opening up of China, as a joint venture between the German and Chinese governments. Germany provided funds and technical assistance to help to develop its style of dual-system VET in Tianjin and in several other cities. The college was linked to a Chinese state-owned enterprise in steel production, which also benefited from German expertise. In turn, the college provided mechanical and electrical technicians and language training for the firm. The college still has a wing of offices for German experts but has now expanded beyond its Sino-German origins as the economy of the area grew to include relationships with many industries and countries. The college now has specialty cooperation programs with Spain, Canada, Australia, and Singapore and an Italian-based European network on lifelong learning.

The college offers nine fields of study, including advanced manufacturing, automation, aeronomics and astronautics, new energy and new materials, automobile technology, information and communications technology, economics and business management, applied languages, and culture, creativity, and design. The head of the college has visited the US to study community colleges' close connection with local economies and the flexible system of transferring credits, which enables students to go back to school for further study or to move on to a university.

### Tianjin Institute of Mechanical Technology

Sharing the same giant educational park is the Tianjin Institute of Mechanical Technology, a Tianjin City Demonstration Secondary Vocational School. It started in the 1950s as part of a state-owned factory, the Tianjin First Machinery Factory, to meet the factory's own need for labor. At the time of the research team's visit, the school had seven thousand students and fifteen majors in the areas of numerical control, automobile systems, information technology, and electronic and mechanical systems. The institute is connected to a large industrial group made up of a lot of different companies. Automobile repair, agricultural equipment production, and mold making are its important specialties. The curriculum is closely linked to the entry-level demands of the local labor market.

Most students come from the local area or nearby provinces and a sizeable number are from disadvantaged backgrounds, especially the children of migrant workers, who attend free of charge. Students come to the school having graduated from secondary school but at very different levels academically. Teachers regularly stay after school to provide help to students who are weaker academically, exemplifying the Chinese saying, "Who loves his children is human and who loves other people's children is a god." Students attend the institute for three years, but a small percentage stay on for two additional years to earn an advanced certificate.

## Beijing Business School

Beijing Business School is an upper secondary model school. Funded by the Beijing Municipal Government and the national government, it is run under the auspices of the Beijing Education Commission. Students come from Beijing as well as other provinces. The school offers courses in business and a wide range of other subjects.

It also plays a number of roles more broadly in the reform and development of VET in China. For example, it provides teacher training for faculty in other VET schools in the field of hotel management, working with Chinese hotels and VET research experts in the development of the training. In addition, it revised its accounting curriculum after analyzing the positions in accounting and the skills and competencies needed in the workplace. This curriculum is now used broadly in China's VET schools. The school is also developing digital resources in accounting and e-business that will be made widely available throughout the country. And as a key school, it has an obligation to work with programs in one or more of the less-developed provinces to improve VET there. A particular challenge facing Beijing Business School is that, since the national government's announcement that it wants to limit the growth of the city of Beijing, focusing on its political and cultural roles but reducing its roles in manufacturing and finance, it will have to significantly change its course offerings.

## Beijing College of Finance and Commerce

Beijing College of Finance and Commerce (BCFC) is one of twenty-seven tertiary vocational colleges in Beijing. It was founded in 1958 as a school for adults. Later, after the Cultural Revolution, it played an important role in training workforces for government and state-owned enterprises. About 60 percent of the managers in the Beijing government ranks and in area state-owned enterprises were trained at BCFC.

At the time of our visit, it trained eight thousand students for a wide variety of occupations in the Beijing area, including teachers of other VET schools in finance and business. BCFC graduates are primarily employed as frontline supervisors, not managers. Only 10 percent of graduates have the opportunity to go on to get a BA, and then often through online learning or self-study. BCFC officials are interested in emulating US community colleges, recognizing the need for better bridges between educational levels and institutions.

BCFC also has a small school of international studies, which organizes joint programs with colleges of further education in other countries. Close to one hundred students have finished three years at BCFC, then gone to the UK or New Zealand for a year and completed a BA. Those students also try to get work experience abroad before returning to China, because Chinese employers prefer people with international experience.

### Shenzhen Polytechnic

Shenzhen is in the heart of Guangdong, a province of one hundred million people and one of the first Special Economic Zones. In the early stages of the opening up of China, the joint ventures between Chinese and foreign firms were in basic manufacturing, most workers had very low education and skill levels, and companies had to invest internally in whatever training was needed to run their businesses. At that time, Shenzhen had a secondary VET school and a university but no tertiary VET institution. In the early 1990s, new types of businesses came in, and with them came a growing need for higher technical skills among the workforce. Shenzhen Polytechnic was created in 1993 as a tertiary VET institution; the first class had 24 students. Today, it has 30,000 students across 5 campuses and offers 80 specialties organized in the following areas: electronic and communication engineering, computer engineering, mechanical and electrical engineering, economics, management, media and communications, art and design, animation, applied foreign languages, construction and environmental engineering, applied chemistry and biological technology, automobile and transportation engineering, medical technology and nursing, and humanities. Shenzhen has been designated a top VET model by the national government.

From the start, there was collaboration between Shenzhen Polytechnic and local industries, especially in the design of curriculum. In the first ten years, as the college was growing quickly, the curriculum was focused on skills for immediate application in the office or on the factory floor. Since then effort has been made to broaden the curriculum to provide a more comprehensive education to ensure that students have a stronger basis for future development, although this sometimes runs up against the national and provincial occupational standards. Although there is close collaboration between Shenzhen Polytechnic and industries in the design of the curriculum, work experience consists mainly of a work placement in a student's last semester. Training of faculty is another important component of the curriculum, as is creating more pathways for students to move on to pursue further degrees. With these kinds of programs, Shenzhen Polytechnic aims to become a university of applied sciences.

## Shanghai Dianji University

Shanghai Dianji University sits on a large campus being built in what will be the new Shanghai Free-Trade Zone. Begun in 1953 as the Shanghai Electrical Machinery Manufacturing School, Shanghai Dianji was raised to university status in 2012. At the time of our visit, it had twelve thousand students, 70 percent of whom were studying engineering at the three-year diploma or the four-year BA levels. Students who graduate from the diploma program can go on for another two years to earn a BA. Shanghai Dianji has twenty-six undergraduate majors and fifteen diploma programs. Its goal is to cultivate field engineers with a focus on energy equipment manufacturing (wind, solar, and nuclear). Graduates have a 100 percent employment rate.

The university has pioneered relationships with state-owned and Chinese private enterprises in the Shanghai area. Each major has a board of ten people drawn from industry and other vocational schools to advise on the curriculum. Some of their schools have "double deans," with one dean drawn from the school and the other employed by industry but working part-time at the college. Faculty spend time in industry, and students have internships. Company officials also become part-time teachers, run short courses, and supervise students when they intern in companies. Companies can also send employees to the college for specific training. These practices are not common but are of increasing interest in China. All these school-enterprise connections are financially subsidized by the Shanghai Municipal Education Commission.

### The Shanghai Construction Group

The Shanghai Construction Group is a state-owned enterprise that was founded in 1953 as the construction bureau of the Shanghai government. Today it is the sixteenth-largest construction company in the world. It has built the most modern skyscrapers in China and now does work outside China, too. It works with the world's most famous architects and employs 20,000 people at the corporate management level, who all have strong technical skills in engineering and architectural design and 9,000 construction site managers, as well as innumerable semi-skilled and unskilled laborers. The company recruits fifteen hundred people per year, 60 percent from universities and 40 percent from the vocational track.

The Shanghai Construction Group also has its own vocational secondary school and vocational college. The company does charge tuition, but poorer students can attend for free. In the first year at both the school and the college, students study math, Chinese, English, engineering, computer-aided design, and mechanics. In the second year, courses relate to construction engineering: costing, construction techniques, and design. In the third year, students do practical work onsite in one of the Group's companies; they rotate through departments and get their expenses paid. Each year, nine hundred students graduate from the secondary school and six hundred from the college. A Shanghai association of construction companies sets the standards for various educational certificates, such as safety, costing, materials, interior design, and landscaping, but there are not yet any unified standards for China. Thirty percent of the secondary school graduates go on to the Shanghai Construction Group's college, and 10 percent of diploma graduates go on to earn a degree at a local university. The Shanghai Construction Group employs about one-third of the college's graduates, and a hundred other companies come to the college to recruit.

The Shanghai Construction Group school has the most up-to-date equipment for tunnel construction and construction simulations. Construction managers from the company teach in the school, and the teachers with more academic engineering backgrounds are sent to work in the construction company in the summer. The curriculum is constantly adjusted to follow new developments in construction; the company houses a research center on innovation in construction. Many senior managers have also studied or had work experience abroad. The company believes in lifelong education; graduates of the secondary vocational school can rise through the ranks and may eventually be sent by the company to get a BA and MBA elsewhere in China or abroad.

The Shanghai Construction Group school and college seem to present a strong VET model. But, as China seeks to reduce the role of state-owned enterprises in the economy, this model of schools run by state-owned enterprises will likely disappear.

### International Benchmarking and Partnerships

Since the beginning of the Open Door Policy in 1978, China has used internationalization as a way of driving internal reform. In the field of VET, China has conducted international benchmarking reviews and created partnerships with a number of countries, in particular Germany, Japan, Singapore, the UK, and Australia, but also Sweden and, more recently, with US community colleges.

In some places, models from other countries are being directly introduced. For example, Singapore has joint projects with institutions in Tianjin and Hanzhou. Warwickshire College in the UK has partnered with a counterpart in Qingzhou, Shandong Province, to offer British-style VET, emphasizing hands-on experience and entrepreneurship. The Tianjin Sino-German

Technical School has been developed with help from the German government from its inception, and some German firms that operate in China, such as Siemens, Volkswagen, and BMW, are providing a small number of German-style apprenticeships. Since 2008, the China Education Association for International Exchange has worked with the American Association of Community and Junior Colleges on leadership development and training, market-oriented curriculum design, and network-building practices for Chinese administrators. And more recently there have been proposals to develop one hundred community colleges in China.

So there is a wealth of experimentation going on. However, none of these international models can be adopted wholesale; they will need to be adapted to the Chinese context. For example, although the German dual-system model is much admired, it is hard to make it work in China. There are large cultural differences between the Chinese veneration of academic learning and the traditional German respect for vocational education. China also lacks the long tradition of close cooperation between VET institutions and private companies that underlies the German apprenticeship system. In Germany, a vocational certificate is required to get a job, whereas in China it's possible to get a job without one. And in Germany, vocational education starts after general education, not during it. With respect to the Singapore model, China lacks the close and easy collaboration between ministries that has enabled Singapore's economic development and educational planning to work hand in hand. And while the market orientation of US community colleges is attractive, China is still transitioning from a planned economy to a free-market economy, so it will be some time before this local market approach to VET will be able to work effectively.

Indeed, China is in a period of intense reform. It aims to develop a world-class education system, to improve labor quality, and increase employment. There are many opinions in China about how to improve VET—from abolishing secondary vocational education and moving all vocational education to the tertiary level, to creating a separate vocational pathway from basic education through to degree level, to blending vocational and general education for everyone and at all levels. Particular attention and debate is currently focused on efforts to reform the university entrance examination to give more opportunities to people from lower-income and rural areas and to students with special abilities, not just those with high general test scores.

## TOWARD A WORLD-CLASS VET SYSTEM

There are several different national models of VET systems. Some, such as Singapore's, are education based; others, such as Switzerland's, are employment based; and still others are a hybrid. Whatever the overall model, studies of VET systems in different parts of the world suggest what will be key characteristics of successful VET systems in the global knowledge economy of the twenty-first century. A top VET system

- provides students with a broad education designed to prepare them to easily gain additional skills and knowledge needed as their career goals, technology, and work organization change over their employed lifetime;
- provides opportunities for students to learn and to practice necessary cognitive and noncognitive skills in an authentic industry setting;
- provides opportunities for students to learn the theory behind the practice;
- creates learning environments in which students can learn and practice on state-of-the-art equipment;
- provides opportunities for students to move from the vocational track to the academic, university track, and vice-versa;
- provides opportunities for students to move up from the lowest levels of occupational preparation to the highest levels of academic and professional preparation, with career guidance along the way;
- provides standards and qualifications widely recognized in the labor market and continually adjusted to the leading edge of industries, including the increasingly global nature of occupations;
- adapts to the level of economic development of the economy in which the student will work and to the level of technological advancement and work organization characteristic of that economy;

- provides a distribution of training slots that is reasonably related to the demands of the economy in terms of occupations and levels of qualifications needed to operate the economy;
- provides instructors who have industry experience and whose knowledge of the industry is fully current with state-of-the-art practice;
- provides incentives adequate to attract the necessary number and quality of instructors for each occupational group and qualification level;
- provides incentives adequate to attract qualified students to each level of the skills training system;
- builds on a basic education system that provides students entering the vocational education system with the skills and knowledge needed to engage productively with the vocational education system; and
- creates a brand that makes vocational education an attractive opportunity to young people who have options.[54]

These principles of international best practice could be used to analyze and improve VET systems in any country. They would need to be adapted to the context of particular countries before being adopted. Historical influences, value systems, concepts of industry involvement, and models of collaboration all vary between countries and need to be taken into account.

Based on our research, we offer the following broad recommendations about what China needs to do to achieve a world-class VET system.

*Create models of systems at different stages of economic development.* Any VET system needs to be matched to the level of economic development. China is so large and has so many stages of economic development that a single unified model is likely not feasible. Rather, VET systems should be substantially designed at the province or city level. Programs, institutions, and skill standards should all be matched to the stage of development of the city/province, but these different levels should be nested within a broader national framework, allowing some students in each province the opportunity to move up the national ladder.

*Build a governance system that is substantially employer driven.* It is critical to build a governance system at every level—national, city/province, and institutional—that engages employers more effectively in the design and implementation of VET. Employers, especially private employers, need to be centrally involved in assessing current and future skill demands and determining the types of equipment and training needed in a rapidly changing market. For example, at the local level, mayors, employers, industry associations, and economic development and education officials could constitute the VET governing board. Government also needs to encourage business recognition of vocational degrees and incentivize businesses to improve the quality of the work-based part of VET.

*Redesign the programs and curricula of VET institutions.* Use industry committees to redesign curricula, creating new structures of experience for students either in real apprentice or other work experience situations or in simulated industry environments in VET institutions. In either model, goods and services could be produced and sold at market rates while students are paid substantially less than adults. Key positions in VET institutions should be held by people with joint appointments in industry or industry associations.

*Create incentives for employer participation and increase standards.* All firms, including state-owned enterprises, should be taxed a training fee used to support the VET system. This tax would be waived for firms that offer youth apprenticeships and a substantial program of continuing education for their adult workers. The waivers would be granted by local boards based on national criteria. VET institutions should also be given subsidies to align themselves with the most globally advanced, highest-productivity firms in the industries in which they offer programs and to continuously upgrade their programs to international standards.

*Build bridges between VET and academic education and higher education.* Education and training need to be conceived of as lifelong pursuits that enable individuals, enterprises, and nations to continually adapt to rapid change.

Bridges and pathways should be built between VET and general academic education and higher education. There are many different models for doing this, including creating applied universities as the capstone of the VET system or developing community college–style institutions that provide students both technical and academic options and flexible credits toward adult education. These could be tried out in different parts of China to see what works best. Whatever the model, the principle should be "no dead ends."

*Address the low public perception of VET.* An explicit campaign must be undertaken to modify the traditional Chinese emphasis on academic learning and diplomas and broader people's conception of the comprehensive abilities of "hearts, hands, and minds."

As China pursues its dream of becoming a "modern, harmonious, and creative high-income society," many changes will be necessary—in the economy, in the legal system, in the financial system, and certainly in the education system. China is on the verge of a transformation as profound as that initiated by Deng Xiaoping in 1978. And virtually everything that China wants to accomplish depends on a dramatic improvement in the productivity of Chinese workers, which, in turn, depends on a dramatic improvement in their education, skills, flexibility, and ingenuity.

## CHAPTER 4

# THE EVOLUTION OF
# CAREER AND TECHNICAL EDUCATION
# IN THE UNITED STATES

*Robert B. Schwartz and Nancy Hoffman*

In 2000, the Organisation for Economic Co-operation and Development (OECD) released a report called *From Initial Education to Working Life: Making Transitions Work.*[1] The United States was one of fourteen countries that participated in the study which preceded the report. To help readers understand the variation among the participating countries, the study team created a typology based on how the countries organized their upper secondary education systems to prepare young people for the transition from school to work. The typology had four categories: *apprenticeship countries* (more than 50 percent of students in apprenticeship); *mixed pathways countries* (fewer than 50 percent in apprenticeship, but most in vocational education); *school-based vocational countries* (more than 50 percent of students in vocational education, mostly school-based); and *general education countries* (more than 50 percent in general education). In the first category were Switzerland and Germany, the "dual system" countries. In the second category were Austria, Denmark, Norway, and the Netherlands. In the third category were most other European countries, including France and the UK. And in the final category, those that rely *mostly* on general education to prepare students for the transition to employment, were countries including Canada, Japan, and the United States.

What "mostly" means in this context is that only about 20 percent of US high school students are vocational "concentrators," meaning that they take at least three courses in a single vocational field during their high school

years. When the OECD revisited the issue of how its member nations prepared young people for work a decade later, it decided not to include the US
in a comparative chart showing the percentage of upper secondary students
in VET (vocational education and training).[2] This decision surprised and
dismayed US vocational policy makers, who, in addition to citing the 20
percent concentrators figure, also pointed to the fact that 75 percent of students take at least one career and technical education (CTE) course. How
could OECD officials conclude that the US had virtually no students in
vocational education? The OECD's answer was that, in its view, the requirement of only three courses was so minimal that it didn't meet the international threshold. By contrast, in Switzerland, a VET student at that time
typically spent three eight-hour days forty weeks a year for three years in an
apprenticeship at a work site and at least another day a week taking classes
at a vocational school.

Why is the secondary-level vocational system in the United States so
limited in scope? It is not because the US has a federal governance system
within which education is principally a state and local responsibility. After
all, the same could be said of Switzerland and Germany, yet those countries
have made explicit decisions to create national upper secondary VET systems within federalist structures in recognition of their link with national
economic and labor market policy. The US system evolved as it did because
of unique features of the nation. Above all, the US's failure to build a strong
national vocational education system at the secondary level reflects a continuing debate about the purposes of K–12 education, a debate that began
in the late nineteenth century.

Despite these challenges, promising VET models do exist in the United
States, and these are now being scaled up through partnerships formed at
the state and regional labor market levels. In this chapter we examine the
development of VET in the US and show how disagreements about the
purposes of education, along with issues of race and class, a historic separation between high schools and postsecondary education, and a lack of connections between schools and the workplace, among other factors, affected
this development. We also look at some promising approaches and show

how the US system is continuing to evolve and offer suggestions for how a high-quality VET system can be implemented within the US context. A strong American-style VET system can be built, one that will enhance the chances that many more young people can prepare for productive careers. If the OECD revisits its study in 2020, it will find that the United States in a different place than it was a decade earlier.

## THE HISTORY OF VOCATIONAL EDUCATION IN THE US

### From the Committee of Ten Report to the Smith-Hughes Act, 1893–1917

The easiest way to understand the historical roots of the debate around vocational education is to contrast two seminal reports about secondary education in America, both sponsored by the National Education Association (NEA), the oldest and largest organization representing US educators. The first of these reports, issued in 1893, resulted from the deliberations of a ten-person committee chaired by Charles William Eliot, president of Harvard University, and made up primarily of university presidents and other higher education leaders. The Committee of Ten was appointed in 1892 and charged with addressing fundamental questions about the purposes and structure of the American public high school. Public high schools were at that time still a relatively new phenomenon on the education landscape, and they were serving fewer than 5 percent of the fourteen-to-seventeen-year-old population. However, the massive wave of immigration that had begun in the 1880s was already well under way, and there was rising pressure to expand access to secondary education. The US economy was also becoming more industrialized, and there were increasing calls to strengthen the connections between schooling and the needs of a rapidly changing economy.

The Committee of Ten's report called for a uniform grade structure—four years of high school after eight years of primary education—and for a college preparatory curriculum for all students: "Every subject which is taught at all in a secondary school should be taught in the same way and to the same extent to every pupil so long as he pursues it, no matter what the probable destination of the pupil may be, or at what point his education is to cease."[3]

The report was seen as a call for reform and modernization in that it argued for the inclusion of the sciences and modern languages alongside the traditional classical subjects and for space in the curriculum for elective subjects. But its primary contribution was the powerful case it made that all high school students deserved access to the same rigorous liberal arts education, not just those headed for college.

By the time the next NEA commission issued its report, in 1918, "The Cardinal Principles of Secondary Education," the recommendations of the Committee of Ten had been overtaken by the economic and demographic changes of the intervening twenty-five years. By 1918, over 25 percent of fourteen-to-seventeen-year-olds were attending high school, and immigration had changed the composition of the high school population dramatically. The schools were seen as the principal vehicle for not only socializing newcomers into American mores and values but also for preparing them for employment in an increasingly industrialized economy.

The Commission on the Reorganization of Secondary Education that issued "The Cardinal Principles" report was very different from the composition of the Committee of Ten. This time it was education professors and school leaders, not university presidents, who issued the prescription for the organization and programmatic focus of high schools. Under the banner of democratization and the recognition of individual differences, the commission articulated a new set of seven objectives for secondary education: health, command of fundamental processes, worthy home membership, vocation, civic education, worthy use of leisure, and ethical character. Of these, the only one that addressed the academic purposes of education was "command of fundamental processes" (literacy and numeracy), which was a far cry from the rigorous academic program the Committee of Ten laid out for all students.[4]

"The Cardinal Principles of Secondary Education" created an opening for those organizations most interested in strengthening the connection between the world of schooling and the world of work. Although "vocation" was only one of the seven principles, a broad business-led coalition had formed around the turn of the century on behalf of vocational education and greater diversification of the high school curriculum, both to engage an increasingly diverse student population and to meet the needs of an increasingly skill-based economy. The coalition included trade union leaders who saw vocational education as a vehicle for dignifying the importance of skilled labor, philanthropists, and social reformers who believed in inculcating the moral value of work, and education reformers who saw hands-on vocational education as an antidote to the stultifying pedagogy that characterized high school instruction at the time.

In 1906 this diverse reform coalition created the National Society for the Promotion of Industrial Education, a lobbying group to promote the expansion of vocational education at the state and local levels and to argue for federal support as well. In response to the society's efforts, Congress appointed in 1914 a Commission on National Aid to Vocational Education, arguing that vocational training "would vitalize general education and democratize schooling by adapting it to the real needs of children, promote industrial efficiency and national prosperity, decrease labour and social unrest, and promote a higher standard of living for workers." The commission recommended federal grants to the states to promote vocational education, with a particular focus on training vocational teachers. It proposed legislation that was later introduced by two of the commission's members, Senator Hoke Smith and Representative D. M. Hughes, both of Georgia, and passed by Congress (with minor modifications) in 1917 as the National Vocational Education Act, subsequently known as the Smith-Hughes Act.[5]

Smith-Hughes was the first federal grants program in K–12 education, providing matching funds to states to support the expansion of industrial education as well as agriculture and home economics. The law created a Federal Board of Vocational Education to distribute funds to states, and states were required to designate an existing entity or create a new state body to administer the funds, thereby acknowledging and abetting an increasing state role in local communities and schools. It gave states flexibility in determining whether to use the funds to support vocational programs in full-time high schools or to support students who enrolled in part-time vocational centers. In the early years following enactment, over 90 percent of the funds went to support programs in part-time centers, but over time federal funding helped support the development of full-time vocational schools as well as the development and expansion of the comprehensive high school, where academic and vocational programs coexisted under one roof.

### Tracking and the Rise of the Comprehensive High School, 1920–1950

The big story of the period 1920 to 1950 was the extraordinary, unprecedented expansion of secondary education in the US, which far outstripped the pace of growth in any other nation at the time. At the turn of the century, only about 5 percent of the high-school-aged population was enrolled in school, and by 1910 that percentage had increased only to 18 percent. But by 1940 the percentage had arisen to an astonishing 73 percent. High school attendance had become the norm; it was no longer reserved only for the handful of young people going on to college. And most young people attended comprehensive high schools, a uniquely American invention.

Although the advocates of vocational education hailed it as a democratizing force, critics warned that the Smith-Hughes Act would encourage the development of a two-track secondary education system, one that would reinforce rather than weaken social stratification, separating those going on to manual labor from those aspiring to the professions. The battle over incorporating vocational programs into existing schools versus creating separate vocational high schools played out most vividly in Chicago, where, even before the federal law was passed, business leaders had argued that only in separate vocational schools could the curriculum be designed to fit the specifications of industry. The education community and the trade unions mobilized against this idea, fearing both an unduly narrow and company-specific training and a retreat from the ideal of the common school, where children from all backgrounds learned to live and work together.

The debate came to a head in 1913 when the Chicago Association of Commerce drafted a bill to separate Illinois schools after grade 6 into vocational and general schools. A pitched battle ensued in the legislature, with the education community arguing it would lead to permanent class divisions. One of the fiercest critics of the proposed separation of the system was John Dewey, the country's leading proponent of applied education, or "learning by doing," who called the legislative proposal "the greatest evil now threatening the forces of democracy in education."[6] Ultimately, the educators and their allies prevailed. The truth is that neither the hopes of the vocational education advocates nor the fears of its critics were fully realized in the three decades following passage of the Smith-Hughes Act. Vocational enrollments never rose much over 20 percent, and most vocational students continued to take the core academic subjects along with their occupational courses.

The themes sounded in the Chicago legislative battle have haunted discussions of vocational education through the decades. Critics have continued to raise concerns about the undue influence of industry in advocating for an overly narrow and utilitarian conception of education, one that may suit the needs of employers at the expense of equipping young people with a sufficiently solid foundation of academic knowledge and skills to be informed, engaged citizens and lifetime learners. Critics have also been quick to point out that while the comprehensive high schools that flourished in the suburbs in the 1940s and 1950s might seem to have been democratizing institutions, the reality was that mostly separate tracks were organized in ways that largely reflected the existing social class structure. The sons and daughters of professional families were assigned to honors or college prep tracks, and the children from low-income and minority families were mostly assigned to vocational programs or to a third "general education" track that resulted in a high school diploma but prepared people neither for college nor work.

### The Legacy of Racial Discrimination

The story of vocational education in America is inextricably linked to issues of race and poverty, and those issues have played out primarily in urban and rural school districts, not in suburbia. While the battles over separate versus comprehensive secondary schools were fought in industrialized urban centers like Chicago, a more fundamental struggle took place in the southern states, where schools remained segregated by law until the 1950s. Despite the rhetoric of "separate but equal," the education of black children in the decades following the Civil War was almost entirely limited to schools designed to prepare them for manual labor, initially in the fields and later in factories.

The manual or industrial training that emerged after the Civil War had a specifically racial theme: how to teach the virtues of hard work to black people, whom many southerners thought had weak moral character and lazy work habits developed during enslavement. Booker T. Washington, the president of Tuskegee Institute and the most prominent black leader in the late nineteenth century, famously argued that black advancement required an acceptance of the social order that prevailed in the South and that black people needed "to learn to dignify and glorify common labor . . . No race can prosper till [sic] it learns that there is as much dignity in tilling a field as in writing a poem."[7] Washington's views were challenged by the leading black intellectual of the period, W. E. B. Du Bois, who pressed the case for an education to prepare black students for exercising the rights and aspirations of fully emancipated citizens through a classical liberal arts education. Because black children were seen by white southerners as fit only for relatively low-level agricultural, industrial arts, or home economics training, while the schools prepared white children for a broader array of academic and vocational choices, it is not surprising that many black leaders today continue to see vocational education as the denial of opportunity rather than a route to upward mobility.

In the North, where by law blacks were entitled to equal educational opportunity, issues of race and class and vocational education played out in more subtle ways. Boston serves as an example. Like many northern urban districts, Boston historically had a mix of citywide and neighborhood-based high schools. Its three leading citywide high schools admitted students by examination and, until quite recently, were the only high schools exclusively focused on college preparation. The eight or nine neighborhood high schools typically offered college, general, and vocational tracks but had low completion rates and even lower postsecondary enrollment rates. There was only one citywide vocational school, Boston Trade, but its reputation was so abysmal that it was closed in the 1970s. There were two avenues for upward mobility in Boston through the 1950s and early 1960s for young people with only a high school education—the trade unions and the civil service—and getting access to those avenues depended at least as much on family connections as on paper qualifications.

It was changing student demographics and a changing economy that together finally brought about change in the schools. Several years of protest by leaders of the African American community—which needed the high schools to function for its children, because they did not have access to the informal networks to place them in the trades or public service jobs—led to a sweeping federal school desegregation order in 1974. The protests cast a searchlight on not only the glaring inequities in access and opportunity based on race but on the reality that the only high school students well-served by the system were those in the three citywide examination schools.[8] Hopes for a modernized and revitalized vocational education system in Boston rested on the construction of a citywide Occupational Resource Center, which opened with much fanfare in the mid-1970s but was never given anything like the resources and support needed to fulfill the ambitions of its advocates. Today called Madison Park Technical Vocational High School, under new leadership it is overcoming its history, building industry-aligned programs in partnership with local employers and higher ed institutions.

It is important to note that during this period there were also much-celebrated examples of strong vocational high schools in other northern urban centers, most notably in New York City. These were typically specialty schools focused on preparing young people for work in a specific industry that had very strong support from industry partners. Aviation High School and the High School of Fashion and Design, established in the 1920s, maintained strong national reputations in the 1960s and 1970s and continue to be leaders in the field. Several such specialty schools exist today as part of a resurgent CTE sector in New York. The city counts 50 CTE schools among its 400 high schools, nearly half of which have been opened since 2010, and there are an additional 220 CTE programs in 75 comprehensive high schools. Together, these CTE high schools and programs serve about 25 percent of New York City's high school population and are increasing in popularity.[9] While New York City has had its own history of troubled racial politics surrounding the schools, especially during the bitter fight over community control in the 1960s, its best vocational schools have continued to enjoy broad community support.

### Federal-Led Expansion in the 1960s

While cities like Boston and New York had their own versions of locally controlled vocational education, many states developed systems of stand-alone vocational schools. Indeed, Massachusetts was the national leader in this regard, when in 1908 it opened three industrial schools. Such schools developed across the US over the following decades.

However, a major expansion of vocational education did not take place until the 1960s, supported in substantial measure by the passage of the Vocational Education Act of 1963 that provided funding to support the construction of area vocational centers and enable comprehensive high schools to grow their vocational offerings. The expansion was fueled by the entrance of a large cohort of students, the baby boomers, into schools. Policy makers believed that more young people would need to be trained for the expanding industrial labor market and that the current supply of vocational programs could not meet this need. This legislation also required states to provide explicitly for disabled, bilingual, low-income, and disadvantaged students living in economically challenged communities. Additionally, it mandated that there be strategies for attracting youth to occupations not traditional for their gender.

The role of this federal law is significant, because in the United States elementary and secondary education (including vocational education) is primarily the responsibility of state and local governments. In fact, over 90 percent of the funds supporting schools comes from state and local taxes. One of the intriguing features of the US system is the disproportionate policy influence federal programs can have despite the government's modest financial contribution to the overall education budgets of states and school districts. This is the case, in part, because there is so little state and local funding deliberately earmarked to support reform and innovation.

## From "Vocational Education" to "Career and Technical Education"

The 2006 reauthorization of the Perkins Act was titled the Carl D. Perkins Career and Technical Education Act.[10] This title change was designed in part to underscore the importance of upgrading and modernizing vocational programs to prepare young Americans to compete in an economy increasingly characterized by globalization and the speed of technology-driven change. The new law introduced some substantive changes as well. Although the law continued to require that 85 percent of funds be distributed to eligible local recipients—school districts, area technical centers, community or technical colleges—there is a new focus on encouraging states to use the 10 percent state set-aside for "leadership activities" to support the development of regional consortia bringing together employers, high schools, and postsecondary institutions. In a recent survey of state CTE directors, forty-two states reported using at least some of their leadership funds to support this kind of partnership activity, while most of this funding remained focused on technical assistance and professional development, two functions essential for program improvement.[11]

Two other aspects of the Perkins Act have marked the transition from vocational education to CTE. One important innovation added in the 1990 reauthorization reflected a new emphasis on career—meaning entry and advancement in an industry, not just preparation for a first job. All Perkins-funded CTE programs are now required to include a component designed to introduce students to "all aspects of the industry" in which their particular program is situated. This means, for example, that high school students enrolled in a certified nursing assistant program should develop some understanding of the larger health-care industry.

A more fundamental shift has been the increasing attention paid to outcomes. This has been part of the larger focus on accountability that has characterized the federal role in education over the past two decades. Although there has been considerable pushback on this aspect of the federal role in the last two or three years, with the pendulum now swinging back from federal to more state control, the insistence on measuring program impact by looking at such indicators as high school graduation and postsecondary enrollment rates, certificate or degree completion, and successful transition into the labor market will only grow stronger. There are a handful of states where the development of longitudinal databases makes it is possible to link wage records to student records so that policy makers and parents can track the returns to academic majors or technical programs for at least a decade postgraduation. As these kinds of data become more available to policy makers and to parents and students, it should provide additional momentum behind the growing movement to reform and modernize CTE programs to better align them with the needs of regional labor markets.

Another key element of the 2006 Perkins Act is the support for "aligned programs of study" that begin in high school and seamlessly connect to majors and specializations in technical and/or community colleges. Although the law now mandates that all local recipients of Perkins funds must offer at least one program of study, nearly half the states require that at least 50 percent of all Perkins funds distributed to localities be spent on programs of study, and twelve states require that all Perkins funds distributed to local secondary programs be used to support programs of study.[12] The revised law ensures that secondary and postsecondary planners work together to create a broad sequence of courses leading to the completion of a two-year degree, certificate, or license.

## VOCATIONAL EDUCATION IN THE US TODAY

The structure of the US education system differs sharply from those of European countries, and, as a result, vocational and technical education operates quite differently as well. In European nations, upper secondary vocational education begins when students are sixteen and ends at when they are nineteen or twenty. In those three or four years, students get the equivalent of the last years of a US high school CTE program and a community college career-focused credential that enables them to enter the labor market directly. Thus, while vocational education is the mission of a single institution in European systems, career and technical education in the US spans two sectors—K–12 and higher education. This cross-sector need for alignment and collaboration makes for a complicated and, some would say, ineffective workforce preparation strategy for young people in the US.

## High School Programs

The "college for all" message that has pervaded education in the last two decades means that the academic side of high schools has received much more attention from policy makers than CTE during this time. Most states have worked to have all students meet the same high school graduation requirements, whatever their post–high school path: four years of English, three of math (Algebra I and II, geometry), three of lab science (biology, chemistry, physics), three and a half of social studies (chosen from US history, world history, geography, economics, and government), and two of a language other than English. In some states, this has become the default course of study, requiring parents who object to opt out of this curriculum for their children. As the 2000 OECD report noted, the implicit assumption is that a rigorous general education constitutes the best preparation for work and career, leaving little time for other coursework.

Programs and courses offering career preparation at the high school level are delivered in many different forms and structures as school leaders attempt to fit career-focused learning into a demanding academic program of study. The comprehensive high school is the predominant structure in both rural areas, where they are regional and serve a dispersed and varied student body, and most suburbs, where there is one (or, at most, two or three) high school. Comprehensive high schools have both academic and CTE tracks, although some proportion of CTE students are placed in the higher sections of academic courses with their college prep peers. In some instances, these large schools have been broken down into smaller learning communities or even separate schools with their own principals housed in a single large building. Such smaller entities, often called career academies, are organized around career themes—media, health care, leadership, social justice, business, information technology, and the like. While they often sound like career-preparation programs, most of these academies are not intended to lead directly to work after graduation. In addition, they rarely have the equipment and resources needed to teach the trades. Instead, the idea is to engage young people in school by providing applied learning that demonstrates the relevance of schooling and therefore stems dropout. At best, they integrate career learning into the traditional disciplines, which may include internships, a partnership with an employer, or a community service opportunity for the purpose of career exploration. In these instances, the boundary between CTE and academics begins to blur. These small programs also pose definitional problems, since students may or may not be counted as CTE participants.

CTE is also delivered through schools devoted primarily to career preparation, although such schools only constitute 4 percent of US high schools: high schools in large urban areas devoted to a single career area (e.g., aviation science, health, engineering, and information technology careers); stand-alone vocational schools offering multiple programs serving either an entire region or a smaller city; and, finally, vocational-technical centers that serve students who are transported there for part of the school day. All these variants share the goal of preparing students to enter further education, most frequently a two-year community college, or, in a decreasing number of cases, to enter the workforce directly from high school. Increasingly, CTE programs provide licensure or industry certifications conferred through assessments set by the state or by a sector organization (e.g., X-ray technician license, CISCO certification). CTE schools are increasingly also mounting demanding science and technology programs in addition to the trades (plumbing, electrical, automotive). Examples include biomanufacturing and cyber security, both courses of study that lead to state certification with clear pathways into two- and four-year degrees.

We offer short profiles of exemplary schools or centers to illustrate the range of institutional models that provide high-quality career-focused education in today's US secondary school landscape.[13] Each serves a substantial proportion of low-income students. Most have impressive high school graduation and postsecondary enrollment rates. Some represent models that have already been scaled, and others models that could be scaled. While all have work-based learning opportunities built into their design and show significant evidence of engagement with employers, none (with the possible exception of Worcester Tech) sees itself as *primarily* in the business of preparing young people for employment immediately after high school—a responsibility that, in the US context, is assigned primarily to postsecondary education, not to high schools.

*Model 1: Worcester Technical High School, a Stand-Alone Urban CTE High School*

In June 2014, President Obama gave his only high school commencement address of the year at Worcester Technical High School on the outskirts of Worcester, Massachusetts, a city of 181,000 and the second largest city in New England. Although in 2006 "Worcester Vo-Tech" was declared a failing school, today it is one of the highest-performing schools in a state known for high academic achievement. The president used his address to highlight the many opportunities available to the largely low-income population. Indeed, 57 percent of students are classified as "high needs" and 44 percent as "economically disadvantaged." The growing interest in CTE that began in the 2000s has brought nationwide attention to Massachusetts's vo-tech schools, as they are called, as being engines preparing young people for the many open technical and technology jobs in the new economy.

A US Department of Education Blue Ribbon School housed in a $90 million state-of-the-art building on a 400,000-square-foot campus, Worcester Tech represents the best of the full-time vocational high school model. Perhaps most impressive is the work experience the 1,400 students gain at Worcester Tech. Students work in profit-making enterprises, both inside the school and externally. The student-run 125-seat restaurant serves meals to the public at reasonable prices. Also operating at the school are a salon and day spa, a sixteen-bay automotive service center, a full-service bank with

ATM, and a state-approved preschool. Partnered with one of the highest-ranked veterinary schools in the country, Tufts at Worcester Tech provides subsidized animal care to low-income families in the Worcester area; students pair with Tufts veterinary medicine students to participate in the treatment of more than 250 animals per month. The carpentry, plumbing, and electrical students built the veterinary clinic, which is housed in a wing of the school; also, the graphic students created the name and designed the logo and brochures, and the painting and design students created the signage. But the school does not neglect important skills, like writing, that are highly valued in the workplace and in college. A current instructional focus in all classes, both academic and technical, is having students demonstrate their ability to write for a variety of audiences. Students are creating writing portfolios and must demonstrate both their ability to write in technical language as well as to do close reading of texts.

For over forty years, Worcester Tech, like all the Massachusetts vo-tech schools, has followed a unique schedule: the first four months of ninth grade, students circulate among each career area offered, after which, with advising, they pick their area of concentration. There on, the schedule alternates—a week of academics, a week of shop. With higher-than-state-average low-income and special education populations, along with the full array of vocational programs, the vo-tech schools offer Advanced Placement courses and dual enrollment for college credit. Today, many of the twenty-six regional vocational high schools and three agricultural schools have waiting lists, show strong results on Massachusetts' state assessments, and boast higher high school completion rates than the state average.

### Model 2: Center for Advanced Research and Technology, a Regional CTE Center

A part-time regional career center located in Clovis, California, near Fresno, the Center for Advanced Research and Technology (CART) provides half-day programs for thirteen hundred eleventh and twelfth graders from fifteen area high schools.[14] While CART uses CTE funds and has some programs that are standard to California's Regional Occupational Programs, nothing is standard about a CART education, from the facility to the approach to learning. With echoes of the Coalition of Essential Schools, a popular high school reform effort in the US begun in the 1980s, CART states that the vision for the school is "to create an environment where the students learn to use their minds well."

The 75,000-square-foot CART building, designed to replicate a high-performance business atmosphere, is organized around four career clusters: professional sciences, engineering, advanced communications, and global economics. Instead of classrooms, teachers, business partners, and invited experts work in large open spaces filled with equipment, work stations, and student work; these spaces are similar to those in a high-tech start-up, a maker space, or a science lab. Within each cluster are several career-specific laboratories in which students complete industry-based projects and receive academic credit for advanced English, science, social science, and technology coursework. Boundaries between disciplines don't exist since students are problem solving and learning just as they would in the real world. Students do everything from testing water in the Sierras, to trying out aviation careers by flying planes, to learning aquaculture. Teaching teams include business and science partners, and many of the teachers themselves have extensive professional experience.

The school's website captures the flavor of CART by featuring "This Week at Cart," short pieces written by students about their current work. Student Amaya DeVore recounted her activity: "My project team and I are raising Chinook Salmon. Aletha and Tom Lang at Aquarius Aquarium decided to take the time to be our mentors for this project. They teach us the necessary techniques to hatch salmon, and learn about the fragility of our planet's aquatic resources and animals. In May we will be releasing our Salmon into the river and they will finally live their life in the open water."[15]

There are no grade or test requirements for admission to CART; students must make the case for themselves as appropriate to the CART philosophy and demands. Through learning plans, individualized attention, and collaboration with business partners, teachers, and parents, students design programs of study that qualify them to pursue the postsecondary path of their choice, from entry-level positions, to industry certification, to university admission. A 2011 study commissioned by The James Irvine Foundation showed that "CART has successfully increased community college and CSU/UC attendance for all students regardless of gender, ethnicity or economic background . . . Results for African American students were particularly dramatic with 68% of students from CART entering community college compared to only 32% of African American graduates statewide."[16]

In 2015, journalists Deborah Fallows and James Fallows visited a number of small towns for Atlantic's Futures Project "to see how people are adjusting to the economic, environmental, and technological opportunities and challenges of this era." CART was among the schools they visited. Deborah Fallows noted, "We have by now visited several career-track high schools and community colleges around the country . . . but have never seen a school quite like CART."[17]

### Model 3: Wheeling High School, a Comprehensive High School

An example of a comprehensive high school with a STEM focus for all, Wheeling High School serves seventeen hundred students from six communities in the northwest suburbs of Chicago.[18] While the programs and career exploration opportunities Wheeling offers may be similar to those in a less diverse, more affluent suburb, the Wheeling student population is 59 percent Hispanic and 31 percent white, with the remaining 10 percent having black and Asian backgrounds, and about 41 percent of the students are low income. In addition, many students speak a language other than English at home. *US News & World Report* recently recognized Wheeling as one of the best high schools in the state of Illinois. On graduation, nearly 90 percent of its students pursue postsecondary opportunities.

Wheeling offers challenging academic coursework, including twenty-four Advanced Placement and college credit courses in business, engineering, architecture, and nanotechnology. Students can also earn industry-recognized certifications in automotive technology, computer technology, health careers, and manufacturing, credentials that can provide access to a job to supplement the costs of further education. Indeed, Wheeling has partnerships with a number of area universities and community colleges, and at one community college students can earn a full associate degree at no cost.

Technology is woven throughout the school. There are fifteen computer labs, Smartboards in classrooms, and a twenty-first-century media library. Also, every student gets an Apple iPad Air to use during their years in the school and to keep after graduation. Wheeling High School also benefits from a unique new Center for Career Discovery, which serves six high schools in District 214. The center facilitates the development and coordination of customized, authentic learning experiences, many outside of classrooms, that provide opportunities to support all students in their skill development and decision-making and with determining their postsecondary goals and future career paths. Students can choose supported, independent, and micro internships, each with different requirements. In addition, students can participate in industry tours, job shadowing, and classes cotaught by an industry professional and school faculty. These experiences provide students the opportunity to observe and engage with professionals in their typical work setting; learn specific job tasks of the person they work alongside; gain insight into the career planning process; identify potential career opportunities with possible majors of study; develop critical thinking competencies and problem-solving abilities; and have the opportunity to improve the ability to communicate, including developing and utilizing networking skills. For example, Wheeling students participating in the engineering and manufacturing program's Project Lead the Way are working with NASA to build brackets and handles for the International Space Station.

### Model 4: Energy Tech, a CTE Early College High School

Energy Tech, a career-focused high school founded in 2013 as part of the City University of New York early college network, specializes in preparing students in engineering and technology fields. Early colleges offer students at risk of not completing a postsecondary credential the chance to earn up to an associate degree while in high school. The average early college student graduates with a year of college credit. Career-focused or CTE early colleges start students on a broad pathway aligned with regional labor market demand.

The students at Energy Tech in Long Island City, Queens, are as diverse as the city's population, and admission is open to all. Asians make up 18 percent of the student body population, blacks 10 percent, Hispanics 53 percent, and whites 15 percent. But as is unfortunately typical in science and tech programs, the student body is 79 percent male and 21 percent female. The small school—fewer than five hundred students—performs well, with 95 percent of the students completing the approved college- and career-readiness curriculum, a percentage substantially above that of either the Borough of Queens or New York City as a whole. Indeed, the school has gained a reputation for excellence in its years of existence, with applications far exceeding spots in the ninth-grade class.

On a typical day at Energy Tech, as the school website explains, some students are engaged in discussion about *Macbeth* and others are in the science and engineering labs testing the solar ovens they designed and built, while still others are constructing prototypes for deliberately complex machines. Later in the day, some students may be off campus learning from a New York City energy company about what the work world entails.

To build a pipeline of young job candidates, Energy Tech partners with Con Edison and National Grid. These companies work closely with the school to provide job shadows and internships and to help shape the school's curriculum by connecting classroom learning to what happens in their industry. The school's industry liaison, who recruits new companies and works with National Grid and Con Edison to develop and manage student experiences, said:

> In addition to all their core academic subjects, and the career and technical education within the engineering, [students are] also getting what . . . we like to call twenty-first-century or leadership skills—how to speak to professionals, how to network, how to have a polished resume, even if you're just getting out there in the workforce for the first time. You're infusing what the work-

force needs right here in this school, making sure we're mapping backwards from the skills that are needed at entry-level jobs to what they're learning in the classes . . . to make sure they're the most competitive candidates for what the engineering and energy industries need for tomorrow.

Energy Tech also partners with nearby LaGuardia Community College to provide free college courses to students starting in grade 10. The school's principal noted that students "will leave us with not only a high school diploma but also an associate's degree and the experiences needed to go directly into competitive STEM jobs or four-year colleges. We believe they will take these skills, understandings, and qualifications, and will go on to solve complex problems and make our world a better place."[19]

### Model 5: Districtwide Career Academies in Long Beach, California

Among the highest-quality career-focused high school reform strategies in the country, Linked Learning is an approach now deeply embedded in nine California districts and expanding elsewhere.[20] A decade of support from The James Irvine Foundation and a multitude of partners, including Jobs for the Future (JFF), has provided districts with technical assistance, capacity building, research, and resources to build out the Linked Learning approach. Certified Linked Learning pathways are built around four elements: rigorous academics, real-world technical skills, work-based learning, and personalized support. California has passed legislation to expand Linked Learning and appropriated $500 million for the California Career Pathways Trust, an initiative that draws in part on the Linked Learning approach.

Starting in 2009, Long Beach Unified School District (LBUSD) embraced Linked Learning as a districtwide structure for redesigning all its high schools, and now almost all its students are currently in career-themed pathways. LBUSD high schools are large, some with more than four thousand students. Prior to Linked Learning, they had been organized into smaller learning communities, but not with industry-connected themes. Today, the high schools have pathways in architecture, construction, and engineering; media and communications; health science and medical technology; engineering and design, manufacturing, and product development; and public service.

Because LBUSD committed to enabling students to experience the real-world applications of their classroom work, the district had to make substantial changes in the way it did business. California State University, Long Beach, established a Linked Learning teacher-training program and in-service workshops to support teachers in providing project-based, integrated academic and career-focused units of study. LBUSD also provides teacher externships in industries to enable teachers to design projects and assignments reflective of the demands of employers. And because of stable and trusted district leadership and the close proximity of both Long Beach City College and Cal State Long Beach, partnership agreements forged between these institutions mean that LBUSD graduates can matriculate into pathways aligned with their high schools' Linked Learning theme.

### Postsecondary CTE Programs

While these five models represent promising approaches to CTE at the high school level, most career and technical preparation occurs at the postsecondary level in community colleges.

The challenge community colleges face is that they have multiple missions, only one of which is career preparation. Their two major missions, transfer and workforce preparation, have their origins in the history of two-year colleges. In some states, junior colleges, as they were once called, developed out of high schools to provide college preparation at a time when private universities wanted to shed the first two years of undergraduate, general education work. They also had a vocational mission to prepare accountants, clerical workers, and salespeople. In the early decades of the twentieth century, two-year programs included private "finishing schools" for young ladies wanting to be stenographers and secretaries should they have to enter the labor market. Public, municipally owned, and private junior colleges continued to grow through the first half of the twentieth century. For much of this period of development, these institutions suffered from a confusion about whether they were "expanded secondary schools or truncated colleges."[21] But the real boom in *public* community colleges came as the birth rate swelled in the 1950s and 1960s and as the GI Bill of 1944 provided support for older students to return to college. The women's movement of the 1960s and 1970s had further impact on community college expansion as women entered higher education in large numbers.

Community college workforce programs fall into two broad categories: noncredit and credit-bearing leading to a degree or certification. Noncredit programs include the myriad revenue-generating programs that community colleges mount to meet employer needs, as well as short-term noncredit credentials for the general population wanting reskilling or upskilling. Credit-bearing programs provide the basic courses or requirements for a major in a four-year institution and for entering the workforce with an associate degree. The best community colleges have designed their workforce programs so that they meet both the transfer and immediate labor market entry goals. For example, Bunker Hill Community College in Boston offers a biomedical engineering degree that prepares students to enter the labor market and to transfer to a four-year institution. The course catalog states that "the Associate of Science in Engineering Program is offered as part of a response to the long-term shortage of skilled workers in the engineering workforce . . . and to address the workforce demands of Greater Boston. The curriculum is structured to mirror the freshman and sophomore years of a university engineering degree . . . The curriculum offers two options: a Biomedical Engineering Option and an Engineering Transfer Option."[22]

### How States Organize CTE

Across the US, how credit-bearing career education is delivered in community colleges and how it is described mirrors the following fuzzy definition—that all learning in community colleges is either immediately or ultimately career focused. States set up career-focused postsecondary education using a variety of designs. An online search for "Massachusetts community colleges CTE" nets information about high school CTE and about vocational high schools' articulation agreements with community colleges but produces nothing about community college CTE, but, of course, every community college mounts career-focused programs. They just don't use the term "CTE." But a search for "California Community Colleges CTE" pulls up a long list of citations, headed by several 2017 news articles announcing the rebranding of postsecondary career and technical education in California and touting the offerings of CTE. This is a consequence of an ambitious five-year effort led by the Vice Chancellor for Workforce Development to make the community college system the principal engine of workforce development for the state. Operating under the banner "Doing What Matters for Jobs and the Economy," the California system has gained substantial support for this mission from employers and legislative leaders, as reflected in substantial investments to increase the capacity of the colleges to carry out this agenda.[23]

This is a shift for California. A 2011 research study about the state's community college system found that 75 percent of students majored in one of three liberal arts areas, with the remaining, largely older, college-ready adults choosing a CTE offering.[24] Consequently, CTE primarily served well-prepared adults, likely many of them career changers with specific career choices already made. As the study points out, most young people were counseled into liberal arts. The study was written as the community college sector was beginning to focus on data that confirmed the low degree-completion rates of community college students. However, the data also showed that students who chose a career-focused program of study—a structured pathway through to a degree with an increasingly specific sequence of courses—were completing at significantly higher rates than those who took the general education courses required for transfer to a four-year degree program.

Georgia has taken a different approach with its postsecondary CTE. It is one of the few states that still has a technical college system comprised of fifty-five institutions focused solely on two-year career preparation programs. The Technical College System of Georgia (TCSG) says it "provides a unified system of technical education, adult education, and customized business and industry training through programs that use the best available technology and offer easy access to lifelong education and training for all adult Georgians and corporate citizens." While the TCSG provides the majority of CTE, some career-focused associate degrees are also awarded at Georgia's public four-year colleges and universities. For example, East Georgia College provides a two-year degree in fire and emergency services, the credits for which can be transferred to the college's bachelor's degree program in fire service management.

All states use federal Perkins funds to supplement their own investments in CTE, but Perkins dollars and requirements have a much greater impact on how career-focused education is carried out at the secondary level than at the postsecondary level, in large measure because public high school education is mandatory and thus more subject to state and federal regulation regarding curricular content, hours in class, distribution of credit, and outcomes. There is much less uniformity in how career education is delivered among the community colleges systems than among secondary schools, and there is little correlation between how a community college system publicizes and carries out career-focused education and the Perkins dollars it receives.

For example, Georgia and California split the funds almost equally between high school CTE and postsecondary programs, while in Massachusetts, with its very strong vo-tech high schools, only a small percentage of Perkins dollars are allocated to the community colleges (73 percent versus 27 percent). In both California and Georgia, college students choose between an academic program and a career program, while in Massachusetts the boundaries are blurred between the two. In fact, all two-year degrees in Massachusetts require students to complete a set of general education courses that allow transfer should the student choose that option. However career and workforce programs are structured, today community colleges, which serve almost half of all college-going students and the majority of low-income students and students of color, are in the spotlight as major engines of upward mobility. Students choosing a pathway are increasingly aware that the economic value is higher for a well-chosen two-year degree than for some bachelor's degrees, and much less of a financial investment. For example, in a recent study for the American Enterprise Institute using Florida data, Mark Schneider and Rooney Columbus showed that of the top-earning sixteen occupations five years after graduation, five require only an associate degree and one just an apprenticeship.[25]

### The Guided Pathways Movement

Community colleges continue to struggle with expectations that they can do everything for everyone seeking a postsecondary education at a low cost. Employers continue to complain that they do not do a good job preparing the entry-level workers they need, even though educators assert that that is just what they are doing. Poll after poll shows a 70–80 percent confidence gap between what employers say and what educators say. There are many reasons for this. Lack of alignment with employer needs is only one of the problems. Employers also complain that community college graduates have not learned on up-to-date equipment or with the most recent technology. But, to put these complaints in context, employers also complain that four-year college graduates have too theoretical an orientation and that all young people lack employability or professional skills.

Today, community colleges are coalescing around the idea that colleges should require students to sign on to a roadmap outlining their path to completion, a plan that shows students just what they will need to do to complete a degree and, at best, that guarantees the courses they need will be available and relevant to labor market needs.[26] Roadmaps are an antidote to the traditional "cafeteria" curriculum model, where the underlying assumption is that more choice means greater satisfaction, when in fact too many choices can be overwhelming and results in students not completing the coursework necessary to earn degrees.[27] Low-income students in particular, who often have very complicated and demanding lives beyond the classroom, are at risk of making uninformed decisions, ultimately wasting both time and money. Wrong choices also take a toll on a student's motivation to succeed.[28] A 2015 study from the Community College Research

Center shows a correlation between students who enter a community college program of study early (taking three courses in their chosen program) and higher completion rates.[29]

This best practice of providing students with a bounded and coherent set of courses within their broad area of interest increasingly falls under two related categories: guided pathway and meta-major. Both build on a strong evidence base that students do much better when they are counseled into a default program of study with a structured schedule rather than encouraged to choose among a bewildering array of courses. *Guided pathway* is the broader term for the roadmap; *meta-major* refers to an array of majors grouped into clusters that that lead to several related career areas. For example, Valencia College in Florida, well-known for its innovative practices and significant completion and job placement rates, describes its eight meta-majors as Arts, Humanities, Communication and Design; Business; Education; Health Sciences; Industry/Manufacturing and Construction; Public Safety; Science, Technology, Engineering, and Mathematics; and Social and Behavioral Sciences and Human Services.[30]

But young people with low skills still face hurdles in entering the most competitive community college career programs. While community colleges are open admission, that does not guarantee entry into the credential program of choice. Nursing is a prime example. Students must complete developmental courses (if needed) and then prerequisites, such as college-level mathematics, composition, anatomy, and physiology before they are accepted into the major. They may also have to take the Test of Essential Academic Skills VI (TEAS VI).

Nursing has limited slots available, and priority often goes to students who already have bachelor's degrees, work experience, and/or no remedial needs or who are transferring in substantial college-level work. Among these are growing numbers of well-prepared students who want to save money by taking their first two years at a community college. The same goes for many medical certificate programs, which tend to cater to adults who already have a bachelor's degree and are changing fields.

*Community Colleges: Looking to the Future*

Like the guided pathway movement, the career pathways movement emerging from CTE is attempting to create a more coherent and up-to-date system, and community colleges are major players in that work. Demographic and economic pressures are also forcing community colleges to change. With a declining number of high school graduates due to decreases in the birth rate, and with increasing numbers of immigrant, older, and first-generation students entering their doors, forward-thinking community college leaders see their task as modernizing their programs and improving completion rates to remain the "go-to" institutions for training the middle-skill and technical workforce that fuels regional economies. They are also increasingly relying on evidence that 80 percent of community college students enter saying they are going to transfer to a four-year college, although only 18 percent complete a four-year degree. Even more worrisome, the 42 percent of students whose associate degree is in liberal arts or general education have very weak outcomes in the labor market. Indeed, those with the liberal arts two-year degree fare little better in the labor market than those with no college degree, while the returns to various certifications and technical associate degrees can yield family supporting wages, career ladders, and good prospects for increasing income.[31]

Community colleges are struggling to manage and thrive in a climate where change is accelerating, demographic shifts are coming, and the old rule about four-year college as the best post–high school choice is eroding. Despite limited and, in many cases, decreasing state support, community colleges are working to improve the quality, array, and accessibility of their career or CTE pathways and to strengthen their advising services for young people who seek a leg up in the labor market. Majors and certificate programs are being revamped in consultation with industry to better serve as engines of workforce preparation. In addition, particularly in systems historically prioritizing the preparation of students for transfer, community colleges are pivoting to refine and improve career-focused programs, as California is doing. To do so, many face challenges in updating and adding the equipment and software to meet employer needs and in implementing "earn and learn" programs that allow students to work in a field linked to their future career while attending school.

Community colleges are also competing with the array of new options for delivering learning at lower cost through technology and short-term prep programs. New providers—boot camps, short-term certificate programs, for-profit vendors—are stepping in with delivery models focused on competencies and skills, unbundling the notion of coherent, vertically organized degree programs. The new providers argue that consumers should choose what they need based on efficiency, cost, and access. More students are willing to abandon the four-year university because the costs are too high and the outcomes in the labor market are unpredictable. This pressure is having a positive impact on community colleges, pushing the best of them to revamp, be creative, and incorporate the latest technologies to improve their outcomes and meet the satisfaction of students and their future employers, and to do so with very limited means.

## THE *PATHWAYS TO PROSPERITY* REPORT AND THE CASE FOR THE NEW CTE

If the growth and development of vocational education in the United States in the twentieth century was driven in large measure by the increasing industrialization of the economy, what is the role of CTE in a twenty-first-century economy in which information, ideas, and innovation are the drivers of growth? Beginning in the 1990s and continuing through the first decade of the new century, US policy makers and their business leader allies argued that the most important thing schools could do to prepare young people for the new economy was to raise academic standards to ensure that all students leave high school with a solid foundation of core academic skills and knowledge. While no one could reasonably argue against this goal, somehow this focus on common high academic standards for all was transformed into the idea that the principal focus of US high schools should therefore be to prepare all students to go on to a four-year college or university. In a world in which "college for all" became the new mantra, high schools focused on students completing more rigorous core academic courses (and intervening with those who were behind), and CTE was seen as unimportant in the quest for college. More families now got the message that mastering the 3Rs was the ticket to college. The percentage of CTE concentrators, students taking three or more CTE courses in a related area, dropped precipitously during this period, from roughly one in three students to fewer than one in five.[32]

In 2011, the Harvard Graduate School of Education (HGSE) published a widely cited report pushing back against the "college for all" movement. *Pathways to Prosperity: Meeting the Challenge of Preparing Young Americans for the 21st Century* challenged the warnings of many economists that the middle of the US economy was "hollowing out" and that we were moving into a world in which there would only be two kinds of jobs: those with high skills, requiring at least a four-year degree, and low-skill, low-wage jobs for everyone else. The report's authors, economist Ronald Ferguson, journalist William Symonds, and Robert Schwartz, cited evidence that at least 30 percent of jobs in the next decade would be in the middle-skills category. The best of these jobs would be technician-level jobs in such sectors as IT, health care, and advanced manufacturing, requiring a strong STEM foundation and some education or training beyond high school but not necessarily a baccalaureate degree.[33]

The pushback against the "college for all" mantra was aided by three other types of evidence. First, while young people and their families clearly heard the message about the importance of college, as reflected in the rising proportion of high school graduates enrolling in four-year colleges and universities, the proportion of young people attaining a baccalaureate degree by their midtwenties remained flat at roughly one in three. Second, it became increasingly clear during the 2008–11 recession that the economic returns for a four-year degree were no longer guaranteed. In 2014, the Federal Reserve Bank of New York reported that over half of BA holders in their midtwenties were underemployed (44 percent), working in jobs that traditionally did not require a four-year college degree, or unemployed (8 percent).[34] Since the end of the recession, those numbers have gotten better, and there is evidence that virtually all of the jobs that have come back since then have gone to college graduates, but the underemployment phenomenon persists.

Third, there has recently been compelling state-level data from Mark Schneider at College Measures that compares the earnings of graduates of four-year degree programs, two-year degree programs, and one-year postsecondary certificate programs after one year, five years, and ten years in the labor market. Schneider found that in some states those with two-year technical degrees were earning about the same as those with four-year degrees even after ten years.[35] His research confirms an analysis done earlier by Anthony Carnevale at the Georgetown Center on Education and the Workforce showing the increasing overlaps among the earnings of those with occupational licenses, certificates, and those with two- and four-year degrees. Carnevale found, for example, that nearly a third of community college graduates were outearning the average BA holder. The headline from both of these studies is that while it remains true in the aggregate that the more education you have the better off you are in the labor market, it is no longer simply a matter of how much education you have but how well your skills match the demands of your regional labor market.[36]

The fourth source of evidence is the experience of other countries, especially the dual system countries, in helping a much larger portion of their youth population make a successful transition from the end of schooling into the labor market. (See especially our discussion of the Swiss VET system in chapter 2.)

## THE CAREER PATHWAYS MOVEMENT

Nearly fifty years ago, US Commissioner of Education Sidney Marland gave an interview in which he explained the distinction between vocational and career education:

> Speaking just in terms of schools, career education—as I see it—would embrace vocational education but would go a good deal further. I suppose all of us are familiar with the situation of a young person finishing high school or even college with no idea of what kind of work he would like to follow. This is

a depressing proposition for the student and in my view a failure on the part of the schools. So what I would hope for is a new orientation of education—starting with the earliest grades and continuing through high school—that would expose the student to the range of career opportunities, help him narrow down the choices in terms of his own aptitudes and interests, and provide him with education and training appropriate to his ambition . . . [The goal is] that every student leaving school will possess the skills necessary to give him a start on making a livelihood for himself and his family, even if he leaves before completing high school.[37]

What is interesting about this explanation is the recognition that all students (not just the young men referenced in Marland's use of gendered pronouns) would benefit from a stronger focus on the world of work and careers, not just those who were enrolled in vocational education. The career pathways movement comes out of the idea that all students must be prepared for *both* college (some form of education or training beyond high school) *and* career. This means that the old dichotomy between "college-bound" and "work-bound" students no longer holds and that high schools need to design programs that integrate academic and career-focused education and provide all students the opportunity to explore both worlds.

While high school CTE programs and career academy programs both embrace the goal of college *and* career, CTE programs tend to prioritize the career goal while academies prioritize the college goal. The common denominator, however, is that both types of programs stop at the end of high school. Career pathways programs are deliberately designed to span both high school and at least the first year or two of postsecondary and end at the point of initial employment. The argument for creating pathways that span the last years of high school and the first year or two of community college is that, given the structure of the American high school and the core curriculum requirements for graduation, the opportunity for students to get either in-depth technical education or an extended leaning experience at a workplace is extremely limited during the high school years. The goal of career pathways programs is to see young people through to the attainment of a first postsecondary credential with value in the labor market and then to help that young person actually get launched into the job market.

In 2012, in response to the demand generated by the *Pathways to Prosperity* report, our respective organizations, HGSE and JFF, joined forces to launch the Pathways to Prosperity Network.[38] While at the time there were a few other national or regional organizations working with networks of high schools on CTE reform or the development of career academies—most notably the Southern Regional Education Board and the National Academy Foundation (NAF)—there was no other organization focused on helping states build career pathways sytems that spanned grades 9–14 and designed to help students attain a first postsecondary credential with value in the labor market. Seven years later the Pathways Network is no longer alone in this field. Thanks in substantial measure to New Skills for Youth, a $75 million grants program launched by the JPMorgan Chase Foundation, there are now several other organizations working with states and localities on career pathways. Consequently, there is now a growing career pathways movement that incorporates CTE but is aimed at a broader career-readiness-for-all agenda. Because we cofounded the Pathways Network and know it best, we use it here to exemplify some of the core principles and practices that characterize the broader career pathways movement.

The Pathways Network began in 2012 with five states. Although each of the five expressed somewhat different motives for joining, one common denominator was a desire to strike a better balance between the narrowly academic purposes of education and the broader career and civic purposes. While the national conversation was moving from "college for all" to "all students graduating high school college and career ready," in most high schools there continued to be much more focus on college preparation, college choice, and admission than on career choice, a problem exacerbated by the notion that the first two years of college could be just about broad liberal arts subjects and that career choice could come later.

We developed a simple five-part framework to guide our work (figure 4.1). The core commitment we asked states to make was to create career pathways systems that spanned grades 9–14 and combine rigorous academics with relevant career-focused education. Around that central commitment we developed four "implementation levers":

- early and sustained career information, advising, and exposure;
- strategies to engage employers as partners and codevelopers;
- identification of employer-facing intermediary organizations to help scale work-based learning opportunities; and
- supportive state policies.

In addition to their agreeing to work on the development of these implementation levers, there were three other key commitments we sought from states. While we encouraged them to begin the work in one or two regions where key assets were already in place (e.g., strong secondary or postsecondary CTE programs, motivated employers), we discouraged them from joining the Network unless their goal over time was to build a statewide career pathways *system*. Because system-building is a long-term process, we also asked states to make a three-year commitment, the minimum time needed to help states lay the path for the system-building journey. And to support the ability of our Pathways team at JFF to work with them, we required states to pay an annual membership fee in return for customized technical assistance and the opportunity to bring a leadership team to semiannual Network institutes designed to promote cross-state learning.

Our states have adopted diverse paths and strategies to initiate the process of building statewide career pathways systems. In Tennessee, for example, the first state to join the Network, it became clear after our initial exploratory visits to two regions that it was a strong CTE state, with virtually all high school students having access to course offerings in two or more traditional CTE fields of study. The challenge, as identified both by key state leaders and employers, was to modernize CTE programs to ensure their alignment with the needs of regional labor markets and to build stronger connections and alignment between secondary and postsecondary programs. In 2014 Governor Bill Haslam launched a major statewide initiative focused on

**FIGURE 4.1   Pathways to Prosperity framework**

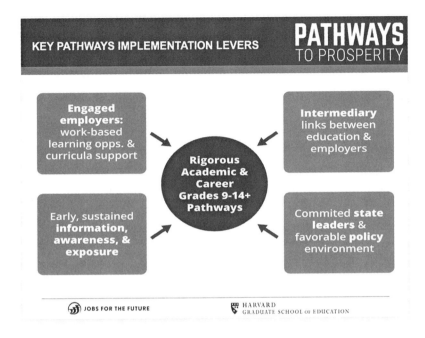

increasing postsecondary attainment in order to attract and retain the kinds of employers needed to grow the state's economy, which only strengthened the case for the modernization and alignment strategy. In the years since Tennessee joined the Network, the state has made substantial progress. A 2017 case study on Tennessee Pathways reported that significant numbers of old CTE programs had been closed, to be replaced by programs in such emerging fields as cybersecurity and human resource management; that 83 percent of high school students had access to at least one of the three priority career clusters the state had identified (IT, health care, and advanced manufacturing); that 77 percent of high schools are now offering dual enrollment courses; and that nearly half of the students who graduated in 2016 were CTE concentrators. This suggests that the work of building a modern career pathways system is well under way in Tennessee.[39]

California, which joined the Network in 2013, chose a different starting point and pathways strategy. Most traditional high school CTE in California takes place in regional occupational centers, not in comprehensive high schools. But since the 1980s, the state has also been a big believer in the career academies model. California Partnership Academies, a state-funded competitive grants program, are small schools-within-schools with an industry focus; they integrate academic and technical education, have industry partners, provide work-based learning, and are focused on preparing all students for postsecondary education. There are currently nearly four hundred such academies across the state.

In 2014, the California Senate, inspired by Long Beach Unified's Linked Learning program and by the Swiss and German youth apprenticeship systems, inserted $250 million in the budget to support the creation of the California Career Pathways Trust (CCPT), a competitive grants program designed to support the development of regional consortia across the state to build nine to fourteen pathways aligned with high-growth, high-demand sectors in each region's economy. In 2015, after a second round of similar funding, there were eighty regional consortia across the state bringing together high schools, community colleges, employer organizations, and workforce boards to provide pathways to postsecondary education and employment for thousands of young people throughout the state.[40] At the same time, the California community college system is rapidly modernizing its CTE programs in ways that will support this state investment.

Tennessee and California represent not only the two principal avenues our Network states and regions have taken in order to move to scale but also the differing strategies of some of the older, best-established national organizations and networks in the broader career education space. The Tennessee approach, modernizing its CTE programs and better connecting them to aligned postsecondary programs, exemplifies the orientation of High Schools That Work (HSTW), a network of over twelve hundred high schools in thirty states that operates under the umbrella of the Southern Regional Education Board.[41] Because CTE programs throughout the South have historically enjoyed strong public support, especially from employers in a predominantly low-skill, low-wage economy, the strategy of working with those programs to upgrade and modernize them to prepare young people to function in an economy demanding a higher level of skills makes political sense. HSTW, rooted in the South for three decades, has made a major contribution in bringing CTE programs in the schools in its network into the twenty-first century.

By contrast, the National Academy Foundation has been the principal source of support for districts and schools seeking to adopt and expand the career academy model. Led from its inception by Sanford Weill, a longtime leader in the financial services industry, NAF has evolved from its origins as a sponsor of one Academy of Finance in New York City to an organization now serving nearly 100,000 students in 675 academies in 5 sectors (engineering, finance, health, hospitality and tourism, and information technology) in 36 states. As NAF has scaled up, it has increasingly focused on districts, not just schools, as the appropriate unit of change, and it has especially focused on trying to deliver on the promise of providing all of its students the opportunity for a significant internship or some other extended work-based learning experience.[42]

As our own work has evolved over these past seven years, and as the Pathways Network has expanded to include four metropolitan regional members, two big city members, and now nine states, our thinking has evolved about the problem of scale and the best ways to help a diverse set members get there. In those states where most students have access to well-developed CTE programs, whether in separate vocational schools, part-time area centers, or comprehensive high schools, the strategy should be modernization, alignment with regional labor markets, and (using dual enrollment and early college designs) enrollment of students in aligned postsecondary technical programs while they're still in high school.

Delaware, which joined the Network in 2014, is the state that has made the most rapid progress in this area, moving from having one small program for high school students in advanced manufacturing housed at Delaware Technical (Del Tech) Community College in 2014 to having more than twelve thousand students across the state participating in career pathways programs in fourteen sectors in 2018. Delaware's goal is to have twenty thousand students in career pathways by 2020, all of which will be aligned with postsecondary programs at Del Tech or other four-year colleges in the state. That goal represents roughly half of the high school cohort in Delaware, which means that this will become the mainstream system in the state, the way most young people will experience high school.[43]

In states that do not have a history of such broad access to traditional CTE programs, a more mixed model approach is needed. For example, Massachusetts has a very strong, well-developed network of regional vocational schools and several excellent district-run vocational schools. The best of these schools outperform the comprehensive high schools in their regions, and they have waiting lists. But these schools and the vocational programs in comprehensive high schools only serve about 20 percent of Massachusetts high school students. While the state has recently made significant investments in equipment and infrastructure to support these schools, its capacity for expansion is extremely limited, and there is little interest at the state level in investing in building additional vocational schools. Consequently, policy makers have recently been focused on how to increase opportunities for students in the comprehensive high schools to experience some form of career-focused education. In 2016, Massachusetts received a New Skills for Youth grant, which it is using to strengthen career advising and generally expand its High Quality College and Career Pathways program.

This leads us to one final example from the Network. In 2016, New York City became the first large city to become a member. While New York has a strong collection of CTE high schools, as well as a large number of other high schools with CTE programs and a small but powerful set of tech-focused early college high schools, what it doesn't have is a strategy to ensure that *all* young people in the city gain enough exposure to the world of work and careers to make an informed choice about the best education or training pathway after high school. This is the problem that prompted leaders from the three key public agencies—the city's education department, CUNY, and the Mayor's Workforce Office—to come together to address through the development of CareerReady NYC: A Compact to Support Universal Career

Readiness. The idea, drawing partly on earlier similar compacts in Boston and Los Angeles, and reminiscent of the case made by Sidney Marland for career education for all, begins by asking, What sequence of career-oriented experiences and activities—in school and out of school, year after year, beginning in grade 6 and continuing through high school graduation and into postsecondary education—would ensure that all young New Yorkers are prepared to meet a serious standard of career readiness? The New York Pathways team believes the most promising strategy to ensure career readiness is to provide all students before high school graduation an opportunity *both* to get started on college *and* to have a well-structured internship or other extended work-based learning opportunity. Reaching universal coverage on these two opportunities will take several years, but New York has two very substantial building blocks: College Now, a partnership between the school system and CUNY that already provides early college experience for nearly 25,000 high school students; and a 70,000-student summer youth employment program that is being redesigned to better align with the city's broader career-readiness agenda.

Outside the Pathways Network, the most interesting development in the broader career pathways field has been the revival of interest in youth apprenticeship. Youth apprenticeship programs adapt the core principles of apprenticeship—paid on-the-job earning combined with classroom instruction aligned with labor market needs—into a structure specifically designed for high school students. Youth apprenticeship first surfaced in the US in the context of the School-to-Work movement in the 1990s, when Wisconsin launched a statewide initiative in 1991. Today youth apprenticeship in Wisconsin is organized through thirty-three regional consortia that bring together employers, school districts, organized labor, workforce development boards, and others. The fields in which student may apprentice have spread well beyond the traditional trades and crafts to include the arts, STEM, information technology, and finance. While the program is based in high schools, students can earn college credits along the way. The program now serves nearly five thousand students and engages more than three thousand employers. The state funds the infrastructure and staffing to manage the program at a cost of about $900 per student.[44] The Wisconsin program offers students two different levels of intensity, both beginning in the junior year. One option provides for 450 hours of workplace learning over two semesters. The other option offers nine hundred hours of workplace learning over four semesters. These workplace hours can readily be accommodated within the typical schedule of a US high school but stop well short of the three full days a week of workplace learning that Swiss students experience in the dual system model.

Colorado is the first state to develop a youth apprenticeship model that more closely mirrors the Swiss approach. After Colorado's governor led a forty-person study tour of the Swiss VET system in 2015, state leaders decided to create a nonprofit intermediary to develop a public/private youth apprenticeship model. CareerWise Colorado, led by the former CEO of a family-owned manufacturing firm, launched its first apprenticeships for 120 students in 2017. The Colorado program is a three-year model. It starts with high school juniors, who spend up to sixteen hours a week in their apprenticeship placement that first year. As seniors they spend up to twenty-four hours a week as the workplace. In the third year they are full-time employees of the firm, earning an industry certification while earning college credits. CareerWise currently offers apprenticeships in five fields: advanced manufacturing, information technology, financial services, business operations, and health care. A sixth field, education, is currently being piloted. Career-Wise, launched with $9.5 million in philanthropic start-up funds and now with a staff of forty, has bold ambitions. It hopes to grow from serving a few hundred students in its early years to serving twenty thousand (10 percent) of the state's high schoolers by 2027.[45]

Beyond Wisconsin, Colorado, and long-standing employer-led programs in North Carolina and South Carolina, there are now a sufficient number of states and regions expressing interest in youth apprenticeship to have led the New America Foundation to create the Partnership to Advance Youth Apprenticeship, a collaborative of eight organizations, including JFF, dedicated to support the growth and development of quality youth apprenticeship models in the US.[46]

## US CTE IN A COMPARATIVE INTERNATIONAL CONTEXT

Despite the presence of such rich and varied career-focused high schools, why has the United States struggled to create its own version of the strong secondary vocational *systems* that we find in countries like Austria, Germany, the Netherlands, Switzerland, and Singapore?

One barrier to devising such a system is the unfortunate legacy of tracking, which too often resulted in shunting low-income and minority youth into low-skill, dead-end jobs that offered little or no potential for upward mobility. Given the widely shared belief in the US in public schooling as the principal engine of social and economic mobility, the tracking of young people into vocational education increasingly came to be seen, especially by the civil rights community, as antithetical to core democratic values.

A second significant barrier is the culture and belief system of most US employers. In countries with strong VET systems, employers and their associations take an active leadership role in the design and implementation of vocational education; they believe that it is in their self-interest to help socialize teenagers into the world of work before they have become entirely the captives of their peer culture. Employers in strong VET system countries are also much more accustomed to acting collectively through their sector associations on recruitment and talent development needs than are US employers. They do this because by sharing the costs of supporting their VET systems, especially the costs of firm-based training, they are much less concerned about "poaching," or losing their investment in someone they have trained to a free-rider competitor. Also, because their sector association has worked closely with the government to ensure that the standards trainees must meet are rigorous and uniform across the country, even if they lose someone they have trained to a competitor, they can be confident that the person they hire will have been trained to the same national industry standard.

It is difficult to overemphasize the importance of national industry standards and a national qualifications system, both for young people and for employers. A European young person completing an apprenticeship in IT, banking, or carpentry, as examples, has a qualification that is portable anywhere in their home country (and increasingly throughout the European Union). In the US, a Registered Apprenticeship credential is similarly portable, but only a tiny fraction of the workforce has such a credential (roughly 500,000 out of a total workforce of nearly 154 million).[47] The two most common and rapidly growing forms of career-related credentials, other than degrees, are occupational certificates, awarded by postsecondary institutions, and occupational certifications, awarded by industry groups. In the absence of national industry standards and a national credentialing or qualifications system, neither young people nor employers have any way of determining the labor market value of such credentials, a huge problem the country is only now beginning to address.[48]

A third challenge the US faces in developing a strong vocational education system has to do with the structure of secondary education in the US. In Europe, compulsory education typically ends at age 15, at the end of lower secondary school, at which point students choose between vocational and general education paths for upper secondary school. In the US, compulsory education ends in most states between ages 16 and 18, meaning that the natural break point in our system comes at the end of high school, not earlier. It's also the case that the US high school has no real counterpart in other countries. While its core function is academic, it also provides a wide range of other programs and services that are essential to its identity, especially in suburban and rural communities. For many young people, the opportunity to participate in school-run activities like athletics, music, and theater is at least as important as the school's academic offerings, and these activities typically enjoy broad parental and community support as well. Given the role that the high school plays in American adolescent life and popular culture, a proposal to allow 40–70 percent of young people to spend their high school years learning mostly in workplaces rather than schools would mean that a major component of community culture would vanish.

A fourth reason the US does not have a strong VET system has to do with the role and structure of higher education in the US. The United States still suffers from the "college for all" messaging problem, which insists that the best option for nearly all young people after high school is the bachelor's degree. In fact, university participation in vocational education has increased in several other countries, and many European universities even limit admission or distribute students among tertiary institutions based on national or state examinations.

Finally, the liberal arts tradition in the US impedes the growth of a comprehensive vocational education system. In Europe, students apply to a faculty within the university (e.g., economics, literature, law, medicine, architecture). Having received a solid preparation in the liberal arts and sciences during their upper secondary years, they are therefore ready to choose a field of study and get started on their career path when they enter a university. In the US, however, broad general studies go on for at least two years of tertiary education. This tradition allows students to put off deep commitment to a career until much later in their schooling.

While it is true that at the elite end of our higher education system admission is very competitive, the reality is that only students seeking a place at a handful of mainly private institutions (e.g., Stanford, MIT, Harvard) have a strong incentive to work hard in high school, since there is a place for them somewhere in the higher education system, no matter how weak their academic record. Middle-class American children are brought up to believe that they will go to college or university after high school, and nearly 90 percent of high school seniors say that is their intention after graduation. Two-thirds of high school graduates actually do in enroll in some form of college after graduation, though only about one in three Americans earn a four-year degree by their midtwenties, with another 10 percent earning a two-year degree.

US policy makers have historically been focused on reducing the high school dropout rate, but the college and university dropout rate is in fact much higher: only 6 in 10 who begin a four-year degree program complete within six years, and fewer than 4 in 10 starting a two-year program complete within three years. While there are multiple explanations for these very high college dropout rates—poor academic preparation, weak college advising and support systems, inadequate financial aid, family obligations, poor time management skills—the consequence is millions of young people reaching their midtwenties with "some college" on their resumes but no academic degree or career qualification, little relevant work experience, and a high likelihood of some student debt. Indeed, many US students work thirty to forty hours per week while going to school to pay not only for tuition but for living expenses. These troubling outcomes are creating rising pressure on higher education institutions to provide stronger career advising services and more internship and other work-based learning opportunities for their students. This adds fuel to the argument that the US needs to reduce its reliance on four-year colleges and universities as the preferred delivery system for equipping young Americans with the skills and credentials to succeed in the labor market.

## THE WAY FORWARD

There are a few lessons for the future to be drawn from this review of the history of vocational education in the US and its evolution into career and technical education.

The first is that, as much as we admire the Singapore and Swiss systems (see chapters 1 and 2, respectively), we think it neither desirable nor feasible to return to a bifurcated world in which students are asked to choose between a college path and a CTE path. We are convinced that virtually all of the jobs that can lead to a livable wage in tomorrow's economy will require at least some form of postsecondary education or training, but not necessarily a four-year degree. We are also convinced that all young people would be much better off if they were provided a more systematic and sustained introduction to the world of work and careers during their middle and high school years so they could make more informed choices among the various postsecondary options open to them.

A second conclusion we have reached is that the knowledge, skills, and dispositions that are most likely to prepare young people for a rapidly changing economy are best acquired through some combination of theoretical and applied learning. In particular, the skills that employers keep telling us they value most—problem solving, teamwork, communication, leadership—are best learned not in classrooms but in well-structured and supported workplace settings, which is one reason we advocate internship opportunities for all.

A third lesson is that while we should definitely focus on strengthening and modernizing traditional CTE programs, as Tennessee and Delaware have done so effectively, we should also be promoting models that can more readily be spread within comprehensive high schools, in particular models like Energy Tech that combine the strengths of career academies and early college high schools.

A fourth lesson, as the New York City example shows, is that while we press ahead to strengthen and expand high-quality CTE and career academy programs, there are limits to the number of students they can serve. There will always be a substantial number of students—in many high schools a majority—who will not be touched by these programs but who should be exposed to the world of work and careers in order to make informed choices about the best path for them after high school. If we are serious about the goal of all students leaving high school prepared for both college and career, the US will need a deliberate, systematic strategy to meet that goal, a strategy that is likely to emerge from the career pathways movement.

Finally, the most important thing we can and must learn from the strongest vocational systems in the world is the critical importance of engaging employers and their associations as codevelopers and co-owners of the career-focused approach. There are very few examples we can point to in our own Pathways Network or elsewhere in the US of demand-driven CTE reforms. Until the demand side of the equation receives equal attention and weight, CTE in the United States will never have the impact on either students or state and regional economies that it has in the Switzerlands and Singapores of the world.

CHAPTER 5

# THE FUTURE OF VET IN A GLOBAL, AI-POWERED ECONOMY

*Marc S. Tucker*

The four countries whose stories are told in the preceding chapters are very different from each other. But those stories have all played out in the same world economy, and that economy has changed dramatically over the last half-century. It is useful to analyze the development of VET in those countries as very different responses to one phenomenon: globalization.

## GLOBALIZATION DRIVES THE DEVELOPMENT OF WORLDWIDE LABOR MARKETS

The development of VET systems since the 1970s in Singapore, Switzerland, China, and the United States, and everywhere else, was profoundly affected by the way the integration of the global economy turned local labor markets into global labor markets almost overnight. Prior to the 1970s, most workers competed with others in a labor market that was local, metropolitan, or regional, only rarely in one that crossed national borders. Thus, the price of labor in any one place reflected the overall productivity of the local or regional economy. Economist Lester Thurow once joked in a meeting of NCEE's board of trustees that it was obvious that American economists were better than British economists because the Americans made more money. Actually, he said, the British economists were at least as good, but the British economy as a whole was not as productive. Wages in a country or in a region within a country rose and fell with the health of the whole economy. So factory workers in the United States made far more money than did factory workers in South Korea or Brazil—but not because they were any more skilled.

Rapid advances in transportation and communications technologies during World War II and in the following decades dramatically reduced the cost of moving goods long distances and made it possible to communicate reliably with any point in the world at practically no cost. Manufacturing companies discovered that they could locate production without regard to where the product would be designed or sold. Also, for manufacturers for whom labor was a big share of the cost of production, and whose workers were mostly unskilled or semi-skilled, this meant that they could locate production in countries where the cost of labor with basic literacy was very low. This would not have worked nearly as well decades earlier, because ordinary workers in many parts of the world were functionally illiterate. But after the war, literacy levels had risen dramatically in the many of the world's poorest countries. To a degree few had realized, large numbers of people in those countries had achieved levels of literacy equal to those of many workers in countries with much higher wages. The stage was set for a massive transfer of low-skill and semi-skilled work to poor countries.

This changed everything. Suddenly, millions of workers in the world's high-wage countries were unemployed and unemployable. The unskilled or semi-skilled labor they had been selling was now a commodity on a newly globalized labor market, and they were charging much more for what they had to sell than global employers had to pay. A giant sorting process ensued. In the rich countries, millions of members of the middle class lost their jobs and were forced to get other jobs that provided less security and paid lower wages, though the returns to those fortunate enough to have more and better education soared. There were growing shortages in the rich countries of people with high skills and growing surpluses of those with low skills.

In September 1977, the CEO of Volvo hired Ira Magaziner, then with the Boston Consulting Group, to conduct a study for Volvo and the Swedish government to find out why key Swedish industries had become uncompetitive after a century or more of steady success. One of those industries was the shipbuilding industry. The managers thought the trouble was with labor.

The unions thought it was poor management. Magaziner, asking where the business had gone, learned that their strongest competitor was South Korea.

After visiting shipbuilders in South Korea, Magaziner told the Swedes that they should give up the shipbuilding business. It would never come back. The South Koreans were using the same advanced technology to build their ships that the Swedes had been using, but that machinery was being effectively operated by low-skill, low-pay workers. He advised the Swedes to tear down their shipyards and, on the ground where they had been, to construct new plants to manufacture products that used advanced technology, which required high-skill labor. The world would pay well for high-tech, high-value-added products that only highly skilled workers could produce, but they would not buy from Sweden high-tech products that low-skill workers could produce much more cheaply elsewhere. He drew them a four-cell matrix:

| high-tech/high skill | low-tech/high skill |
| --- | --- |
| high-tech/low skill | low-tech/low skill |

If Sweden wanted to continue to provide broadly shared prosperity to its citizens, Magaziner said, it would have to develop public policies that would enable it to concentrate on the development of products and services that used leading-edge proprietary technologies, offered innovations that customers all over the world valued highly, and employed highly educated and very skilled workers who would be treated not as cogs in a machine but as knowledge workers whose skills and ideas were valued by their employers. Following Magaziner's prescription, Sweden tore down its shipyards and steel mills and replaced them with car factories and cell phone manufacturers.

In the high-wage countries around the world, the compensation of those who worked with their heads soared as companies figured out Magaziner's matrix for themselves and as the compensation of those with low skills and low literacy nose-dived. The message went out to parents in many of those countries that the future belonged to those with a university education. VET was increasingly viewed as the education of last resort for those who were no good at academics. This was the case even in rich countries with first-rate VET systems. In Europe, many countries had invited guest workers to come from countries with poor education, poor technical skills, and failing economies to take low-skill manufacturing jobs in their booming economies in the 1960s and 1970s. As these factory jobs became less attractive to many native workers, the lower ranks of the VET programs began to fill with the children of these immigrants. This combined with the increased desire of native-born parents to send their sons and daughters to university to lower the status of VET even further.

## NATIONAL COMPETITIVE STRATEGIES AND THE FATE OF VET

Nations reacted to the spread of the forces of globalization differently. Their responses were largely based on where they were on the spectrum of economic development, a trajectory that starts with a country being in poverty and ends with that country becoming a rich nation. The strategy each country chose to compete in a world turned upside-down by the creation of a global market for labor, of course, proved critical in determining how fast a country would move along that trajectory and how far it would get. And there were some countries, most notably the United States, that did nothing at all.

Two of the four countries studied in this volume, China and Singapore, were both very poor in the 1960s. Newly independent Singapore set out to get rich using its low-cost, low-skill workforce as the big draw for foreign investors in the newly globalizing labor market. China set out to get rich a decade later using the same strategy, putting globalization into high gear. Both countries built the massive, high-quality infrastructure, including deep-water ports, needed by global manufacturers interested in employing large numbers of highly disciplined, hard-working unskilled and semi-skilled factory workers. Both created tax-free zones for manufacturing firms and worked hard to find investors to fill them with factories.

From the beginning, Singapore kept raising the skills of its workforce and using those skills to attract firms that were willing to pay higher wages for the higher-skill labor they needed. The government's Economic Development Board understood the logic behind Magaziner's matrix very well and was determined to move Singapore toward a "high-tech/high skill" position as quickly as possible, step by logical step. It was important to the government to create an economy that could provide broadly shared prosperity to its people, because there was no shared national identity to bind the new nation together. In its first move, it placed a high priority on VET, with the training of the carpenters, masons, electricians, and plumbers needed to kick-start the economic development process. But in only a few years raising academic and especially technical engineering skills across the board and building a strong postsecondary education system to support that goal took the highest priority, leaving VET far behind and the educational option of last resort for those with low academic skills. The ethnic Chinese did much better in Singapore's schools than did the minority populations, and the government saw this difference in educational options as the very kind of threat to broadly shared prosperity and political stability that its founders had most feared. The government recognized that the economy would be dysfunctional if it had a strong high-skills sector and a weak middle-skills sector; it could only deliver the goods if both sectors were world class. In response, the Singaporean government made an enormous investment of both money and political capital to build a world-class VET system.

China, a vast country, had to start somewhere, and that turned out to be the coastal provinces, the logical place to build goods for export. Like Singapore's leaders, Deng Xiaoping and his colleagues knew that China would be more prosperous, but would never get rich, using other countries' designs and copying their products, so they set in motion a long-range plan to make China a global leader in science and critical technologies by investing heavily in schooling, postsecondary education and research and development. China did not make a similar push in the area of vocational education, however. This has resulted in a success in primary and secondary academic education in a number of the coastal provinces but also in a VET sector that is largely disconnected from the industries China is counting on to move its economy forward and that is populated by students who see it as a last resort and staffed by teachers who often have little or no useful experience in the occupations they are training their students for. Some of the best job training was being done at several of China's state-owned companies, but these companies are increasingly doing less and less training. The foreign-invested firms are not being encouraged by the government to train young people, and private Chinese firms have shown little interest in training their future workers.

To some degree, the success of Shanghai and other coastal provinces in international comparisons of student academic performance is related to the millennia-old conviction of Chinese parents that doing well on the school academic exams is the key to future well-being. The converse of that proposition, however, is that working with one's hands and getting those hands dirty in the process is viewed as low class and low status. To some extent, then, the price of China's academic success may be a low status for VET, which could be a growing problem for China's economic growth and political stability.

Yet, there is evidence that the government in Beijing sees the danger. Very large sums have been invested over the last ten years or so in new physical facilities and equipment for VET schools. Considerable emphasis has been placed on the creation of new VET models in many parts of the country. A thousand flowers are indeed blooming. It is also the case that the one of the highest priorities for the central government is making China the world leader in certain key technologies—especially artificial intelligence (AI), robotics, quantum computing, and machine learning—as quickly as possible. They are working hard to build the skills needed at every level of their economy to make good on this goal. So, while China appears to be far behind a number of other countries in VET, and VET seems to have very low standing in the eyes of most Chinese parents, educators, and students, the government seems to be determined to catch up.

Experienced China watchers are unanimous in their conviction that it is both easy and unwise to underestimate the probability that the central government will be able to reach the kind of very ambitious social and economic goals it has repeatedly set for itself and achieved. And culture is not destiny. Singapore, which is largely run by ethnic Chinese who share the same values as the mainland Chinese, saw the danger that China now faces—unemployed university graduates and growing shortages of the highly skilled technicians needed to run a modern economy—and met the challenge by building a vibrant, high-tech, first-rate VET system that is proving to be more and more attractive to young Singaporeans and their parents.

One could easily argue that Singapore and China make a good pairing, because only a few decades ago both countries were very poor and both chose to start their economic climb by selling cheap labor and deep water ports, their principal assets. But one could make just as good a case for pairing Singapore and Switzerland. As Nancy Hoffman and Robert Schwartz note in chapter 2, there was a point at which leading Swiss industrialists gathered together to consider the future of their country and concluded that they wanted to live in a country with broadly shared prosperity. They decided that that could be achieved only if the Swiss workforce was among the best educated and mostly highly skilled in the world, and they then married that competitive advantage to worldwide technological leadership in a few selected industries.

The Swiss deliberately built on a strong tradition of manufacturing excellence and an equally strong commitment by businesses to the development in their firms of the skills of the nation's young people. The Swiss also decided to have few traditional universities, make them world class, and limit the number of professional programs they offered. The decision to limit the scope of traditional university education made room for a flourishing and attractive VET sector, and the decision by Swiss firms to invest heavily in VET in their own firms provided the means by which Swiss young people could get a first-rate applied education that was just as plausible a way to the top ranks of Swiss society and a professional degree. Like Singapore, Switzerland had a clear commitment from the beginning to a design for its economy that could provide broadly shared prosperity for all of its people.

A less obvious pairing, at least on the surface, is that of the United States and China, which are more usually seen as opposites from almost every point of view. Yet both are large countries with enormous variations in almost every relevant dimension of politics, demography, geography, economic strategy, and vision. And there are further parallels that are very revealing in the context of vocational education and training.

Both China and the US are usefully viewed not as one economy but as collections of economies. In China, some provinces, mostly those along the coast, are economic powerhouses, technologically vibrant, home to highly educated workforces, and getting wealthy quickly. Others, mostly in the interior, look like the coastal provinces did decades ago: relatively poor and with much lower education levels, many fewer professionals, and much-less-advanced technology.

The same is true in the United States. It is mainly the coastal states that are home to many of the world's most advanced economies, while other states have economies that are more like those found in many third world countries. It is as if the states had decided individually how to respond to the globalization of the world economy. Some states that were already home to leading research universities and high-tech firms and had high performing school systems chose, not surprisingly, to behave like Switzerland and Singapore and invest heavily in their education systems and making their states attractive to highly talented professionals worldwide. They were willing to raise their taxes, which were already high, to make their states worldwide leaders in technology, research, and education. Also like Singapore and Switzerland, they did not mind being high cost if that meant they could be a leader in the global market for technological leadership and high-quality products and services. But other states did not see themselves as competitors in the market for high-skilled labor and high-quality products and services. They had long lagged far behind the leading states in both education and technology. And their politics were dominated by business interests that competed not on the basis of quality but on price, which required keeping wages and taxes as low as possible.

All of the states were interested in VET, but their visions were very different. The poor states competing on the price of labor were used to attracting businesses with concessionary tax rebates and the offer of free job training.

And because the firms they were after were looking mainly for relatively low-skill, low-cost labor, the training they wanted was not for high-skill, high-technology jobs but for relatively low-skill, low-technology jobs, and it was also often designed to provide firm-specific skills that the worker could not easily take to another employer. The rich states, however, built a VET system that attracted top-performing high school students by offering a curriculum that combined challenging academics with hands-on experience with high technology. This vision for VET, as seen in the example of Massachusetts, was more like Switzerland's and Singapore's than it was like many other states'.

The United States has different economic systems that are spread out along a continuum, and these varying systems offer different visions of VET. As Schwartz and Hoffman point out in chapter 4, there are a number of states, like Tennessee, whose political leaders are working hard to move their states from a low-skills equilibrium to a high-skills equilibrium.

Transitioning an economy from attracting low-skill, low-pay employers to one that attracts high-skill, high-pay employers is anything but easy. Economists describe each kind of economy as typically being in a kind of equilibrium and therefore very hard to change. Economies in a low-skill equilibrium are dominated by firms whose interests lie in keeping taxes and compensation as low as possible. Because that is true, they have little or nothing to invest in education and skills development. Because most of the available work is low skill and low pay, the students they do educate to high standards tend to leave. And because so little is offered to highly educated and skilled workers, firms do not attract workers from the outside. It becomes very hard for far-seeing political leaders to change all of this because they are afraid that raising education and skill levels will not only raise taxes but will also lead to demands for higher pay, which will destroy their business model. The opposite is true in economies powered by high technology and high skills. With this equilibrium, there is strong support for the kind of high-skills, high-pay economy that can lead to broadly shared prosperity and a modern, high-quality VET system.

Another similarity between the United States and China is their approach to the development and spread of education and training policy. They both tend to issue very broad policy statements from the center and then follow up on these mandates not by controlling in detail how they are implemented at lower levels but instead by calling for experimentation everywhere. "Let a thousand flowers bloom" is how Deng Xiaoping began the opening up of China in 1978. As many things are tried in many places, government at different levels takes note, with guidance very slowly emerging based on what seems to work. This style of development is likely not to come up with the one best way for everyone but, rather, will determine the best way for different places at different times. It is messy but flexible.

Yet another important similarity between China and the US is related to the fear Peter Drucker expressed—that the US might adopt the kind of VET systems that the Northern and Central Europeans have.[1] According to Drucker, the great advantage of the US in global trade is its innovation and flexibility, both of which could be severely compromised by a form of VET that requires an elaborate system of formal credentials that change only slowly and are often set to standards that represent not leading-edge practice but average practice. Drucker and others contend that the American belief that anyone with drive, ambition, and discipline can pick up what they need to do the next job, and ought to be free to do whatever the market will reward, is the right idea. Such a system, messy and chaotic as it is, in which education and training institutions of all kinds are constantly offering a wide range of learning opportunities in a fiercely competitive market, will adjust much more readily to market opportunities than one that is highly regulated and governed by a complex system of occupational standards that can seriously interfere with the capacity of an economy to adjust to new technologies and more efficient forms of work organization.

Could it be that the weakness of the American VET system as viewed by experts and the failure thus far of the Chinese to develop a serious VET system are actually advantages for those countries in the global labor market?

## THE AI EFFECT

Another factor that must be taken into account by designers of VET systems today is the rapid advance of artificial intelligence and related technologies and their influence on the future of work.

In 1990, for every job the United States was losing to globalization, ten were being lost to automation. As the price of labor has risen since then in emerging countries, much of the manufacturing that moved to countries with low-priced labor has moved back to the US, but many of the jobs have not. The people doing them have been replaced by machines. Even the coastal provinces of China, the principal destination for the jobs that left the US for low-cost producers, are now the scene of vast installations of robots and other automated machinery replacing millions of Chinese manufacturing workers, who are still making much less money than their American counterparts.

Over the last twenty years, digital equipment of all kinds has become vastly more capable and much less expensive. The most vulnerable workers are those in high-wage countries doing relatively routine work that can be captured in a set of standard instructions written in code. A very large number of people who participate in VET around the world do work of this kind, among them cooks, servers, retail clerks, factory workers, truck and bus drivers, legal researchers, warehouse workers, farmworkers, and stocktakers. Researchers have calculated that about half of the jobs now being done in the American economy could be done by automated equipment today.[2] Some observers, alarmed by these developments, have predicted that many workers will become permanently redundant as technology takes their jobs and they are no longer productive members of the community. They are proposing various schemes to provide these former workers with a basic minimum income paid for by taxes on the owners of the increasingly automated production equipment.

Entire industries are being destroyed or rebuilt using these technologies. Retail department stores and malls are in trouble because many people prefer to order from digital retailers from the comfort of home. The people who work in the warehouses those digital retailers are building are themselves being replaced by automated machines. Giant mines are now being built where ore is mined by automated equipment, taken to the surface by automated equipment, transported to a deep-water port by automated equipment, and put on the boats by automated equipment for transport to distant ports. Pictures that used to be taken on film that used to be processed by tens of thousands of people working in processing centers are now shared digitally using services that make a handful of people fabulously wealthy but employ no one else. Cars with technologically sophisticated drive trains that used to be built by people with very strong technical skills are now being replaced by much simpler electric vehicles that do not require very many people with strong technical skills for their construction or maintenance.

Big companies that used to employ thousands of people are now employing many fewer people as regular employees and hiring many others on a temporary or part-time basis as needed so that they can take advantage of these new technologies as they come on line. Meanwhile, many of their former employees are becoming independent entrepreneurs, taking on part-time clients from many different firms at one time. As the technologies advance, they have to learn new jobs and relearn old ones to stay current. But because the firms can no longer capture the benefits from training their employees, they have less and less incentive to invest in training and retraining them. That means that they expect their new hires and their contract workers to come with all the skills needed to do what is often highly technical work—which means the worker has to spend time and money acquiring new skills in technologies and forms of work organization that are changing so fast that their investment could be wasted.

Some people see the arts as a refuge from the depredations of these technologies. But software can now write popular and classical music that experts cannot distinguish from the best music composed by humans. Programs are now available that will produce diagnoses of medical problems that are more accurate than those of expert doctors. News outlets now publish stories describing sporting events that are written by software, not human journalists. Software is being written that can learn how to solve very complex problems faster and more accurately than any human being is able to. Some global banks are letting their very high-priced investment bankers go and employing programs to make their investment decisions instead. And software is now available that can write software better than expert software developers!

These technologies are advancing very quickly, and they will certainly have profound effects on global labor markets. It is very difficult, however, to anticipate exactly what those effects will be or what the makers of education and training should do about them, because lead times for the implementation of education and training policy are long and the technological changes are taking place quickly.

## BROADLY SHARED PROSPERITY

When we look across the whole skein of VET strategies used by the United States, China, Singapore, and Switzerland, what do we see, and what should we conclude about VET policy and practice?

First, the question of vision in relation to the relative price of labor on the global labor market is crucial. The only nations, states, and provinces that really have the option of competing on the price of labor and staying in a low-skills equilibrium are those jurisdictions in which labor prices are very low compared to global prices for low-skill labor. The future is grim for jurisdictions in a low-skill equilibrium in which wages are nevertheless high in a global context, as in many American states, or moving higher, as in many provinces in China. If they cannot break out of their low-skill equilibrium and move through the middle-income trap, they will get poorer and poorer.

The alternative is moving toward broadly shared prosperity, which requires a very high standard for primary and secondary education for all students, because in high-wage countries the incentives for employers to automate all the routine jobs that can be automated will only grow stronger and stronger, so the jobs that used to be available to people with only a typical high school education will become fewer and fewer. To provide a balanced workforce in which everyone can prosper, high-wage nations pursuing broadly shared prosperity will have to think hard about how they will create an economy with a good balance between people in middle-skill jobs and others in high-skill jobs—all of whom are making enough money to live well and feel that they are making a strong contribution so they can live in dignity.

On this point, the Swiss and Singaporean models stand out as exemplary. Both have made an explicit all-in commitment to these goals and have developed very effective policies and institutional structures to support that commitment. Both countries have established a very high standard for primary and secondary education. Both have developed a small number of first-class research universities to provide a supply of top-notch researchers, engineers, managers, and political leaders to support an advanced technology-driven, globally competitive economy. Both have built a combination of first-class upper secondary VET programs closely aligned with applied universities in Switzerland and polytechnics in Singapore that are capable of providing their economies with a world-class cadre of middle-skill and high-skill workers.

The biggest difference between these countries' VET models is that the Swiss model is employer based and the Singaporean model is school based. Both models, however, are built on the assumption that students come into the VET system with language and mathematics literacy that is very high compared to VET students almost anywhere else in the world. The question is where students pick up the theory that goes with the work they are training for and the skills needed to actually do that work to a high standard.

Yet, the difference is not as large as it might seem, because the Singaporean government invests so much in building inside the VET schools workplaces that look and feel like their counterparts outside the schools and because many of these simulated workplaces sell their products and services to real customers, often at market prices. Also, Singapore is moving aggressively and imaginatively to create more opportunities for its VET students to work and learn in real workplaces in the real economy.

The Swiss system is built around carefully specified descriptions of skills and knowledge that apprentices are expected to develop for each occupation for which training is available. The length and content of the training are fully specified. Instructors are trained and licensed by the state to common standards. Employers can offer apprenticeship slots only if they meet certain detailed specifications, and they must pay apprentices wages at levels regulated by the state. Also, training required for an apprentice in the regulations but not offered by the employer must be offered by an intermediary organization.

This complex architecture, which grew out of the medieval guild system, begs the question, Does it build an inherent conservatism into the system that makes it, as Drucker suggests, slow to adjust to increasingly rapid changes in technology and work organization? It also raises the issue of what the right balance is between the chaos of the US system and the order of the Swiss system in the kind of environment likely to be created by advancing digital technologies.

A few years ago, I found myself on a plane with a senior engineer from Siemans, one of the world's leading automation companies, automating everything from factories to entire cities. He had been trained as an engineer in East Germany, behind the Iron Curtain, and while working at Leitz, a company long admired for its high-quality lenses and cameras and precision instrumentation, he had been given a lead role by the Soviet government in the design of the inertial guidance systems used to guide nuclear-tipped missiles to their targets. When the Iron Curtain came down, Siemans had recruited him, and there he became a high-level manager, sent all over the world to turnaround factories that were in trouble for a variety of reasons. He had just completed a succession of assignments in Germany and the United States and was on his way to take over a factory in China. I asked him to compare these three countries, in terms of the strengths and weaknesses of their labor forces.

The Germans, he said, offered first-rate engineering and a first-rate front-line labor force. If you were after a beautifully engineered and beautifully built product, he said, Germany was the place to go. China, in his estimation, was very good at making standard products well at a competitive cost. The engineering was solid, if not imaginative. The manufacturing was not up to the same standard as in Germany but was usually perfectly adequate and a good buy at the low Chinese price. He said that the United States was the place for imaginative engineering that often met the German standard but was typically more creative or innovative. But you would not go there for quality manufacturing, because American labor was well below the German standard and very expensive compared to what one could get at the same price elsewhere.

This insider's take on the current labor forces serves as a warning for China as its labor gets more expensive: its engineering will have to be more creative and its labor better skilled as its products and services get more expensive. It is also a warning for Germany, because its gift for precision in design and manufacturing will be no substitute for imagination and flexibility in a world increasingly torn apart by digital technologies. The Germans are superb makers of high-performance gasoline- and diesel-powered automobiles, but that may be of no help in a world of electric cars that are much simpler to build. And this is also a warning to American workers that their talent for creativity and innovation will only benefit a small number of engineers whose designs will be built not in the United States but elsewhere in the world unless ordinary workers in the US can develop the high level and range of technical skills that alone will justify high salaries and wages in a truly global economy.

This comparative assessment also sheds some light on the validity of Drucker's warning. Drucker was right in thinking that the flexibility and innovative capacity of the US economy would prove to be invaluable assets. He was also right when, in the late 1970s, he said that the future of work in the advanced industrial countries would be "knowledge work," work that calls for high levels of complex skills and knowledge and the ability of the workers at all levels to exercise the kind of judgment normally accorded only to professionals.[3] But Drucker was wrong to think that the American worker would be better positioned than the workers of Germany or Switzerland for the future he anticipated. The US workplace was more profoundly affected by the mass production model of industrialization than any other country, and that was a model in which workers needed only very modest literacy or skills and were expected to do as they were told—the very opposite of the knowledge worker model.

It was the legacy of the implementation of that model that my engineer seatmate was commenting on. Indeed, data from the Organisation for Economic Co-operation and Development now show that the typical American worker is the least well educated of all the workers in the advanced industrial nations.[4] The poor education of America's front-line workforce is compounded by the poor quality of its VET system. The result, as Schwartz and Hoffman note, is that US employers complain bitterly that American workers lack a strong work ethic, high levels of literacy, and the kind of technical skills needed in today's economy.

So, if Drucker was wrong to hold up the US nonmodel of VET as the model for the future, what is the right model?

## A FIRST-RATE PRIMARY AND SECONDARY EDUCATION SYSTEM

Because digital technologies will do more and more of the low-skill routine work, the first requirement for building a strong VET system is to dramatically raise the literacy standard—language, mathematical, scientific, and technical literacy—to which the bottom half of the future workforce will be held. But language, mathematics, science, and technology are not enough. Because new technologies are already causing dislocations in national economies that have direct political consequences, and those dislocations are certain to increase in intensity, it is essential that the high-wage countries give their future citizens the political and historical knowledge and skills they will need to construct societies that will work for them. Thus, the inescapable foundation for a well-functioning VET system in the future will be a first-rate primary and secondary education in the liberal arts.

This broad educational base is not just a matter of literacy and political awareness. It runs much deeper than that. Recall that the digital technologies are creating a new workforce that will be increasingly self-employed in a gig economy that demands learning new skills for new jobs all the time, often jobs that come not seriatim but all at the same time. Recall, too, that the worker in this gig economy will have no employer who is likely to pay for that or give the worker the time to do it. That will put an enormous premium on learning complex new things quickly and constantly. This means is that our conception of a basic, compulsory education will have to change.

Most industrialized nations have long had one primary and secondary system for its elites and another for everyone else. The one for the elites—seen as the society's future leaders—emphasized leadership qualities like the ability to work independently, teamwork, analytical skills, the ability to synthesize a lot of material from many different sources, problem solving, goal setting, and strategic thinking. It is not at all clear that the reality matched this aspiration in more than a few places in any one country, but it is now clear that these skills are needed by almost everyone, not just the elite.

Some argue that the advance of digital technologies means that the need for the kind of knowledge and cognitive skills that schooling has long been about will recede into the background as the machines outdo humans in those arenas and as the need for distinctly human qualities like ethical judgment, compassion, warmth, and social skills will come to the fore. This argument is made by those who think that the machines will not put people out of work but instead will become complements to, rather than competitors of, humans. Maybe. That is not clear. It is entirely likely that value and ethical judgment will be ever more important, but it is less clear that we will not have to do much thinking. My guess is that we will have to do much better and more effective thinking.

All of this suggests that the demands on our schools to provide what amounts to an elite liberal arts education to all our students will grow increasingly strong, if only to build the capacity our future workers will need to learn quickly and well. Learning quickly and well is a function of the degree to which our education has given us the frameworks we need to absorb and use new information. Those frameworks are both the conceptual structures of the subjects we study in school and the big ideas behind those frameworks. Once we understand those big ideas and have understood the frameworks at a fairly deep level, we can more readily apply what we have learned to real-world problems, draw on multiple bodies of knowledge all at once, learn new things much more quickly, and, by applying the frameworks from one field to problems and challenges in another, create and innovate freely.

This is the heart of a liberal education. A liberal education used to be the birthright of our elites. Now it will have to be the birthright of all our children. And it will have to be provided in record time, mostly during compulsory education.

## THE T-SHAPED CURRICULUM

Preparing a large and growing proportion of the professional and technical workforce to learn how to do not just new tasks but whole new jobs with a lot of technical content to a high standard very quickly will be a very heavy lift for national mass education systems. It will amount to raising achievement in terms of both the content and the quality of the academic program to the extent that it essentially changes the shape of the curve of student achievement, radically compressing it and then shifting it far to the right. It will require a T-shaped curriculum, with one leg being a strong broad liberal arts curriculum and the other leg being mastery of a technical subject at a high level. As part of the curriculum, each student would complete their education having at least one technical qualification, whether that qualification was a medical degree or an emergency medical technician certificate, which would allow them to get started in the workforce. We are headed toward a world in which the vast majority of students will get at least two years of education beyond grade 12.

What I see happening in the education and training of high-status professionals is instructive. These are the careers that one attains by taking the university track, not the VET track. But preparation for these careers has been evolving in interesting ways.

For example, in recent years the education of doctors has been transformed. It used to be the case that the undergraduate education of a doctor was followed by years of coursework in the related sciences and medical disciplines, like pathology. And it was only after years of such courses that a young doctor could put on a white coat, start doing rounds under the supervision of a clinical professor, and become a resident. That whole approach assumed that there was a more or less fixed body of medical knowledge to be learned that would make one a competent doctor, and the student's job was to learn it before learning the practice of medicine.

Now a student's medical education begins with a combination of short courses and rounds, during which the group of students is presented with a carefully chosen case, told to come up with a diagnosis and prescription, and given access to libraries, labs, and doctors as resources. They progress from simple cases to more complex ones, with coaching at every step. They get most of what used to be provided in the full courses, but now they get it when they need it. Most important, they learn how to figure out what they need to know and how to find it, and they learn how to work with colleagues. They learn that the field is developing so quickly that there is no way they can learn everything they need to know before they start working as doctors. Most important, they learn the theory and the practice side by side, not in sequence. They gain a much deeper understanding of the theory and a better-developed capacity to apply what they are learning—they know it better and can use it more adeptly. And they are prepared for a lifetime of learning.

Engineering education has been going through a similar revolution, as have other high-status professional fields. Mixing the understanding of the theory with its application turns out to be a better way to learn both the theory and how to use the theory for some practical purpose. You can, of course, learn how to perform a task by rote, without learning the theory behind it, but application is much easier when you understand *why* and not just *what*. And the practitioner who knows not just what to do in normal circumstances but why that strategy works will be much better prepared when the unexpected or unusually complex case is encountered. Most important, the practitioner who knows why is far better prepared to learn how to use new technologies and even contribute to their development.

The idea of the T-shaped curriculum conjures up an image of a strong academic education and a strong VET education, separate but coupled. It suggests not just that students will need both forms of education, whether they are going to be doctors or emergency medical technicians, but that the boundaries between these two forms of education need to be blurred. VET needs a stronger academic component, but in a form that is designed to be illuminated by the relevant applications.

The right response is to set a high standard for the common education that all students are supposed to complete by the end of lower secondary school and to do everything possible to make sure that the majority achieve that standard, no matter what they plan to do afterward. Then introduce a T-shaped curriculum to provide a broad and deep general education designed to make it very easy to learn almost anything quickly and well and to master the technical skills and knowledge needed to succeed at the entry level to a career.

In building such a system, the education and training that facilitate and support these trajectories should be designed so that it is possible to move laterally, to change destination. The institutional structure should also allow students who want to pursue a largely intellectual approach to the curriculum to do so, but the system should be designed so that, to the extent possible, the academic instruction requires constant application of theory to real-world problems. The curriculum should also address the development of the social and emotional skills needed to be successful, as well as the cognitive and technical skills.

The choice should not be between VET and a university track but between an applied form of education and a more intellectual form of education that involves less application. Both forms of education should lead to tertiary education, with various credentials offered along the way, so that a student can work at various points along the trajectory and also return for more advanced study and credentials.

## BUILDING SKILLS-STANDARDS SYSTEMS THAT WORK

In the United States, anyone with a pickup truck and a ladder can go into business as a roofer. That would be illegal in Germany, however, where one must be a master roofer to do that, and one cannot become a master roofer without demonstrating conclusively that one knows everything there is to know about every kind of roofing material and every approved method of roof construction. We'd all like some assurance that the roofer we hire is competent, so why wouldn't we want the German system?

This is a crucial question for the development of VET systems. If young people are to be trained for demanding, complex work, it is essential that they be provided a curriculum that imparts the skills that employers are looking for, not those that educators would like to teach. Those responsible for providing training need a specification of the desired skills to develop an effective curriculum. Students need to know what skills are desired in order to choose among potential training providers. Firms need to know whether students have been trained and assessed against industry standards in order to judge the competence of job applicants. One would think, though, that this is a simple challenge to meet; just ask the employers to come up with the standards for the jobs in their industry. But it is not that simple.

In the 1990s I learned from New Zealand's minister for economic development about the country's institution of the world's newest and most powerful occupational skills standards authority, which was charged with setting a very wide range of occupational, educational, and training standards. She recounted how she had recently been visited by one of the authority board members, the head of Toyota's operations in New Zealand, who told her that Toyota was on its way to dominating the auto industry worldwide by instituting radically different methods of organizing the work of assembling cars. Toyota was relying on the judgment of its front-line workers rather than treating them like cogs in the machine, and using robots would do most of the physically hard work. The other automakers in New Zealand, however, were still building cars the way Henry Ford made them and saw no reason to change. He told her that Toyota was pulling out because it would lose its competitive advantage if it went back to the old methods, if it followed the authority's standards.

This was exactly what Drucker warned against: standards that simply encode average practice will retard the development of the whole economy. In considering this case, the answer, I thought, was not to abandon standards for VET but to find a way to create standards that will drive industries forward, not encase them in the past. With standards like that, a nation can ensure that students are being trained for leading-edge practices and will be the people in their companies who introduce others to those practices and, as a result, make the whole economy more competitive. But how, I wondered, can a country create standards that most firms in that industry were uncomfortable with?

In Switzerland, the government relies on the industry associations to set the skills standards, just like in New Zealand. But New Zealand had long been a supplier of raw materials in a mercantile system controlled by Britain, so it had very few domestic manufacturing companies that were at the leading edge of anything. The big Swiss firms had made a pact to be number one, two, or three globally in any industry they chose to compete in, so the companies that dominated the standard-setting bodies were already defining the state of the art. Singapore was determined to offer a state-of-the-art workforce, so it created a skills-standards system, advised by industry, that was based not on those standards used by the firms *in* Singapore but on those used by the global companies the government wanted to attract *to* Singapore. Denmark's skills-standards system is similar to Germany's, but local groups of industrial firms can apply to the government for the right to use their own standards if they can make a case that they are more advanced and will make Denmark more competitive. If the government approves an exception on this basis, it gives the industry association the option of revising that set of standards. The result is that skills standards are constantly revised to reflect what leading businesses are doing to adjust their technologies and work organizations to suit the changing markets.

A good skills-standards system drives the economy forward; it does not frustrate industrial ingenuity and development.

## WORK-BASED LEARNING

No VET system will be effective if the students do not get the opportunity to work in places that are as much like the area in which they are seeking employment as possible. In chapter 3, Vivien Stewart describes VET institutions in China where students are taught by teachers who have no experience doing the work they're training their students to do, and it is not hard to find students in the United States in auto repair and maintenance programs who are practicing on cars that have no computers in them.

It's not just a matter of acquiring the technical skills needed to hit the ground running in a first job. In chapter 4, Schwartz and Hoffman's description of VET in the United States points to the high social, personal, and economic costs of the high unemployment rates among young people in a society that provides very few opportunities for a smooth transition from school to work. In such a society, students' opportunities to mature as individuals, to learn what it means to be employed, to develop the work habits that make them employable, and to experience the pride that comes from doing work well are all stunted. For students who grow up in poverty, the opportunities to develop the kind of networks that lead to good first jobs and better second and third jobs are similarly limited. As they get through their teens and into their early twenties without a decent regular job, they lose hope and become increasingly unattractive to employers who prefer to hire someone right out of school or someone with a strong work record. Work-based training in the US is largely limited to the apprenticeship programs offered by the building trades unions, and most firms have little or no interest in taking on responsibility for training young people.

The Swiss system of employer-based learning that Hoffman and Schwartz describe in chapter 2 is very attractive. Swiss parents and students select that pathway through their system in very large numbers, and Swiss employers sing its praises and, at their own expense, provide the work-based learning experiences that make it hum. The modern Swiss VET system has evolved and changed greatly from the guilds of medieval times, but it still rests on the willingness of employers to offer opportunities for work-based learning.

China had its own version of the medieval system when it required employers to provide a wide range of social, educational, and training services, as well as housing and food, to their workers. Each firm trained all the workers it needed by taking on the sons and daughters of their employees as apprentices. But after Deng Xiaoping upended that system, the state-owned companies terminated their apprenticeship systems, and the private companies have assumed very little responsibility for training young people at all.

That leaves the Singapore model of work-based training, which relies mainly on creating virtual employer-based training sites in the VET schools. This is an expensive undertaking, but it is paying off handsomely for the Singaporeans. In fact, the Singapore government is moving aggressively to find more ways to increase opportunities for young people to combine work in real employer work sites with learning.

## WHO IS RESPONSIBLE FOR THE VET SYSTEM? IS ANYONE IN CHARGE?

Effective VET at a national scale requires the active engagement of many players. It lives at the intersection of national economic goal setting, economic development, national manpower planning, primary and secondary education, tertiary education, business, and labor.

In the United States and China, educators typically dominate decision-making, and business and labor play largely subsidiary roles. In Singapore, the economic agencies of government dominate. In Switzerland, the business interests play the central role. In many countries, each of these stakeholders occupies their own posthole and pursues their own interests separately. In countries with effective VET systems, the government acts to coordinate and sometimes lead in the development of coherent, powerful strategies that bridge these interests and engage the players in ways that are effective for the students and the economy as a whole. That is very difficult to do. Countries that aspire to build world-class VET systems would do well to look at how the countries with the most effective VET systems govern those systems.

In many countries the VET system is an afterthought, not the main game. But as the advance of AI, robotics, and other related technologies gathers steam, destroying not just jobs but entire industries, ever larger groups of workers who are being dispossessed by these technologies, feeling they have nothing to lose, that neither capitalism nor democracy has done anything for them, could easily decide that willing autocrats have more to offer. And so a well-designed VET system could provide a path to well-being for millions of people who might otherwise not just face grim futures themselves but also be more than willing to bring down the whole system.

It is precisely because VET sits at the intersection of the workings of the education system and the real economy that it could play such an important role in determining the fate of individuals and nations.

# NOTES

## Chapter 1

In writing this account, I drew heavily on three books: Chan Chin Bock, I. F. Tang, S. Dhana, Chua Soo Tian, et al., *Heart Work: Stories of How EDB Steered the Singapore Economy from 1961 into the 21st Century* (Singapore: Singapore EDB and EDB Society, 2002), which offers fascinating stories that take the reader step by step, company by company, technology by technology, and training strategy by training strategy through the process by which the EDB lifted the country up to its current status as a world-class economy; Mickey Chiang, *From Economic Debacle to Economic Miracle: The History and Development of Technical Education in Singapore* (Singapore: Times Editions, 1998), the best one-volume account of the whole history of VET in Singapore up to 1988; and Lee Sing Kong, Goh Chor Boon, Birger Fredriksen, and Tan Jee Peng, eds., *Toward a Better Future: Education and Training for Economic Development in Singapore Since 1965* (Washington, DC: International Bank for Reconstruction and Development and the World Bank, 2008), which features very good chapters, written by key participants, on each of the major aspects of technical education in Singapore in recent years, including compulsory education and the university system. The following articles and other resources also proved valuable: "Case Study on Institute of Technical Education (ITE) Singapore" (report, Asia-Pacific Economic Cooperation, 2010); "Emerging Asia Can Teach the West A Lot About Emerging Government," *The Economist*, March 19, 2011; Gundy Cahyadi, Barbara Kursten, Marc Weiss, and Guang Yang, "Singapore's Economic Transformation" (presentation, Global Urban Development, Prague, June 2004); Sean Cavanagh, "Singapore Crafts Vocational Ed with Industries in Mind," *Education Week*, July 14, 2009.

1. US Central Intelligence Agency, *The World Factbook: East Asia/Southeast Asia: Singapore*, https://www.cia.gov/library/publications/the-world-factbook/geos/sn.html.

2. According to the Singapore Tourism Board, growth was 49.7 percent in 2010. See https://www.stb.gov.sg/statistics-and-market-insights/marketstatistics/x1annual_report_on_tourism_statistics_2010_2011.pdf.

3. Goh Chok Tong, "1981 Budget Statement" (speech to Parliament, Singapore, March 6, 1981), http://www.nas.gov.sg/archivesonline/data/pdfdoc/gct19810306s.pdf.

4. Goh Chok Tong, "Shaping Our Future: Thinking Schools, Learning Nation" (speech, 7th International Conference on Thinking, Singapore, June 2, 1997), http://ncee.org/wp-content/uploads/2017/01/Sgp-non-AV-2-PM-Goh-1997-Shaping-Our-Future-Thinking-Schools-Learning-Nation-speech.pdf.

5. Hsien Loong Lee, "Our Future of Opportunity and Promise" (speech, National Day Rally, University Cultural Center, Singapore, August 22, 2004), http://ncee.org/wp-content/uploads/2017/01/Sgp-non-AV-3-PM-Lee-2004-Our-Future-of-Opportunity-and-Promise-Teach-Less-Learn-More.pdf.

6. Song Seng Law, "Vocational Technical Education and Economic Development," in *Toward a Better Future: Education and Training for Economic Development in Singapore Since 1965*, ed. Sing Kong Lee, Chor Boon Goh, Birger Fredriksen, and Jee Peng Tan (Washington, DC: World Bank; Singapore: National Institute of Education, 2008), 114–34.

7. Chiang, *From Economic Debacle to Economic Miracle*.

8. Bock et al., *Heart Work*, 165.

9. Institute of Technical Education, *Established Enough to Lead Yet Young Enough to Dance: ITE Highlights 2012/13* (Singapore: Institute of Technical Education, 2013).

10. OECD, "Singapore: Rapid Improvement Followed by Strong Performance," in *Strong Performers and Successful Reformers in Education: Lessons from PISA for the United States* (Paris: OECD, 2010), 167.

11. "Emerging Asia Can Teach the West A Lot About Emerging Government," *The Economist*, March 19, 2011.

12. Bhagyashree Garekar, "ITE Wins Prestigious Harvard Award," *Straits Times*, September 25, 2007, http://news.asiaone.com/News/Education/Story/A1Story20070926-27077.html.

13. "Emerging Asia."

14. Betsy Brown Ruzzi, "Tucker's Lens: Interview with Bruce Poh, CEO, Institute of Technical Education, Singapore," April 2, 2015, NCEE, http://ncee.org/2015/04/tuckers-lens-interview-with-bruce-poh-ceo-institute-of-technical-education-singapore/.

15. Ibid.

16. Ibid.

## Chapter 2

1. While High German is the language of instruction in German-speaking Switzerland, people speak the unwritten language, Schweizerdeutsch, which is sufficiently distinct from German that even a listener who knows neither language can hear the difference.

2. OECD, *Economic Policy Reforms 2012: Going for Growth* (Paris: OECD, 2012), http://dx.doi.org/10.1787/growth-2012-en.

3. These are averages usually cited. For salaries for each profession, see http://www.berufsberatung.ch/dyn/46447.aspx.

4. Samuel Muehlemann, Harald Pfeifer, Gunter Walden, Feliz Wenzelmann, and Stefan Wolter, "The Financing of Apprenticeship Training in Light of Labor Market Regulations," *Labor Market Economics* 17, no. 5 (2010): 799–809.

5. See, for example, Zurich University of Applied Sciences, http://www.zhaw.ch/en/zurich-

university-of-applied-sciences.html; University of Applied Sciences and Arts Northwestern Switzerland, http://www.fhnw.ch/homepage?set_language=en; SERI, "Universities of Applied Sciences," 2014, http://www.sbfi.admin.ch/fh/index.html?lang=en.

6. SERI, "Vocational and Professional Education and Training in Switzerland 2018: Facts and Figures," https://www.sbfi.admin.ch/sbfi/en/home/services/publications/vocational-education-and-training.html.

7. Mirjam Strupler and Stefan C. Wolter, *Die duale Lehre: eine Erfolgsgeschichte—auch für die Betriebe: Ergebnisse der dritten Kosten-Nutzen-Erhebung der Lehrlingsausbildung aus der Sicht der Betriebe* (Zurich: Rüegger, 2012).

8. SERI, "Vocational and Professional Education and Training."

9. SwissMEM, "Training and Innovation," http://www.swissmem.ch/en/industry-politics/training-and-innovation.html.

10. Ibid.

11. For more information, see Center for Young Professionals in Banking (CYP), https://cyp.ch/en/.

12. "Systemic Innovations in the Swiss VET System: Country Case Study Report" (report, OECD/CERI Study of Systemic Innovation in VET, Paris, 2008), http://hdl.voced.edu.au/10707/127031.

13. Sheilagh C. Ogilvie, *Institutions and European Trade: Merchant Guilds, 1000–1800* (Cambridge, UK: Cambridge University Press, 2011).

14. R. James Breiding, *Swiss Made: The Untold Story Behind Switzerland's Success* (London: Profile Books, 2013).

15. Alan Cowell, "New Records Show the Swiss Sold Arms Worth Millions to Nazis," *New York Times*, May 29, 1997, http://www.nytimes.com/1997/05/29/world/new-records-show-the-swiss-sold-arms-worth-millions-to-nazis.html.

16. Ursula Renold, "Wo das Männliche anfängt, da hört das Weibliche auf": Frauenberufsbildungsdiskussionen im Spiegel der sozio-ökonomischen Entwicklung (1860–1930)" (PhD diss., University of Bern, 1998).

17. Patrick A. Puhani, "The Rise and Fall of Swiss Unemployment: Relative Demand Shocks, Wage Rigidities, and Temporary Immigrants" (discussion paper, University of St. Gallen, Switzerland, 2002).

18. Kathrin Hoeckel, "Vocational Education and Training Made in Switzerland" (unpublished paper, 2013).

19. Bruno Lavin and Paul Evans, eds., *The Global Talent Competitiveness Index 2018: Diversity for Competitiveness*, 2018, https://www.insead.edu/sites/default/files/assets/dept/globalindices/docs/GTCI-2018-report.pdf.

20. "State School System," September 16, 2018, https://www.swissinfo.ch/eng/state-school-system-/29286538.

21. See "Youth in Europe," Eurostat, http://epp.eurostat.ec.europa.eu/statistics_explained/index.php/Youth_in_Europe; "Age Dependency Ratio: Young (% of Working-Age Popu-

lation) in Switzerland," Trading Economics, http://www.tradingeconomics.com/switzerland/age-dependency-ratio-young-percent-of-working-age-population-wb-data.html.

22. See https://lenews.ch/2017/06/20/for-the-first-time-many-swiss-commercial-apprenticeship-positions-are-vacant/.

23. Melissa Eddy, "Swiss Voters Reject Move to Restrict Immigrants," *New York Times*, November 30, 2014, http://www.nytimes.com/2014/12/01/world/europe/swiss-voters-reject-move-to-restrict-foreign-workers.html?_r=0.

## Chapter 3

1. Weiping Shi, "Better Skills, Better Career, Better Life: Recent Developments of TVET Policies in China" (PowerPoint presentation, UNESCO Third International Congress on TVET, Shanghai, May 14–16, 2012); Hao Yan, "China's Vocational Education and Training: The Next Key Target of Education Promotion" (background brief, East Asian Institute, National University of Singapore, 2010).

2. World Bank, *China 2030: Building a Modern, Harmonious and Creative Society* (Washington, DC: World Bank, 2013).

3. Justin Y. Lin, *Demystifying the Chinese Economy* (Cambridge, UK: Cambridge University Press, 2012).

4. Orville Schell and John DeLury, *Wealth and Power: China's Long March to the Twenty-First Century* (New York: Random House, 2013).

5. Ibid.

6. Ezra F. Vogel, *Deng Xiaoping and the Transformation of China* (Cambridge, MA: Belknap Press of Harvard University Press, 2011), 7.

7. Nicholas Lardy, *Sustaining China's Growth After the Global Financial Crisis* (Washington, DC: Peterson Institute for International Economics, 2011).

8. Ibid.

9. Ibid.

10. "China GDP Annual Growth Rate," *Trading Economics*, January 21, 2019, https://tradingeconomics.com/china/gdp-growth-annual.

11 Vogel, *Deng Xiaoping and the Transformation of China*

12. Lin, *Demystifying the Chinese Economy*.

13. World Bank, *China 2030*.

14. "Biggest Banks in the World 2018," *Global Finance Magazine*, November 2018, https://www.gfmag.com/magazine/november-2018/biggest-banks-world-2018; "Fortune Global 500 List 2018," *Fortune Magazine*, https://www.fortune.com/global500/list.

15. World Bank, *China 2030*.

16. Ibid.

17. Houkou has its origins in the household registration system of ancient China, but it was revived and enforced in the 1950s by the Chinese government to limit mass migration from rural areas to cities. The economic development of China's eastern cities beginning

in the 1980s has encouraged millions of migrant workers to move to these cities, but, lacking an urban houkou, they have not had access to urban education, health, and welfare services. The system is widely seen in China as unfair and discriminatory, and it causes tremendous churn in the labor market. The system is gradually being dismantled to allow rural migrants to obtain a residence permit and access services in the cities in which they work.

18. Stephen Roach, *Unbalanced: The Co-Dependency of America and China* (New Haven, CT: Yale University Press, 2014).

19. Li Yang, "Rebalance 'Less Important' Than Innovation," *China Daily*, March 20, 2014.

20. Lardy, *Sustaining China's Growth*.

21. World Bank, *China 2030*.

22. Ibid.

23. Elizabeth C. Economy, *The Third Revolution: Xi Jinping and the New Chinese State* (Oxford, UK: Oxford University Press, 2018).

24. *National Medium- and Long-Term Education Reform and Development Plan (2010–2020)* (Beijing: Ministry of Education of the People's Republic of China, 2006).

25. Cong Cao, Richard P. Suttmeier, and Denis F. Simon, "China's 15-Year Science and Technology Plan," *Physics Today* 59, no. 12 (2006): 38–43, doi:10.1063/1.2435680.

26. ShanghaiRanking Consultancy, "Academic Ranking of World Universities, 2018," http://www.shanghairanking.com/ARWU2018.html; Dennis Simon and Cong Cao, *China's Emerging Technological Edge* (New York: Cambridge University Press, 2009).

27. Chinese National Bureau of Statistics, "2017 Migrant Workers Monitoring Survey Report," http://www.stats.gov.cn/tjsj/zxfb/201804/t20180427_1596389.html.

28. Shi, "Better Skills, Better Career."

29. Zhenyi Guo and Stephen Lamb, *International Comparisons of China's Technical and Vocational Education and Training System* (Dordrecht, the Netherlands: Springer, 2010).

30. Vogel, *Deng Xiaoping and the Transformation of China*.

31. Ministry of Education, *Educational Statistics in 2017*, http://en.moe.gov.cn/Resources/Statistics/edu_stat2017/national/201808/t20180808_344687.html.

32. Zhenguo Yuan, "China: Promoting Equity as a Basic Education Policy," in *Education Policy Reform Trends in G20 Members*, ed. Yan Wang (New York: Springer, 2013).

33. Guo and Lamb, *International Comparisons*.

34. Yuan, "China."

35. Yan, "China's Vocational Education and Training."

36. Institute of International Education, "Open Doors Data," 2018, http://www.iie.org/research-and-publications/open-doors/data.

37. Yang, "Rebalance."

38. Eric Fish, "How the Asian Financial Crisis Led to China's Massive Graduate Unemployment," *Asia Blog*, June 8, 2017, https://asiasociety.org/blog/asia/how-asian-financial-crisis-led-china%E2%80%99s-massive-graduate-unemployment.

39. MyCOS, "My China Occupational Skills," http://en.mycos.com.

40. Bai Tiantian, "Sweeping Gaokao Reform Pledged," *Global Times*, September 5, 2014, http://www.globaltimes.cn/content/880101.shtml.

41. Ma Jun, "The Development and Reform of Chinese Secondary Vocational Education in the 21st Century," in *Initiatives to Foster Chinese TVET and TVET Teacher Training*, ed. Frank Bunning, Kai Gleissner, Mi Jing, and Sun Yang (Magdeburg, Germany: Deutsche Gesellschaft fur Internationale Zusammenarbeit, 2018).

42. Yan, "China's Vocational Education and Training."

43. Ibid.

44. Minxuan Zhang and Jinjie Xu, "Toward China's Modern TVET System: Take Shanghai as Special Experience" (PowerPoint presentation, 2014).

45. Ibid.

46. See the acknowledgments to this volume for a list of the interviewees.

47. AMCHAM China, "2014 China Business Climate Survey Report," http://www. amcham china.org/businessclimate2014.

48. "Chinese Official Urges Modern Vocational Education," Xinhua News Agency, March 26, 2014, http://news.xinhuanet.com/english/china/2014-03/26/c_133216011.htm.

49. Z. He, "Review of Vocational Education Policy in China During the Past Thirty Years" (report, Research in Education Development, Tangshan Industrial Vocational Technical College, Tangshan, Hebei Province, March 2009), http://www.tsgzy.edu.cn/kyc/onews. asp?id=372.

50. Ibid.

51. "Third Plenary Session Communique of the 18th Central Committee of the Communist Party of China, 2014," China.org.cn, January 15, 2019, http://www.china.org.cn/china/thirdplenarysession/2014.

52. Vogel, *Deng Xiaoping and the Transformation of China*.

53. Zhang and Xu, "Toward China's Modern TVET System."

54. Center on International Education Benchmarking, "Characteristics of a World Class VET System," http://www.ncee.org/programs-affiliates/center-on-international-education-benchmarking/characteristics-of-the-worlds-top-vet-systems/

## Chapter 4

In contrast to our chapter on Switzerland (chapter 2), in this chapter we are writing about our own country and a field in which we have both worked for many years. Consequently, we were able to rely heavily on our own knowledge and experience and on a wide variety of excellent reports and studies, many of which are cited in the endnotes. For advice on sources for the historical section of the chapter, we would like to acknowledge the advice of James R. Stone, longtime director of the National Research Center on Career and Technical Education. For the school profiles in the high school section of the chapter, we relied primarily on written material and on conversations with colleagues from the Pathways to Prosperity Network who know these schools well.

1. OECD, *From Initial Education to Working Life: Making Transitions Work* (Paris: OECD, 2000).

2. OECD, *Learning for Jobs* (Paris: OECD, 2010), https://read.oecd-ilibrary.org/education/learning-for-jobs_9789264087460-en#page1.

3. National Education Association of the United States, *Report of the Committee of Ten on Secondary School Studies: With the Reports of the Conferences Arranged by the Committee* (Washington, DC: NEA, 1894), 17.

4. See https://www3.nd.edu/~rbarger/www7/cardprin.html.

5. "Report of the Commission on National Aid to Vocational Education," in *American Education and Vocationalism: A Documentary History 1870–1970*, ed. Marvin Lazerson and W. Norton Grubb (New York: Teachers College Press, 1974).

6. "Introduction," in Lazerson and Grubb, eds., *American Education and Vocationalism*, 37.

7. Howard D. Gordon, *The History and Growth of Career and Technical Education in America* (Long Grove, IL: Waveland Press), 34.

8. On race and schooling in Boston during this period, see Peter Schrag, *Village School Downtown: Boston Schools, Boston Politics* (Boston: Beacon Press, 1967).

9. Tamar Jacoby and Shaun M. Dougherty, *The New CTE: New York City as Laboratory for America* (New York: Manhattan Institute, 2016).

10. In 1984 the law was renamed the Carl D. Perkins Vocational and Applied Technology Act to honor the longtime chair of the House Education and Labor Committee, a staunch and highly effective advocate for vocational education.

11. Advance CTE, "How States Use Perkins—The Basics," https://cte.careertech.org/sites/default/files/How_States_Use_Perkins-The_Basics-2018.pdf.

12. Ibid.

13. Robert Schwartz and Nancy Hoffman, "High-Quality Career and Technical Education," in *Education for Upward Mobility*, ed. Michael Petrilli (Lanham, MD: Rowman & Littlefield, 2016).

14. See http://cart.org/what-is-cart/; "A Model for Success: CART's Linked Learning Program Increases College Enrollment," January 2011, http://irvine.org/images/stories/pdf/grantmaking/cart%20findings%20report%20final.pdf.

15. "This Week at CART," http://cart.org/this-week-at-cart-amaya-de-vore/.

16. Press release, January 11, 2011, The James Irvine Foundation, https://www.irvine.org/blog/multi-year-study-reveals-cart-attendance-dramatically-increases-likelihood-of-students-college-attendance-across-ethnicity-gender-and-economics.

17. Deborah Fallows, "Reinventing High School: How Fresno Prepares the Kids in the Middle," *The Atlantic*, March 11, 2015, https://www.theatlantic.com/education/archive/2015/03/reinventing-high-school/387190/.

18. See https://whs.d214.org; https://www.theatlantic.com/education/archive/2015/03/reinventing-high-school/387190/.

19. See http://www.energytechschool.org/content/information.

20. California Collaborative on District Reform Meeting 17 summary, College and Career Readiness for All: Linked Learning in Long Beach, November 7–8, 2011, http://www.cacollaborative.org/sites/default/files/CCDR_Meeting_17_Summary_Final.pdf.

21. Arthur Cohen, *The American Community College*, 6th ed. (San Francisco: Jossey-Bass, 2013), 12.

22. Bunker Hill Community College, "College Catalog," 2019, 178–79.

23. See http://doingwhatmatters.cccco.edu.

24. Colleen Moore and Nancy Shulock, "Sense of Direction: The Importance of Helping Community College Students Select and Enter a Program of Study," 2011, http://edinsightscenter.org/Publications/Research-Reports-and-Briefs/ArticleType/ArticleView/ArticleID/2028.

25. Mark Schneider and Rooney Columbus, "Degrees of Opportunity: Lessons Learned from State-Level Data on Postsecondary Earnings Outcomes" (report, American Enterprise Institute, Washington, DC, October 2017).

26. "AACC Pathways: The Pathways Project," American Association of Community Colleges, http://www.aacc.nche.edu/Resources/aaccprograms/pathways/Pages/default.aspx.

27. Barry Schwartz, "More Isn't Always Better," *Harvard Business Review* 84, no. 6 (2006): 22.

28. See Barry Schwartz's September 14, 2014, TED talk, "The Paradox of Choice," https://www.ted.com/talks/barry_schwartz_on_the_paradox_of_choice.

29. Thomas Bailey, Shanna Smith Jaggars, and Davis Jenkins, *What We Know About Guided Pathways* (New York: Community College Research Center, Teachers College, Columbia University).

30. See http://valenciacollege.edu/academic-affairs/new-student-experience/meta-majors.cfm.

31. Mark Schneider, "The Value of Sub-Baccalaureate Credentials," *Issues in Science and Technology* 31 (Summer 2015): 31–34.

32. Table H127, National Center for Education Statistics, *Career/Technical Education (CTE) Statistics*, 2009, https://nces.ed.gov/surveys/ctes/xls/h127_2009.xls.

33. Anthony Carnevale, Nicole Smith, and Jeffrey Strohl, *Help Wanted: Projections of Jobs and Education Requirements Through 2018* (Washington, DC: Georgetown University Center on Education and the Workforce, 2010).

34. Jaison R. Abel, Richard Deitz, and Yaqin Su., "Are Recent College Graduates Finding Good Jobs?" *Current Issues in Economics and Finance* 20 no. 1 (2014).

35. Schneider, "The Value of Sub-Baccalaureate Credentials."

36. Carnevale et al., *Help Wanted*.

37. The interview with Sidney P. Marland Jr. from *American Education* is reprinted in Lazerson and Grubb, eds., *American Education and Vocationalism*.

38. For more information about the Pathways Network, see http://www.jff.org/initiatives/pathways-prosperity-network.

39. See Richard Kazis, "Balancing Bold State Policy and Regional Flexibility: Pathways Tennessee" in Robert B. Schwartz and Amy Loyd, eds., *Career Pathways in Action: Case Studies from the Field* (Cambridge, MA: Harvard Education Press, forthcoming).

40. For an early report on the implementation of CCPT, see http://www.jff.org/sites/default/files/publications/materials/CCPTImplementationReport_03717_0.pdf.

41. See https://www.sreb.org/high-schools-work.

42. See https://naf.org.

43. See Robert Rothman, "Getting to Scale through Strategic Pathways: Delaware Pathways" in Robert B. Schwartz and Amy Loyd, eds., *Career Pathways in Action: Case Studies from the Field* (Cambridge, MA: Harvard Education Press, forthcoming).

44. See https://dwd.wisconsin.gov/youthapprenticeship/.

45. See https://www.careerwisecolorado.org.

46. See https://www.newamerica.org/education-policy/partnership-advance-youth-apprenticeship/.

47. See https://www.bls.gov/news.release/empsit.a.htm.

48. The foundation-funded Credential Engine is a promising new initiative designed to respond to this challenge. See https://www.credentialengine.org/about.

## Chapter 5

1. Peter Drucker, *The Age of Discontinuity: Guidelines to Our Changing Society* (New York: Harper & Row, 1969).

2. Louise Walsh, "Humans Need Not Apply," *Research Horizons* 36 (June 2018): 36–37; James Manyika, Susan Lund, Michael Chui, Jacques Bughin, Jonathan Woetzel, Parul Batra, Ryan Ko, and Saurabh Sanghvi, "Jobs Lost, Jobs Gained: Workforce Transitions in a Time of Automation" (report, McKinsey & Co., December 2017).

3. Drucker, *The Age of Discontinuity*.

4. OECD, *Skills Matter: Further Results from the Survey of Adult Skills* (Paris: OECD, 2016), http://www.oecd.org/skills/piaac/Skills_Matter_Further_Results_from_the_Survey_of_Adult_Skills.pdf.

# ACKNOWLEDGMENTS

## Chapter 1
## The Phoenix: Vocational Education and Training in Singapore

*Marc S. Tucker*

This chapter was based on many visits I made to Singapore, beginning with the 1989 visit cited in the text, but profited in particular from a visit I made with Betsy Brown Ruzzi, Robert Schwartz, and Vivien Stewart in June 2012 that focused exclusively on Singapore's vocational education system. My colleagues and I are indebted to Professor Lee Sing Kong, director of Singapore's National Institute of Education, and his staff for arranging that visit.

The following people kindly shared their time with us during our visit. *From the Office of the Prime Minister*: Mr. Tharman Shanmugaratnam, Deputy Prime Minister, Minister for Finance, and Minister for Manpower. *From the Ministry of Education*: Ms. Ho Peng, Director General; Mr. Wong Siew Hoong, Deputy Director General; Mr. Lim Shung Yar, director, Human Resource Strategy and Leadership; Mr. Manogaran Suppiah, executive director, Academy of Singapore Teachers; Dr. Poon Chew Leng, deputy director, Research and Evaluation; Dr. Cheong Wei Yang, director, Planning Division; Mr. Lim Tze Jiat, deputy director, Planning and International Cooperation. *From the National Institute of Education*: Professor Lee Sing Kong, director; Professor Low Ee Ling, associate dean, Programme and Student Development; Mr. David Hogan, principal research scientist, Education Research Office; Ms. Patricia Campbell, head, Public, International and Alumni Relations; Ms. Valerie Sim, assistant head, Public, International and Alumni Relations. *From the Institute of Technical Education*: Mr. Tan Seng Hua, Deputy CEO (Academic); Ms. Sabrina Loi, Deputy CEO (Corporate); Mr. Goh Mong Song, deputy principal, ITE College West; Ms. Jenn Tan, head, International Development and Relations. *From Ngee Ann Polytechnic*: Mr. Chia Mia Chiang, principal; Mr. Mah Wee Beng, deputy principal.

*From the business community*: Ms. Chan Yit Foon, Senior Vice President of Human Resources, Marina Bay Sands; Mr. James Eyring, COO, Organisational

Solutions; Mahboob Alam, Associate Director of Asia Headquarters and Asia Practice, Leader for Employee Relations, Diversity, HR Analytics, Procter & Gamble; David Kiu, Senior Manager of Government Affairs, Procter & Gamble Asia; David Fernandez, managing director, Emerging Asia Research, J. P. Morgan. *And others*: Mike Thiruman, president, Singapore Teachers Union; Sandra Davie, senior writer, *Singapore Straits Times*.

A number of officials from the Institute of Technical Education (ITE) prepared PowerPoint presentations that I relied on in writing this chapter: Sabrina Loi, Deputy CEO (Corporate); Bruce Poh, director and CEO; Tan Seng Hua, Deputy CEO (Academic); and Yek Tiew Ming, principal, ITE College West.

## Chapter 2
## Gold Standard: The Swiss Vocational Education and Training System
*Nancy Hoffman and Robert B. Schwartz*

This chapter is based on several visits we made to Switzerland in 2010, 2013, and 2014 to study that country's vocational education and training system. Marc Tucker and Betsy Brown Ruzzi accompanied us on the June 2014 visit. We are indebted to the many people who gave their time generously to arrange our visits, explain the system, bring together practitioners and students, and help us navigate the many interconnected components of VET.

We especially thank Dr. Ursula Renold, head of Research Division Education Systems at the Swiss Economic Institute in Zurich; and Professor Dr. Stefan C. Wolter, managing director of the Swiss Coordination Centre for Research in Education and professor of Economics at the University of Berne, where he also heads the Centre for Research in Economics of Education. Not only did they both spend hours arranging several visits, but they also visited us in Boston and learned enough about the US education system to help us think about what in the Swiss system might be transferable or adaptable.

During our 2014 visits, Dr. Renold and the staff of Research Division Education Systems at the Swiss Economic Institute far exceeded our expectations in arranging our schedules and accompanying us as we traveled. Many people were kind enough to share their time with us in June 2014.

*From the business community*: Urs Honegger, CEO, PriceWaterhouseCoopers; Susanne Ruoff, CEO, Swiss Post; Jasmin Staiblin, CEO, Alpiq; Lukas Gaehwiler, CEO, UBS Switzerland. *At the VET Center of Manufacturing Industries, Baden*: Ingo

Fritschi, CEO, LIBS, and several of his apprentices. *At the VET School, Baden*: Ruedi Siegrist, principal; Hanspeter Vogt, vice principal, IT Department. *At the State Secretariat of Education, Research and Innovation (SERI)*: Claudia Lippuner and Jérôme Hügli, international education project managers. *At the Swiss Federal Institute of Vocational Education and Training (SFIVET)*: Dalia Schipper, director general. *At the School of Engineering, University of Applied Sciences and Arts (FHNW), Brugg-Windisch*: Jürg Christener, director; Sarah Hauser and Manfred Vogel, Computer Science Department, School of Engineering. *At the VET School, Interlaken*: Urs Burri, principal; Stefan Schmid, teacher, and several of his apprentices; Robert Brügger, teacher, and several of his apprentices; Jörg Wyss, teacher, and several of his apprentices. *At the Residential and Nursing Home, Interlaken*: Rita Rüegsegger, instructor, and several of her apprentices. *At the PET College in Hospitality, Thun*: Géraldine Schué, deputy principal, and students. *At the Swiss Economic Institute*: Lino Guzzella, rector and president-elect; Jan-Egbert Sturm, director; Johanna Kemper, doctoral student. *At the University of Zurich*: Uschi Backes-Gellner, Department of Business Economics. *At the Confederation of Swiss Employer Associations*: Valentin Vogt, president. *At SwissMEM*: Hans Hess, president. *At the Center for Young Professionals in Banking*: Alexia Böniger, CYP, and several apprentices. *At VSEI, Professional Association of Electricians and Electro-Installation Companies*: Adrian Sommer, master expert, Career Guidance Center; Patrick Cotti, CEO; Fredy Christen, head, Information and Publications.

## Chapter 3
## Made in China: Challenge and Innovation in China's Vocational Education and Training System

*Vivien Stewart*

This case study of China comes out of several visits to China in 2013 and 2014 by the study team of Marc Tucker, Vivien Stewart, Betsy Brown Ruzzi, and Nancy Hoffman. As a team, we spent time in secondary vocational schools and tertiary vocational education colleges and visited with chambers of commerce, foreign-invested firms, and Chinese private and state-owned enterprises. We also met with economic and education researchers and government policy makers at the national, province, and city levels. We are grateful to all the people who took the time to meet with us and share their perspectives on China's economic and educational development.

We especially thank Dr. Zhang Minxuan, then president of Shanghai Normal University and a member of the Center on International Education Benchmarking's International Advisory Board, and Liu Yufeng at the Central Institute for Vocational and Technical Education in Beijing, who set up a number of visits. The American Chamber of Commerce was also extremely helpful in facilitating meetings with employers in the four cities we visited: Shenzhen, Tianjin, Shanghai, and Beijing. Dr. Lin Qin of the National Institute of Education Sciences in Beijing arranged the school visits in Tianjin.

We are indebted to many people who were kind enough to share their time and insights with us: Kenneth Jarrett, president, American Chamber of Commerce, Shanghai; Zhang Minxuan, president, Shanghai Normal University; Cui Liquiang, director, Vocational Skills Testing Authority, Shanghai Department of Human Resources and Social Security; Qiao Gang, president, Shanghai Business School; Zhao Qianghua, manager general, Human Resources, Shanghai Construction Group; Li Hui, professor, School of Finance and Business, Shanghai Normal University; Liu Jianghui, professor, School of Finance and Business, Shanghai Normal University; Xu Jinjie (Maggie), Center for International and Comparative Education; Bai Xinyue, CEO, Teach for China; Hu Guoyong, professor, Shanghai Normal University; Xia Huixian, dean, School of Education, Shanghai Normal University; Yang Xiuying, principal, Shanghai Technical Institute of Electronics and Information.

*At the Shanghai Municipal Education Commission*: Lao Xiaoyun, director, Division of Vocational and Adult Education; Lei Song, Division of Vocational and Adult Education. *At the Shanghai Academy of Environmental Sciences*: Yang Guo, director, Institution of Vocational and Technical Education. *At East China Normal University*: Weiping Shi, professor and director, Institute of Vocational and Adult Education. *At Shanghai Dianji University*: Ruofan Yang, vice president, also party representative of Shanghai to the National Congress; Wudon Wang (Kevin), director, International Affairs Department; Jun Kiu, assistant dean, School of Mechanical Engineering; Tianyu Liu, associate professor, School of Electrical Engineering. *At the Shanghai Institute of Health Sciences*: Wang Charles, director, International Exchange Office; Tang Lei, Vice President of Academic Affairs. *At Shanghai Jianfeng Vocational College (a Shanghai Construction Group school)*: Hui Xu, president; Xiufan Yang, headmaster. *At the Ministry of Education, Central Institute for Vocational and Technical Education*: Wang Jiping, former director general; Liu Yufeng, director, Division of International Cooperation and Comparative Education. *At Beijing Business School*: Xiaohe Shi, general secretary; Guocheng Liu, deputy principal; Li Ji, director, Institute for Vocational and Adult Education at the Beijing Academy of Educational Sciences; Dayong Yuan, assistant research fellow. *At Beijing Vocational College of Finance and Commerce*: Wang Changrong, president; Teng Long, Vice President for the School of International Education; Lu Yizhong, Vice President in Charge of Teaching; Yong Pan, director, Foreign Affairs Office, School of International Education; Qingying Xu, teacher, School of International Education. *At the National Institute of Educational Sciences*: Qin Lin, Research Center for International Comparative Education, National Institute of Educational Sciences. Li Ji, head, Institute of Vocational and Adult Education, Beijing Academy of Educational Sciences; Jian Zheng, International Education Cooperation and Benchmarking Research Division, Vocational and Technical Education Research Center, Ministry of Education.

*At Beijing Normal University*: Liu Yufeng, director, Division of International Cooperation and Comparative Education; Qiding Yu, professor, Faculty of Education, Institute of Vocational and Adult Education, and executive director, National Academy for Vocational Education. *At Boeing Tianjin Composites Company*: Jeff Foster, operations manager; Doug Gisselberg, manager, Production Support Department; Liu Rayman, production manager; Zhang Harry, quality manager; Huan Zhang, assistant general manager. *At Tianjin Sino-German Vocational and Technical College*: Li Dawei, president and board chairman; Zhang Xinghui, president. *At Tianjin Institute of Mechanical and Electrical Technology*: Song Chunlin, president and secretary of the party. *At Shenzhen Polytechnic*: Runhui Yang, vice president; Fan David, associate professor and deputy director, International Office; Shen Tong, manager, International Office; Wu Nian Xian, deputy director, Education Department of Guangdong Province; Lee Ricky, professor, Education Research Center Guangdong Province; Xidong Wen, professor and vice president; Zhiming Dou, professor of teaching; Lanpig Liu, professor, Center of the VET Research Center. *Education reporters*: Shaoxiao Dong, Shanghai Station, *China Education Daily*; Feng Zhao, director, *Shanghai Education*.

*Economists*: Wang Qian, director, Research, China Investment Corporation; Li Hongbin, C. V. Starr Professor of Economics, Tsinghua University. *At the American Chamber of Commerce China*:_Wang Patrick, vice president, Government Affairs; Jin He, Senior Program Officer for Education, Ford Foundation; David Tulloch, Economic Officer, US Embassy; Jonathan Ostroff, Abacare Group; Gong Sherry,

Hogan Lovells LLP; Ira Cohen, executive director, China Programs, University of Maryland. *Tianjin Business Leaders:* He Amanda, assistant chapter manager, American Chamber of Commerce Tianjin; Li Anna, chapter manager, American Chamber of Commerce Tianjin; Luo Rossi, senior associate, TriVista Business Services Co.; Eelco Van Kuilenburg, business development manager, Euro-Com International; Ruth Lycke, CEO China, InVision; Olivier Rochefort, general manager, Hotel Nikko Tianjin; Wei Chen, vice president, China site manager, Xerox; Liu Catherine, Director of Sales and Marketing, Hotel Nikko Tianjin; Jeff Foster, operations manager, Boeing; Michael Hart, managing director, Jones LaSalle. *Shenzhen business leaders*: Hon David, CEO, Dahon Technologies, and governor of the American Chamber of Commerce South China; Mo Tony, director, Human Resources, Lenovo Electronics; Sun Summer, senior manager, Human Resources, Lenovo Technologies; Lim David, senior director, Human Resources, Walmart Global Sourcing; Hou Ellen, senior manager, Human Resources, Walmart Global Sourcing.

# ABOUT THE EDITOR

**Marc S. Tucker** is the founder, former CEO and president, and, currently, a senior fellow at the National Center on Education and the Economy. A leader of the standards-driven education reform movement, Tucker has been studying the strategies used by the countries with the most successful education systems for three decades. He created New Standards, a precursor to the Common Core; the National Board for Professional Teaching Standards; and the Commission on the Skills of the American Workforce and its successor, the New Commission on the Skills of the American Workforce. He also created the National Institute for School Leadership and was instrumental in creating the National Skill Standards Board.

Tucker authored the 1986 Carnegie Report, *A Nation Prepared: Teachers for the 21st Century*, coauthored the report of the Commission on the Skills of the American Workforce, *America's Choice: High Skills or Low Wages*, and was lead author of *Tough Choices or Tough Times,* the report of the New Commission on the Skills of the American Workforce. Tucker has coauthored or edited numerous books, including *Thinking for a Living: Education and the Wealth of Nations* (Basic Books, 1992); *Standards for Our Schools: How to Set Them, Measure Them, and Reach Them* (Jossey-Bass, 1998); *The Principal Challenge: Leading and Managing Schools in an Era of Accountability* (Jossey-Bass, 2002); and *Surpassing Shanghai: An Agenda for American Education Built on the World's Leading Systems* (Harvard Education Press, 2011).

In 1994 Tucker was commended by President Bill Clinton for his contributions to the design of the Clinton administration's education and job training proposals in the Rose Garden ceremony celebrating the passage of the legislation authorizing the program. In 2014 he was awarded the James Bryant Conant award by the Education Commission of the States for his outstanding individual contribution to American education.

# ABOUT THE CONTRIBUTORS

**Betsy Brown Ruzzi** is vice president of the National Center on Education and the Economy (NCEE) and director of its Center on International Education Benchmarking. Since 2011 Brown Ruzzi has directed NCEE's effort to help countries around the world understand the principles, policies, and practices that top-performing countries use to drive their education systems, and as such she has been centrally involved in the research represented in this book. She oversees a grant program supporting scholars from around the world to study the practices of countries whose students regularly top the PISA league tables. She helps states redesign their primary and secondary education systems to match the performance of the world leaders in education. Brown Ruzzi also manages the NCEE's outreach and public relations work, including its website, newsletter, blog, and other social media. Most recently she managed the research, publication, and outreach for its studies: *Strong Performers and Successful Reformers in Education: Lessons from PISA for the United States* (OECD, 2011); *Surpassing Shanghai: An Agenda for American Education Built on the World's Leading Systems* (Harvard Education Press, 2011); *Fixing Our National Accountability System* (NCEE, 2014); *Chinese Lessons: Shanghai's Rise to the Top of the PISA League Tables* (NCEE, 2014); *The Phoenix: Vocational Education and Training in Singapore* (NCEE, 2016); and *What Does It Really Mean to Be College and Career Ready?* (NCEE, 2013). During her career at NCEE, she has helped create the National Institute for School Leadership, the National Skill Standards Board, the Commission on the Skills of the American Workforce, and the National Board for Professional Teaching Standards, all initiatives to improve the academic performance of our nation's students and strengthen the skills of our workforce. Brown Ruzzi has also worked on Capitol Hill, in the British Parliament, and in the Massachusetts governor's office.

**Nancy Hoffman** is a senior adviser at Jobs for the Future (JFF), a national nonprofit in Boston focused on improving educational and workforce outcomes for low-income young people and adults. In 2012 she cofounded with Robert Schwartz the Pathways to Prosperity Network, which seeks to ensure that many more youth complete high school, attain a postsecondary credential with currency in the labor market, and get launched on a career. Hoffman, who holds a BA and a PhD in comparative literature from the University of California, Berkeley, has held teaching and administrative posts at a number of US universities, including Brown, Temple, MIT, and UMass, Boston, and currently she coteaches the New Pathways for College and Career Readiness course at the Harvard Graduate School of Education. She also serves on the Massachusetts Board of Higher Education. Hoffman has served as a consultant on VET systems for the education policy unit of the OECD. Her book *Schooling in the Workplace: How Six of the World's Best Vocational Education Systems Prepare Young People for Jobs and Life* (Harvard Education Press, 2011) is a result of that work. She is an editor of three JFF books: *Double the Numbers: Increasing Postsecondary Credentials for Underrepresented Youth* (Harvard Education Press, 2004); *Minding the Gap: Why Integrating High School with College Makes Sense and How to Do It* (Harvard Education Press, 2007), and *Anytime, Anywhere: Student-Centered Learning for Schools and Teachers* (Harvard Education Press, 2013). She is also the author of *Women's True Profession: Voices from the History of Teaching* (Harvard Education Press, 2003). Her most recent book, coauthored with Robert Schwartz, is *Learning for Careers: The Pathways to Prosperity Network* (Harvard Education Press, 2017).

**Robert B. Schwartz** is Senior Research Fellow and Professor of Practice Emeritus at the Harvard Graduate School of Education (HGSE). Prior to joining the Harvard faculty in 1996, he served in a variety of roles in education: high school teacher and principal; education adviser to the mayor of Boston and the governor of Massachusetts; director of The Boston Compact; and education program director at The Pew Charitable Trusts. From 1997 to 2002 Schwartz served as founding president of Achieve, Inc., a nonprofit organization created by governors and corporate leaders to help improve performance in US schools. More recently he has contributed to two OECD studies, *Learning for Jobs* (2010) and *Strong Performers and Successful Reformers in Education* (2010) and coauthored the influential 2011 HGSE report *Pathways to Prosperity*, which calls for more attention to career and technical education. In 2012 he cofounded with Nancy Hoffman a national network of now fifteen states, metro regions, and large cities committed to act on the analysis and recommendations outlined in the *Pathways* report. He is also the coauthor, with Nancy Hoffman, of *Learning for Careers: The Pathways to Prosperity Network* (Harvard Education Press, 2017).

**Vivien Stewart** is the senior adviser for education and former vice president of education at the Asia Society, where she promotes the study of Asia and other world regions, cultures, languages, and global issues in America's schools and builds connections between US and Asian education leaders. In the US this has included working with a network of state education leaders, creating a national initiative to expand the teaching of Chinese, and developing a model network of internationally oriented schools. Internationally, she developed a series of benchmarking exchanges to share expertise between American and Asian education, business, and policy leaders on how to improve education to meet the demands of globalization. Stewart writes extensively on education internationally. Her book *A World-Class Education: Lessons from International Models of Excellence and Innovation* (ASCD, 2012) describes what the US can learn from high-performing education systems around the world. Prior to working at the Asia Society, Stewart directed the children, youth, and education programs at Carnegie Corporation of New York and led the development of reform agendas in early childhood education, urban school reform, science education, teaching as a profession, and healthy adolescent development. She has also served as a senior policy adviser to the UN High Commissioner for Refugees and has been a visiting scholar at the Teachers College, Columbia University. In addition, she is a trustee of a number of national and international organizations, including the National Center on Education and the Economy.

# INDEX